The

Series editors: Alec Motyer (OT)
John Stott (NT)
Derek Tidball (Bible Themes)

The Message of Jonah

The Bible Speaks Today: Old Testament series

The Message of Genesis 1 – 11
The dawn of creation
David Atkinson

The Message of Genesis 12 – 50
From Abraham to Joseph
Joyce G. Baldwin

The Message of Numbers
Journey to the promised land
Raymond Brown

The Message of Deuteronomy
Not by bread alone
Raymond Brown

The Message of Judges
Grace abounding
Michael Wilcock

The Message of Ruth
The wings of refuge
David Atkinson

The Message of Chronicles
One church, one faith, one Lord
Michael Wilcock

The Message of Nehemiah
God's servant in a time of change
Raymond Brown

The Message of Job
Suffering and grace
David Atkinson

The Message of Psalms 1 – 72
Songs for the people of God
Michael Wilcock

The Message of Psalms 73 – 150
Songs for the people of God
Michael Wilcock

The Message of Proverbs
Wisdom for life
David Atkinson

The Message of Ecclesiastes
A time to mourn, and a time to dance
Derek Kidner

The Message of the Song of Songs
The lyrics of love
Tom Gledhill

The Message of Isaiah
On eagles' wings
Barry Webb

The Message of Jeremiah
Against wind and tide
Derek Kidner

The Message of Ezekiel
A new heart and a new spirit
Christopher J. H. Wright

The Message of Daniel
The Lord is King
Ronald S. Wallace

The Message of Hosea
Love to the loveless
Derek Kidner

The Message of Joel, Micah and Habakkuk
Listening to the voice of God
David Prior

The Message of Amos
The day of the lion
Alec Moyter

The Message of Jonah
Presence in the storm
Rosemary Nixon

The Bible Speaks Today New Testament *and* **Bible Themes**
series are listed at the back of this book

The Message of Jonah

Presence in the Storm

Rosemary A. Nixon

InterVarsity Press

InterVarsity Press
P.O. Box 1400, Downers Grove, IL 60515-1426
World Wide Web: www.ivpress.com
E-mail: mail@ivpress.com

Inter-Varsity Press
38 De Montfort Street, Leicester LE1 7GP, England
World Wide Web: www:ivpbooks.com
E-mail: ivp@uccf.org.uk

InterVarsity Press® is the book-publishing division of InterVarsity Christian Fellowship/USA®, a student movement active on campus at hundreds of universities, colleges and schools of nursing in the United States of America, and a member movement of the International Fellowship of Evangelical Students. For information about local and regional activities, write Public Relations Dept., InterVarsity Christian Fellowship/USA, 6400 Schroeder Rd., P.O. Box 7895, Madison, WI 53707-7895.

Inter-Varsity Press is the book-publishing division of the Universities and Colleges Christian Fellowship (formerly the Inter-Varsity Fellowship), a student movement linking Christian Unions in universities and colleges throughout the United Kingdom and the Republic of Ireland, and a member movement of the International Fellowship of Evangelical Students. For information about local and national activities write to UCCF, 38 De Montfort Street, Leicester LE1 7GP, England.

USA ISBN 0-8308-2426-X

UK ISBN 0-85111-898-4

Printed in the United States of America ∞

British Library Cataloguing in Publication Data

A catalogue record for this book is available from the British Library.

Library of Congress Cataloging-in-Publication Data

Nixon, Rosemary A.
The message of Jonah: presence in the storm: whither shall I go from Thy spirit? or whither shall I flee from Thy presence? Psalm 139:7/ Rosemary A. Nixon.
p. cm.—(The Bible speaks today)
Includes bibliographical references.
ISBN 0-8308-2426-X (U.S. pbk.: alk. paper)—ISBN 0-85111-898-4 (U.K. pbk.: alk. paper)
1. Bible. O.T. Jonah—Commentaries. I. Title. II. Series.
BS1605.53.N59 2003
224'.9207—dc21

2003008332

P 17 16 15 14 13 12 11 10 9 8 7 6 5 4 3 2 1
Y 17 16 15 14 13 12 11 10 09 08 07 06 05 04 03

Contents

To Dorothy
and to the memory of Edwin
with gratitude

General preface

The Bible Speaks Today describes three series of expositions, based on the books of the Old and New Testaments, and on Bible themes that run through the whole of Scripture. Each series is characterized by a threefold ideal:

- to expound the biblical text with accuracy
- to relate it to contemporary life, and
- to be readable.

These books are, therefore, not 'commentaries', for the commentary seeks rather to elucidate the text than to apply it, and tends to be a work rather of reference than of literature. Nor, on the other hand, do they contain the kind of 'sermons' which attempt to be contemporary and readable without taking Scripture seriously enough.

The contributors to The Bible Speaks Today series are all united in their convictions that God still speaks through what he has spoken, and that nothing is more necessary for the life, health and growth of Christians than that they should hear what the Spirit is saying to them through his ancient – yet ever modern – Word.

Alec Motyer
John Stott
Derek Tidball
Series Editors

Author's preface

It is said that travel broadens the mind. The message of Jonah is inextricably bound up with an extraordinary journey which took him westward into the Mediterranean, down into the belly of the great fish, then eastward into the area we now know as Iraq. His travelling Companion, however, seems to have been less interested in the wild geography of the terrain he crossed and more concerned with the unruly contours of Jonah's heart. The extent to which the narrow-minded prophet was changed by his travelling remains uncertain. Indeed, the book itself leads us to think that the journey is not yet over.

It is some years since Jonah first appeared on my horizon. Initially inspired by the fine teaching of the late Joyce Baldwin, the journey took me from a north London parish to St John's College with Cranmer Hall, Durham, to be tutor in Old Testament Studies. All the while seeking to plumb the depths of this strange character, it was in moving to live and work in the parish of central Gateshead that I heard the book of Jonah addressing me, plumbing my own depths and beginning to interpret some of the intricate complexities lurking there. Here lay the discovery that at the heart of mission lies the challenge of change.

After a lifetime in the Church of England, the challenge to journey further north to serve in the surprisingly different context of the Scottish Episcopal Church presented itself. Here was a small church with a huge task. Adept at change and skilled in the fine tools which ensured it was handled creatively, this little Christian community, untrammelled by the hierarchies of establishment, showed gracious courage and faith in the great God who constantly calls us out of our settled places to venture with him into the unknown.

The use of some Jewish thinking on Jonah reflects part of a journey which took me to London, Jerusalem Gateshead and Edinburgh. I was enriched in those places by encountering the contributions of Jewish thought, and the powerful reminder of how our

God speaks through people of very different cultures. Here, too, was the important reminder that our Christian roots reach deeply into ancient Hebrew Scripture.

And where would Jonah's travels have taken him without the whale? The animal wisdom we meet in the book is around us all the time. In order to enjoy Western lifestyle to the full we use, and sometimes misuse, humble animals for our convenience and well-being. Enjoying canine companions among my faithful friends for many years has opened new windows into God's rich gift of life. Their outrageous antics, fun-loving obedience, unfailing presence and earthy company bring joy, humour and realism to life.

This small volume has been nourished by friends and colleagues, students and parishioners in Bristol, London, Durham, Jerusalem, Gateshead, Edinburgh and Cleadon who have been, and like Jonah remain, part of my life's journey. Special thanks must go to the Scottish Episcopal Church for granting me a sabbatical term, colleagues at the Theological Institute who took on the extra work, and the church of All Saints', Cleadon. Finally, without the prized support and the valuable suggestions of Alec Motyer, and the enduring encouragement and critical support of Judith Brearley, this book would not have been written.

ROSEMARY NIXON

Chief Abbreviations

AB	Anchor Bible
AV	Authorised Version
BS	*Bibliotheca Sacra*
HUCA	*Hebrew Union College Annual*
IDBSup	*Interpreters' Dictionary of the Bible, Supplementary Volume*
IntB	The Interpreters' Bible
JBL	*Journal of Biblical Literature*
JSOT	*Journal for the Study of the Old Testament*
LXX	Septuagint (Greek Old Testament)
NIV	New International Version
NRSV	New Revised Standard Version
RSV	Revised Standard Version
RV	Revised Version

Bibliography

Works listed here are referred to in the footnotes by the author's surname, or surname and date.

Akerman, James S., 'Jonah' in *The Literary Guide to the Bible*, ed. Robert Alter and Frank Kermode (London: Fontana Press, 1989).

Alexander, T. D., *Jonah: An Introduction and Commentary*, Tyndale Old Testament Commentaries (Leicester: Inter-Varsity Press, 1988).

Alter, R., *The World of Biblical Literature* (London: SPCK, 1992).

Archbishop of Canterbury's Commission on Urban Priority Areas, *Faith in the City: A Call for Action by Church and Nation* (London: Church House Publishing, 1985).

Assembly of Rabbis of the Reform Synagogues of Great Britain (eds.), *Forms of Prayer for Jewish Worship III Prayers for the High Holydays Days of Awe*, eighth edition 5745 (London: Reform Synagogues of Great Britain, 1985).

Augustine, *City of God*, Book 18 (Oxford: Oxford University Press, 1963).

Bewer, Julius A., *The Book of the Twelve Prophets*, ICC Series (Edinburgh: T. and T. Clark, 1949).

Bickerman, E. J., *Four Strange Books of the Bible* (New York: Schocken Books, 1967).

Blank, Sheldon H., 'Doest Thou Well to Be Angry? A Study in Self-Pity', *HUCA 26* (1955).

Bolin, Thomas M., *Freedom Beyond Forgiveness: The Book of Jonah Re-examined*, *JSOT* Supplement Series 236, Copenhagen International Seminar 3 (Sheffield: Sheffield Academic Press, 1997).

Bonhoeffer, D., *The Cost of Discipleship* (London: SCM, 1959).

Brockington, Leonard H., 'Jonah', *Peake's Commentary on the Bible*, ed. M. Black and H. H. Rowley (London: Nelson, 1962).

Brueggemann, W., *Israel's Praise* (Philadelphia: Fortress Press, 1988).
Buber, M., *I and Thou* (New York: Charles Scribner's Sons, 1970).
—, *Knowledge of Man* (New York: Harcourt, Brace and World, 1933).
Calvin, J., *Commentaries on the Twelve Minor Prophets* (Edinburgh: Calvin Translation Society, 1847).
Childs, B. S., *Introduction to the Old Testament as Scripture* (London: SCM Press, 1979).
Clements, R. E., 'The Purpose of the Book of Jonah', *Congress Volume* 1974, *VTSup*. 28 (Leiden: Brill, 1975).
Cohen, A. H., 'The Tragedy of Jonah', *Judaism* 21 (1972).
Craigie, P. C., *The Twelve Prophets Vol. 1 Hosea, Joel, Amos, Obadiah and Jonah* (Edinburgh: Saint Andrew Press, 1984).
Eaton, J., *Mysterious Messengers: A course on Hebrew prophecy from Amos onwards* (London: SCM, 1997).
Eissfeldt, O., *Amos und Jona* (Berlin: Evangelische Verlagsanstalt, 1964).
Ellul, J., *The Judgment of Jonah* (Grand Rapids: Eerdmans, 1971).
Frye, N., *The Great Code: The Bible and Literature* (London: Routledge & Kegan Paul, 1982).
Gibson, J., *Genesis*, Volume 1, Daily Bible Study (Edinburgh: Saint Andrew Press, 1981).
Good, E. M., *Irony in the Old Testament* (Sheffield: Almond Press, 1981).
Gunn, D. M., and D. N. Fewell, *Narrative in the Hebrew Bible* (Oxford: Oxford University Press, 1993).
Hayman, P., 'Rabbinic Judaism and the Problem of Evil', *Scottish Journal of Theology*, Vol. 29 (October 1976).
Henry, M., *Commentary in One Volume* (London: Marshall, Morgan and Scott, 1960, first published 1708).
Heschel, A. H., *The Prophets* (New York: Harper Row, 1962).
Holbert, J. G., *Deliverance belongs to YHWH: Satire in the Book of Jonah*, *JSOT* 21 (Sheffield: Sheffield Academic Press, 1981).
Hooker, M. D., *The Signs of a Prophet* (London: SCM Press, 1997).
Jenson, P., *Reading Jonah*, Grove Biblical Series B14 (Cambridge: Grove Books, 1999).
Jeremias, J., *Jesus' Promise to the Nations* (London: SCM Press, 1958).
Knight, G. A. F., and F. W. Golka, *Revelation of God* (Edinburgh: Handsel, 1988).
Koyama, K., *Mount Fuji and Mount Sinai* (London: SCM Press, 1984).
LaCocque, A. and P.-E. Lacocque, *Jonah: A Psycho-Religious*

Approach to the Prophet (Columbia, South Carolina: University of South Carolina Press, 1990).

Landes, George M., 'Jonah, Book of', *IDB Sup.* (Nashville: Abingdon, 1976).

—, 'The "Three days and Three Nights" Motif in Jonah 2:1', *JBL* 86 (1967).

Lewis, C., 'Jonah, a Parable for our Time', *Judaism* 21 (1972).

Limburg, J., *Jonah*, Old Testament Library (London: SCM Press, 1993).

Luther, M., 'Lecture on the Minor Prophets II', *Luther's Works*, 19, ed. H. C. Oswald (St Louis: Concordia, 1974).

Magonet, J., *Form and Meaning: Studies in Literary Techniques in the Book of Jonah* (Sheffield: Almond Press, 1983).

—, *A Rabbi's Bible* (London: SCM Press, 1991).

—, *Bible Lives* (London: SCM Press, 1992).

—, *The Subversive Bible* (London: SCM Press, 1997).

McGowan, J. C., *Jonah*, Jerome Biblical Commentary (London: Geoffrey Chapman, 1968).

Miles, J. R., 'Laughing at the Bible: Jonah as Parody', in Y. T. Radday et al., *On Humour and the Comic in the Hebrew Bible* (Sheffield: Sheffield Academic Press, 1990).

Moltmann, J., *The Crucified God* (London: SCM Press, 1974).

Motyer, J. A., *The Prophecy of Isaiah* (Leicester: Inter-Varsity Press, 1993).

Nolan, A., *Jesus before Christianity: the Gospel of Liberation* (London: Darton, Longman and Todd, 1977).

Radday, Y. T., and A. Brenner, *On Humour and the Comic in the Hebrew Bible* (Sheffield: Sheffield Academic Press, 1990).

Roth, L., *Man and God in the Old Testament* (London: Allen and Unwin, 1955).

Ryken, L., Wilhoit, J. C., Longman III, T. (eds.), *Dictionary of Biblical Imagery* (Leicester: Inter-Varsity Press, 1998).

Salters, R. B., *Jonah and Lamentations* (Sheffield: JSOT Press, 1994).

Sasson, J., *Jonah*, AB 24B (Garden City, New York: Doubleday, 1990).

Scott, R. B. Y., 'The Sign of Jonah', *Interpretation 19* (Richmond, Virginia: Union Theological Seminary and Presbyterian School of Christian Education, 1965).

Skinner, J., *Prophecy and Religion* (Cambridge: Cambridge University Press, 1922).

Smart, J. D., *Jonah*, IntB Vol. 6 (New York: Abingdon, 1956).

Smith, G. A., *The Book of the Twelve Prophets* (London: Hodder and Stoughton, 1901).

Stanton, G. B., 'The Prophet Jonah and his Message', *BS* (1951, pp. 363–376).

Stuart, D., *Hosea-Jonah*, Word Biblical Commentary 31 (Waco, Texas: Word Books, 1987).
Trible, P., *Rhetorical Criticism: Context, Method and the Book of Jonah* (Minneapolis: Fortress Press, 1994).
Watts, J. D. W., *The Books of Joel, Obadiah, Jonah, Nahum, Habakkuk and Zephaniah* (Cambridge: Cambridge University Press, 1975).
Wiesel, E., *Five Biblical Portraits* (London: Notre Dame Press, 1981).
Wiseman, D. J., 'Jonah's Nineveh', *Tyndale Bulletin 30* (1979).
Wolff, H. W., *Obadiah and Jonah: a Commentary* (Minneapolis: Augsburg Publishing, 1986).
Woods, F. H., and F. E. Powell (eds.), *The Hebrew Prophets* (Oxford: The Clarendon Press, 1917).

The Hands of God

It is a fearful thing to fall into the hands of the living God.
But it is a much more fearful thing to fall out of them.

Did Lucifer fall through knowledge?
oh then, pity him, pity him that plunge!

Save me, O God, from falling into the ungodly knowledge
of myself as I am without God.

Let me never know, O God
let me never know what I am or should be
when I have fallen out of your hands, the hands of the living God.

That awful and sickening endless sinking, sinking
through the slow corruptive levels of disintegrative knowledge
when the self has fallen from the hands of God
and sinks, seething and sinking, corrupt
and sinking still, in depth after depth of disintegrative consciousness
sinking in the endless undoing, the awful katabolism into the abyss!
even of the soul, fallen from the hands of God!

Save me from that, O God!
Let me never know myself apart from the living God!

(*D. H. Lawrence, 1885–1930*)

Introduction

Jonah must be the best known of the twelve minor prophets.[1] His story is told in countless children's books, the famous episode of the fish undoubtedly being its most memorable feature. Perhaps the main reason for our familiarity with the book is that it offers a totally different kind of experience for the reader from that of other prophetic books. It is a story with character delineation and lots of surprises! It starts off, like the others, in a familiar way with God calling a prophet to a particular task (1:1–2), but thereafter it is a tale of the unexpected. Were we not so familiar with the book we would be shocked, and indeed rightly so, to discover a prophet *refusing* to do God's will. Voting with his feet, Jonah hotfoots it to Joppa to catch a ship to the ends of the earth. The voyage is sabotaged by a vicious storm; when urged to pray for deliverance, something even atheists are known to have done in times of crisis, the prophet remains silent. The pagan mariners are the ones who turn to God offering urgent prayers and supplications. Meanwhile the 'hero', or perhaps more aptly the 'anti-hero', has gone from the innermost part of the ship into the innermost part of the great fish, where he remains for three days and nights thanking God for his deliverance. But it remains unclear just what he has been delivered from, even after the fish spews him out alive and well.

Without further ado, he sets off to Nineveh and, unlike any other prophet, is utterly successful: the people of Nineveh, from greatest to least, repent and turn to God. As a result of this good news, Jonah suffers paroxysms of rage. He cannot live with a God like this. He longs to die. His death wish is assuaged when God provides a plant to protect him from the heat of the sun – but only temporarily. A worm destroys the plant in the night, and Jonah, exposed to the sun and the sultry east wind, longs once more to die. Jonah's anger has

[1] Hosea, Joel, Amos, Obadiah, Jonah, Micah, Nahum, Habakkuk, Zephaniah, Haggai, Zechariah and Malachi.

not gone away. Nineveh has repented. Yahweh has repented. But Jonah is unmoved. He has no lasting memory of God's salvation to sustain him. He has no pleasure in his own deliverance from death. The reader might well be puzzled that Jonah's rescue from a watery grave appears to have no effect on his subsequent attitude. At the close of the story he remains as much an awkward figure as he was at the beginning. We could speculate that his response to Yahweh's final question would be similar to his response to Yahweh's initial call. It seems as though God is intent on his work of salvation despite the stubbornness of his people. Jonah was unwilling to change, but God was willing to take risks for the sake of his love.

Not surprisingly, this short book, comprising a mere forty-eight verses, has tantalized and intrigued scholars and commentators from the start. Although on the surface the story appears fairly simple and straightforward, it soon becomes apparent that underlying it a complex and fascinating web is spun by an author drawing on a range of resources as he grapples with conflicting perceptions of God. The result is an exquisite gem, unique in the pages of holy Scripture and unparalleled in contemporary writings.

Just as a mist sometimes descends as we scale a mountainous peak, obscuring our view, so it can be as we approach the peaks of scriptural revelation. It is as though a miasma robs us of the glories of the truth revealed. We may be teased, even tormented, by questions such as: 'Is it literally true?' 'Did it happen in history?' As we focus on the book of Jonah our questions tend to revolve around Jonah and the fish. Could a man live inside a fish for three days? Is his physical deliverance a miracle or is it a hyperbole? Is it a serious theological statement or a red herring? In what sense is this story true and what is its meaning? As we set our questioning in the context of the book as a whole and give our attention to hearing the word of God through its pages, we may begin to see the story afresh. The prophet himself appears to have had no difficulties at all being swallowed and spat out by a great fish in chapter 2, but from the beginning of chapter 1 to the end of chapter 4 Jonah had huge problems with a great God. He knew the truth about God, that he was merciful and gracious, slow to anger and abounding in steadfast love, always ready to forgive and desist from punishment (4:2), but the implications of this truth were too great for him to contemplate. In consequence he remained at the level of awkward and endless debate in the face of God's word, fired by self-righteousness and unbelief.

But God had questions too. He addressed Jonah through questions on the lips of pagans: 'What kind of person are you?' and 'What kind of God do you worship?' (1:8). God asks Jonah, 'Do you do well to be angry?' (4:4, 9) and 'Should not I pity Nineveh, that great city?' (4:11). So while we, the readers, question some of the extraordinary features of this little story, we too are being questioned by the God who questions Jonah. With consummate skill the author has loaded this brief narrative so that it reflects back onto the reader a range of questions. Does he intend to challenge his readers about the nature of the God of Israel and its implications for action? Or is he underlining the sovereignty of God over all things? Is he reflecting on what is involved in being the 'chosen people'? Or is he dealing with an 'unbelieving believer'? In common with the little book of Nahum, the book concludes with a question on the lips of God (4:11). It remains unanswered. All who read are invited to answer for themselves. For many the question posed here is harder to answer than the questions posed by the episode of the great fish.

'The great fish'

Although we shall encounter the fish in various parts of our study, it may be helpful at this point to say that writers with equal regard for the Bible as the fully inspired Word of God have, as we shall see, frequently taken contrasting stances on the fish. Some are convinced that a parabolic understanding is necessary to do justice to the true nature of sacred Scripture, while others are convinced that only a literal and historical view safeguards the honour due to the Bible as God's written Word. All would agree that the eternal Creator, while transcending time and history, yet intervenes to shape human history, fashioning the chaos of humanity by the constant and faithful brooding of the Holy Spirit. Not only does such history enable community and identity, but God's action in history is a way of mapping all his dealings with humankind and, as such, is crucial to faith. In adopting a parabolic approach to the story of Jonah, sacred history is not being denied. Rather, in the context of the overall sweep of history the parable is seen as a sure means of disclosing God's ways with his people, whether they know him (Jonah) or not (Nineveh).

Although ways of understanding the fish may have the effect of polarizing readers of the Bible, the central importance of being open to hearing God's word is the overriding concern. As we shall discover, one of the themes of Jonah is that God uses the unfamiliar, even the despised, in order to address his people. By being open to different possibilities we may be enabled to hear God's living word in new ways.

Approaching an interpretation

Early church

Not surprisingly, difficulties in interpreting Jonah are not new. The Jewish historian Flavius Josephus (*c.* AD 1) includes the story in his history of the Jewish people, suggesting he understood Jonah to be a significant person in Israel's story. New Testament reference is made to the 'sign of Jonah' (Matt. 12:38–42; 16:1–4; Luke 11:29–32), suggesting a particular understanding of the book. Some early Christian commentators such as Origen (AD 185–254), Gregory of Nazianzen (AD 330–89) and Theophilact (AD 1070–81) favoured allegorical interpretations. This was in fact a common and acceptable way of interpreting many parts of the Old Testament. Indeed, the method may have allowed the early Christians to incorporate the Hebrew Scriptures into their canon of Scripture. They clearly saw little difficulty in doing this, being untroubled by the modern concept of history which so bedevils some contemporary approaches. They regarded Jonah as a prototype of the crucifixion leading to resurrection. Augustine of Hippo (AD 354–430) drew on the same themes of death and resurrection, while favouring a more literal interpretation: 'For why was he [Jonah] three days in the whale's belly and then let out, but to signify Christ's resurrection from the depth of hell on the third day?'[2]

While seeing Jonah as a type of Christ, Jerome (AD 345–419) believed the purpose of the book was to encourage Jews to repent, a view followed in an eleventh-century Jewish liturgy, *Mahzor Vitry*. Another early Christian view, which was also reflected in Matthew 12:41, saw the repentance of Nineveh as a source of great shame on Israel: 'The men of Nineveh will arise at the judgment with this generation and condemn it; for they repented at the preaching of Jonah, and behold, something greater than Jonah is here.' This interpretation was picked up by some in the early church and used to denigrate the Jews. On the other hand, some early Gentile churches understood themselves as 'Nineveh' in the story; they were pagans accepted by God. On this view Jonah represented narrow-minded Jews who disagreed with the salvation of Gentiles. Some medieval interpreters blended these views: they said Jonah was not opposed to the repentance of Nineveh, but his zeal for Israel took priority. This view is reflected in some Gospel accounts of Jesus' own self-understanding (Matt. 10:5; Mark 7:27).

[2] Augustine, *City of God*, Book 18, chapter 13.

Jonah appears in an early prayer used by Gentile Christians between AD 150 and 248. The prayer was originally Jewish and was adapted for use by the Christian community:

> Now also, yourself, O Master God, accept the entreaties on the lips of your people, who have come out of the Gentiles, who call upon you in truth, even as you received the gifts of the righteous in their generation: Daniel in the hole of the lions; Jonah in the belly of the whale; the three children in a furnace of fire . . . And now, therefore, receive the prayers of your people, offered up with full knowledge to you through Christ in the Spirit.

Reformation

Martin Luther (1483–1546) referred to Jonah as

> a queer and odd saint who is angry because of God's mercy for sinners, begrudging them all the benefits and wishing them all evil . . . And yet he is God's dear child. He chats so uninhibitedly with God as though he were not in the least afraid of Him – as indeed he is not; he confides in him as a father.[3]

He adds,

> In view of this [the repentance of Nineveh], I am tempted to say that no apostle or prophet, not even Christ himself, performed and accomplished with a single sermon the great things Jonah did. His conversion of the city of Nineveh with one sermon is surely as great a miracle as his rescue from the belly of the whale, if not an even greater one.[4]

Although John Calvin (1509–64) was to argue that Jonah did not want to go to Nineveh because he was afraid of being known as a prophet whose word did not come true, his dominant theme concerns God's love and mercy. Commenting on the Lord's care of the sleeping prophet, he writes, 'We hence see that the Lord often cares for his people when they care not for themselves, and that he watches while they are asleep.'[5]

[3] Luther, *Jonah*.
[4] Ibid., p. 37.
[5] Calvin, p. 54.

Modern

Until recently, the tendency among modern scholars has been to regard the books of Jonah and Ruth as religious tracts whose purpose was to challenge prevailing attitudes of Jewish exclusivism after the exile (597–538 BC). Exclusivist attitudes are said to be reflected in the writings of Ezra and Nehemiah, for example in Nehemiah 13:23–30. By contrast, the books of Jonah and Ruth show very different attitudes towards non-Jews. For instance, Ruth was a Moabitess who married Boaz from Bethlehem and became the great-grandmother of King David. In his day, Nehemiah declaimed against intermarriage with the Moabites.[6] The suggestion is that Jonah and Ruth were 'tracts for the times', written by a minority group with the specific purpose of challenging such exclusivist attitudes.

Literary studies

Most recent interpretations of the book of Jonah, however, have drawn attention to its striking literary features. Many of these are clear even in translation, so can be seen by the reader of the English texts. They include repetition of certain words and phrases, the use of key words with multiple meanings and a paralleling of events in the overall shaping of the book.

Repetition

Repetition is a literary device which impacts on the reader or listener, heightening the tension and climax of events. It is interesting to notice the way the author heightens the tension in the story. Referring to the storm in 1:4 he writes 'and there was a mighty tempest on the sea', in verse 11 'the sea grew more tempestuous', and in verse 13 'for the sea grew more and more tempestuous against them'. Another example of this technique is found in 1:5, 'the mariners were afraid', verse 10, 'Then the men were exceedingly afraid', and verse 16, 'Then the men feared the LORD exceedingly.'

There are other instances of such repeated phrases. Jonah 'went down' to Joppa (1:3), 'went down' into the boat (1:3), 'went down' into the deepest part of the boat (1:5), and finally 'went down' to the land of death (2:6). It is as though the writer is pointing to something more than Jonah's physical flight from God's call. As we shall see, the implication of his going away from God's presence is his descent into

[6] Neh. 13:25.

the place of death. In another example, the Lord says to Jonah, 'Arise' (1:1), the captain of the ship calls him to 'arise' (1:6), the Lord calls Jonah a second time, 'Arise' (3:2), and the king of Nineveh 'arose' from his throne (3:6). The word seems to echo through the story as a reminder of Jonah's call and a challenge to his descent. Another word occurring with notable frequency is 'great' (1:2, 4, 12, 17; 3:1, 5; 4:11). Is this intended as a humorous hyperbole, or perhaps as a clue to the fact that Jonah was up against something greater than himself?

Some key words

Some key words have many shades of meaning. For example, the Hebrew word *rā'â* translated 'wickedness' in 1:2 means 'calamity' (NIV) in 1:7, 'trouble' (NIV) in 1:8, 'evil' in 3:8, 'wickedness' and 'destruction' (NIV) in 3:10, and Jonah's 'displeasure' (NIV) in 4:1, while in 4:2 it refers to the 'calamity' (NIV) which God might inflict on the unrepentant. Another example is the word rendered as 'fear' or 'afraid' in chapter 1. It describes the mariners' reactions to the storm in 1:5, Jonah's account of his relationship to God in 1:9, the mariners' response to Jonah in 1:10, and their response to God in 1:16. Using words in this way could suggest that the writer is playing with subtleties of meaning in order to create questions and open up fresh avenues of thought and insight. In the first example there may be an underlying question concerning the localization of 'evil'; is it in Nineveh, in God or in Jonah? In the second there is a question about what it means to 'fear God'.

Highlight

Another technique the writer uses is to highlight significant elements in the story by putting particular stress on them. For example, 'the men were exceedingly afraid' (1:10), Nineveh was 'exceedingly great' (3:3), Jonah was 'exceedingly . . . angry' (4:1), and then he was 'exceedingly glad' (4:6). Is the writer aiming to draw our attention to these parts of the story, or is he using exaggeration to make a point?

Contrast

Contrast, such as Jonah going west after being called to go east, and going 'down' in response to being called to 'arise'; comparison, such as the king of Nineveh sitting penitently in sackcloth and ashes while the prophet sits in comfort waiting for disaster to fall; and irony, such as Jonah's response to astonishing success with fury and a longing for death – all these combine to create a story with a power far beyond its length.

Opposites

'Sea' and 'dry land' are opposites, like heaven and earth, light and darkness, great and small, good and evil. The statement of opposites in this way is intended to denote the inclusion of all the reality that lies between them. This literary device is commonly found in Scripture. The technical term for it is 'merismus'.

Structure

To these details we must add the observation that there is an overall structure to the story in which several parallel elements appear. For example, chapters 1–2 find parallels in chapters 3–4. The main features can be set out as follows.[7]

Chapters 1–2		*Chapters 3–4*	
Word of God to Jonah	**1:1**	Word of God to Jonah	**3:1**
Response of Jonah	**1:3**	Response of Jonah	**3:3–4a**
Gentile response	**1:5**	Gentile response	**3:5**
Action of captain	**1:6**	Action of king	**3:6–9**
Sailors and Jonah	**1:7–15**	Ninevites and God	**3:10**
Disaster averted	**1:15c**	Disaster averted	**3:10c**
Response of sailors	**1:16**	Response of Jonah	**4:1**
God and Jonah	**2:1–11**	God and Jonah	**4:2–3**
God's response	**2:11**	God's response	**4:6–11**

Through these parallels we can see that the entire sequence is both initiated and concluded by God. In the story the responses of Jonah and the Gentiles are contrasted, Jonah appearing not to fear God while the Gentiles show an appropriate fear. Throughout, God's concern is directed towards deliverance. No distinction is made between the wickedness of Nineveh and the evil which shapes Jonah.

Chiasmus

Mention must be made of one final literary feature, the 'chiasmus'. This common literary device is frequently found in the pages of Scripture. The word 'chiasmus' derives from the letter X, *chi* in the Greek alphabet. The basic pattern follows two diagonal lines which, like the *chi* X, cross at the centre. For example:

[7]Trible, p. 110.

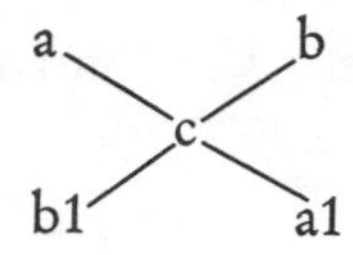

It reflects to some extent ordinary human communication. For example, a simple exchange between people can be presented like this:

A How are you? **B** Not so good.
C Why's that?
B1 I've lost my job. **A1** I am sorry to hear that.

A and A1 begin and end the conversation. The kindly enquiry (A) elicits information (B). More information is offered (B1) in response to a central question (C). A concluding response (A1) rounds off this bit of conversation.

The chiastic form is most frequently represented in a step-like pattern:

A How are you?
  B Not so good.
    C Why's that?
  B1 I've lost my job.
A1 I am sorry to hear that.

This simple device illustrates how human conversation progresses from one step to the next. The form developed significantly in a culture where story-telling and memorization were key elements in the life of the human community. It is not surprising, therefore, that in Scripture similar patterns are frequently found. For example, the words of Isaiah 55:8–9 are in chiastic form and may be set out in a step-like structure:

A For *my thoughts* are not *your thoughts*,
  B neither are *your ways my ways*, says the LORD.
    C For as the heavens are higher than the earth,
  B1 so are *my ways* higher than *your ways*
A1 and *my thoughts* than *your thoughts*.

Setting the words out in this way highlights the theme: 'my thoughts and your thoughts' (lines A and A1) and 'my ways and your ways' (lines B and B1). The central line (C) is key to understanding the extent of the difference between God and humankind.

The chiasmus can be seen in short phrases or in longer passages. It is easier to see the literary correspondences in the longer passages when they are set out in this step-like structure. Using this device, we can see that the key to understanding a passage may be at its centre.

In the book of Jonah several instances of this chiastic pattern can be seen, confirming the belief that the book is a finely honed piece of literature. For example, the first words uttered by the prophet appear in verses 9–10a of chapter 1. Their significance is underlined by the place they occupy in the narrative – that is, at the centre:

A Introduction (1:1–3)
    B The build-up of the storm (1:4–8)
        C *Jonah speaks* (1:9–10a)
    B1 The stilling of the storm (1:10b–15)
A1 Conclusion (1:16)

The events leading up to Jonah's first speech are mirrored as the first part of the story comes to an end. The sequence suggests a build-up (1:1–8), a climax (1:9) and a resolution (1:10–16). From this design we can deduce that Jonah's first words are significant to the meaning of the story.

A chiastic form also dramatically describes the king of Nineveh's response to God's word in 3:6:

A He arose from his throne,
    B removed his robe,
    B1 covered himself with sackcloth,
A1 and sat in ashes.

The book of Jonah in the canon of Scripture

When studying any book of Scripture it is important to have some sense of how it relates to other books in the canon. As we come to the book of Jonah we find affinities in its style and content with books in all three parts of the Hebrew canon, namely the Torah, the Prophets and the Writings.

Torah

In the book of Genesis we find stories portraying a dialogue between God and humankind. There are similarities between the stories of

Adam and Cain,[8] who hide from God's presence, and the story of Jonah, as he tries to get as far away as possible from God. There are contrasts between Abram's debate with God over the fate of Sodom and Gomorrah[9] and Jonah's debate with God over the fate of Nineveh. In the book of Exodus there are similarities between Israel's preference for the comfort of captivity in Egypt[10] and Jonah's preference for the security of being in his own country. Neither Israel nor Jonah wanted to be called out to something new and potentially uncomfortable.

Prophecy

1. Style of prophetic writing

In the great majority of biblical books named after a prophet, the reader is given some historical marker. For example, we can glean from Isaiah clues about the setting in which the prophet worked: Isaiah 1:1; 6:1 and chapter 7 refer to people and events which are corroborated elsewhere, either in Scripture or in other contemporary records. Moreover, from this lengthy text we also get glimpses of events which shape the prophet's life: 6:1–11; 7:3–17; 8; 20:1–5 all give information about both international and internal political crises as well as the religious attitudes which the prophet was called to address. Although there are many important themes running through the book of Isaiah, however, no story about the life of the prophet himself is given. By contrast, the book of Jonah provides no reference to external events corroborated elsewhere. The most significant political event, the repentance of Nineveh, is unknown from any other source. Names of kings are not given and Jonah's words give no clue to the historical setting of the book. Instead, the writer of Jonah offers a story in which the prophet's dialogue with God is the central feature. From this we recognize that these two prophetic books are different in style – which suggests we should adopt a different approach towards Jonah from that we adopt towards Isaiah.

2. Prophetic experience

While noticeable differences exist between Isaiah and Jonah, we find an area of similarity between Jonah and Jeremiah. Curiously, although described as 'a prophet' in 2 Kings 14:25, Jonah son of Amittai is not spoken of as a prophet in the book of Jonah itself. It is

[8] Gen. 2:8; 4:9–16.
[9] Gen. 18:20–23.
[10] Exod. 16:2–3.

God calling Jonah that indicates his prophetic task. The interest of the narrator lies in Jonah's response to his call rather than in his message or even in the book's historical setting. It is at this point we see a similarity between Jonah and Jeremiah. In the long text of Jeremiah, we find disclosures of the personal cost of being called by God and we are given a unique insight into Jeremiah's inner response to God's call. These disclosures, which have become known as the 'confessions' of Jeremiah, are found in Jeremiah 11:18–12:6; 15:10–21; 17:14–18; 18:18–23; 20:7–12 and 14–18. They reveal a man torn by the pain of speaking God's words to Jerusalem and yet torn by not speaking them.[11] The word 'confessions' does not appear in the biblical text, but came to be used by commentators seeking to understand the prophecy of Jeremiah. Of these so-called confessions, Skinner writes:

> The characteristic of the confessions is that in the form, frequently of monologue, but more frequently of strangely ingenious and arresting colloquy with God, they lay bare the inmost secrets of the prophet's life, his fightings without and fears within, his mental conflict with adversity and doubt and temptation, and the reaction of his whole nature on a world that threatened to crush him and a task whose difficulty overwhelmed him.[12]

In his dialogue with God, Jeremiah accused the Lord of overpowering him. We see here the cost of being called by the Lord God to be a prophet in Israel. Jonah faced a similar, costly struggle, although it is expressed in a different way from that in the book of Jeremiah.

3. *A prophetic theme*

An important theme which Jonah also has in common with Jeremiah, a sixth-century prophet in Jerusalem, is that of repentance.[13] The prophet Joel,[14] a possible contemporary of Jeremiah, also majors on this theme. On Yom Kippur, the Jewish Day of Atonement, the book of Jonah is read urging repentance.

4. *Similarities and contrasts*

As well as these affinities between Jonah and other prophets, there are also similarities between Jonah and Elijah, a ninth-century prophet in Israel. In 1 Kings 19:2ff. we read about Elijah fleeing from

[11] Jer. 20:9.
[12] Skinner, p. 202.
[13] Jer. 18:5–11, especially verse 11; cf. Jonah 3:8.
[14] See Joel 1, especially verses 13–20.

the death threat issued by Queen Jezebel. He goes first to Beersheba, requesting that he might die (v. 4). After being refreshed by sleep and food he journeys on to the mountain of God at Horeb (v. 8ff.). Here he pours out his heart to God, who then recommissions him for the work he is called to do. In similar vein, Jonah flees – not from a wicked Canaanite queen, but from the King of heaven and earth. He descends to Sheol (2:2), taking the way of death before being recommissioned in 3:1. Despite the similarities, however, the significant difference between the two prophets lies in their individual response to God's call. Jonah is portrayed as one who struggled, like a fish caught in a net, to avoid God's call, while Elijah, despite tremendous difficulties, remained obedient to God's call.[15] The unusual conclusion to the book of Jonah leaves the reader in a state of suspended animation as the prophet continues in a mood of resistance to God's all-embracing mercy. By contrast, the story of Elijah concludes with the prophet being translated into God's nearer presence.

Jonah's struggle to flee the presence of God flies in the face of a notable passage in Amos 9:2–3, where Amos asserts the total impossibility of escaping God:

> Though they dig into Sheol,
>   from there shall my hand take them;
> though they climb up to heaven,
>   from there I will bring them down.
> Though they hide themselves on the top of Carmel,
>   from there I will search out and take them;
> and though they hide from my sight at the bottom of the sea,
>   there I will command the serpent, and it shall bite them.

Despite this claim, Jonah sets out to do the impossible, to defy gravity, to flee the presence of God. A mirror image of the passage in Amos 9 is found in Psalm 139:7–10, where the psalmist meditates on the implications of the impossibility of escaping God's presence.

> Whither shall I go from thy Spirit?
>   Or whither shall I flee from thy presence?
> If I ascend to heaven, thou art there!
>   If I make my bed in Sheol, thou art there!
> If I take the wings of the morning
>   and dwell in the uttermost parts of the sea,
> even there thy hand shall lead me,
>   and thy right hand shall hold me.

[15] 2 Kgs. 2:1ff.

Here is a hint that the sovereign Lord will overcome even death (*Sheol*), a theological theme which echoes through Jonah, Amos, Hosea and Isaiah of Jerusalem.[16]

Writings

Among the so-called 'Writings',[17] the subject matter of the book of Jonah is somewhat akin to that of the book of Job. Both books display little interest in an historical setting and both place considerable emphasis on the dialogue between the main character and God. The two books also have in common the theme of God's relationship to the Gentiles; in Jonah this interest is focused in the sailors and Nineveh, while in the book of Job it is Job himself who is a Gentile.[18]

Who was Jonah?

Jonah son of Amittai is mentioned in two Old Testament texts. Both 2 Kings 14:25–28 and the book of Jonah make reference to the full name of the prophet, and both texts link the prophet to the theological theme of divine mercy. These links provide sufficient grounds for assuming a relationship between the prophet in the book of Jonah and the man in 2 Kings 14:25–28. Although likely, however, this identity cannot be guaranteed.[19]

With the exception of the psalm in Jonah 2:2–9, both these accounts are written in the third person. Unfortunately and unusually, the writer of the book of Jonah makes no direct historical allusions, for example by referring to Jeroboam II (781–746 BC) or to Jonah's other connections with Israel. Had he done this, much scholarly debate and uncertainty concerning the identity of Jonah may have been obviated. It is fair to say, however, that the prophetic author of the book of Jonah used the name, experience and reputation of the prophet from 2 Kings 14:25–28. Inspired by the Spirit of God, the chief concern of the prophetic writer was to set out the message of Jonah in a most glorious and memorable way. The theme of divine mercy which permeates and undergirds the scriptural testimony has undoubtedly gained

[16] Jonah 2; Amos 9:2; Hos. 13:14; Is. 25:8.

[17] The name given in the Hebrew Bible to the books of Psalms, Proverbs, Job, Song of Solomon, Ruth, Lamentations, Ecclesiastes, Esther, Daniel, Ezra, Nehemiah and Chronicles.

[18] Job 1:1, 'A man in the land of Uz', is likely to refer to a Gentile. See also reference in Ezek. 14:14.

[19] Eissfeldt, pp. 11–12.

added focus and poignancy having been set in the framework of a particularly disobedient prophet.

The book handles theological and spiritual issues which transcend specific historical periods. It might seem natural to assume that the story of an eighth-century prophet called Jonah would be set in eighth-century Israel, but as we have already noted, it is the theological affinities between Jonah and other prophets which point to a core of concerns clustering around, but by no means limited to, the events of the eighth century. Questions of repentance, the relationship between the chosen people and the rest of humankind, and dialogue between the human soul and its Creator all transcend a single historical setting. Concerning the book, B. S. Childs writes, 'It serves as a critical prophetic judgement on Israel in line with the rest of the prophetic witness of the Old Testament.'[20]

Hebrew prophecy is a profoundly distinctive phenomenon in world faiths. Perhaps its most significant feature is the way it throws the relationship between God and his covenant people under the spotlight. In the book of Jonah we appear, at first sight, to be caught up with an intriguing storyline. But the story itself is prophecy. Uniquely among the prophets, it addresses the relationship between God, who is undoubtedly the main character and hero of the story, and Jonah, his stiff-necked prophet. It is most likely that the prophetic writer, under the Spirit of God, saw this memorable story addressing the people of Israel. As a lengthy prophetic oracle addressed to God's people it was intended that they should recognize themselves in the person of Jonah son of Amittai. The final question is addressed to them.

His name – Yonah

His name, Jonah ben Amittai, or Jonah the son of Amittai, means 'Dove son of faithfulness'. It conjures up the image of a gentle creature with strong homing instincts. The dove is easily put to flight, seeking secure refuge in the mountains.[21] Hosea, speaking of Israel's eventual return from exile, describes her as a homing bird (*yônâ*).[22] In a more humorous vein he speaks of Israel being a 'silly' dove when she flees, seeking her home in Egypt or Assyria.[23] When in deep trouble, the psalmist longs for wings like a dove so that he could escape to find shelter elsewhere.[24]

[20] Childs, p. 426.
[21] Ps. 55:6–8; Ezek. 7:16.
[22] Hos. 11:11.
[23] Hos. 7:11.
[24] Ps. 55:4–8.

My heart is in anguish within me,
  the terrors of death have fallen upon me.
Fear and trembling come upon me,
  and horror overwhelms me.
And I say, 'O that I had wings like a dove!
  I would fly away and be at rest;
yea, I would wander afar,
  I would lodge in the wilderness, (*Selah*)
I would haste to find me a shelter
  from the raging wind and tempest.'

We can imagine such feelings inspiring Jonah's flight from what proved to be the source of all his troubles, namely God's call.

While in some sense Jonah was dove-like in that he longed for the security of home, he was also the 'son of Amittai'. We do not know who Amittai was, but we do know that his name means 'truthful', 'trustworthy', 'faithful'. Using the same root, Jeremiah 23:28 contrasts the true prophet with the false: the true prophet is one who will 'speak God's word faithfully'.

His home town – Gath-hepher

In 2 Kings 14:25 we are told that Jonah came from Gath-hepher. This is a Hebrew name meaning 'winepress of digging'. Referred to in Joshua 19:13, it was situated on the border of Zebulun and Naphtali, a few miles north-east of Nazareth. Today it is identified with Khirbet ez-Zurra and nearby Meshhed el-Meshhed ('martyr's grave'). In local tradition it has long been associated with Jonah. In the fourth century AD Jerome said the prophet's tomb was not far from Sepphoris, a location which corresponds to that of Gath-hepher.

Jesus and Jonah

Jonah's connections with Galilee remind us of the later prophet from Galilee, Jesus of Nazareth. Gath-hepher, a small village situated in the Galilean hills between Cana and Nazareth, must have been known to Jesus. We can imagine his interest in this man called Jonah, his perplexing struggle with God, his reluctant obedience and the uncertain outcome of his mission. Maybe Jonah offered some insight into the costliness of obedience. Jesus, like Jonah, was tempted to flee the rigours of God's call. But while Jonah remained faithful to the ways of his own people, Jesus transcended the comparable theology and devotion of his day, represented by the great and the good commonly known as scribes and Pharisees. He walked where Jonah walked, but lived a new life. Jonah remained faithful to what he knew, responding in fear and anger to that which threatened his security. Jesus was faithful to the God who called him, even though it led to his execution by crucifixion. Theology such as this, which did not lead to success or acclaim, but to apparent failure and death, is theology which bows in humility before the Creator and Redeemer God.

As we shall see, the ancient Hebrew tradition which gave shape to the book of Jonah critiques Jonah's attitude towards the Gentiles. By fulfilling that ancient stream of revelation, Jesus' life contrasts with that of Jonah. His teaching draws on the gracious inclusiveness of God's love and he spurns the temptation to play safe by seeking the comfort of the familiar.

While Jesus of Nazareth was a trailblazer, a man who walked by faith in God, Jonah of Gath-Hepher was a homing pigeon, an anti-hero. His chief instincts were to run away, to sleep, to hide, to die, to be angry, to be comfortable, to inhabit a predictable and familiar world. Jonah son of Amittai is the 'dove of faithfulness'. He is faithful to the familiar ways of his fathers. On his door is a large notice which says 'Do Not Disturb'. And yet he is a prophet in Israel.

So the story of Jonah from Gath-hepher, and the Jewish tradition which subsequently grew up around him concerning his miraculous restoration from death to life,[25] could well have helped shape the thinking and teaching of Jesus of Nazareth. His reference to 'the sign of Jonah' suggests that, in the contemporary Jewish tradition on which Jesus was drawing, Jonah had come to be associated with judgment, repentance and resurrection. These themes coincided very considerably with Jesus' life and teaching.

This little book ends with a question. God asks Jonah, 'And should not I pity Nineveh?' As he looked towards the great city of Nineveh, the prophet remained silent. As Jesus looked at the great city of Jerusalem from the Mount of Olives some centuries later, his response was quite different.

The 'sign' of Jonah

In the way that Moses, the true prophet, had performed signs in Egypt,[26] so we read in the Synoptic Gospels of people asking Jesus

[25] 'Lives of the Prophets', an early Jewish text discussed in Hooker, chapter 2.
[26] Exod. 7:9ff.

for a sign. They could see that he was like a prophet, but they wanted an authenticating miracle, a sign, which would prove to them that he was a true prophet of God. His response was decisive: only one sign would be given to those who demanded a sign, and that was 'the sign of Jonah'. This is referred to in three passages.

The first comes in Matthew 12:39–42:

> But he answered them, 'An evil and adulterous generation seeks for a sign; but no sign shall be given to it except the sign of the prophet Jonah. For as Jonah was three days and three nights in the belly of the whale, so will the Son of man be three days and three nights in the heart of the earth. The men of Nineveh will arise at the judgment with this generation and condemn it; for they repented at the preaching of Jonah, and behold, something greater than Jonah is here.'

Here Jesus speaks of Jonah as the sign. His three days and nights in the belly of the whale is spoken of as prefiguring Jesus' three days and three nights in the heart of the earth. Ultimately, the 'sign' which would validate Jesus' teaching would be his resurrection. But Jesus does not leave it there. In the way that Jonah's deliverance from the fish was a 'sign' to the prophet himself that he could not escape God's word, so it was with these religious leaders; even if they rejected the Christ they would not be able to escape God's word. Unlike the scribes and Pharisees, the people of Nineveh did not seek a sign to persuade them of the truth of God's words through Jonah; they knew it for themselves. It was their response which validated God's call through the prophet. In speaking to the scribes and Pharisees, Jesus implies that they could learn something from the Ninevites, who repented when they heard God's word. The Ninevites were able to recognize the authority of God's word when they, the considered experts, could not.

The second reference is in Matthew 16:4:

> 'An evil and adulterous generation seeks for a sign, but no sign shall be given to it except the sign of Jonah.' So he left them and departed.

In Matthew's second mention of the 'sign of Jonah', no explanation is offered. This suggests that the Pharisees and Sadducees to whom Jesus was speaking would know what was meant. As in Matthew's earlier passage, we see religious leaders in their role as guardians of the flock seeking to test Jesus. There is a not-too-distant echo here of Psalm 95:8–9. Where hearts are hardened, signs count for little.

For the religious leaders, Jesus' works of healing and grace, as recounted in Matthew 15, were reckoned insufficient validation of his claims. But in the same way that the repentance of Nineveh was sufficient authentication of Jonah's ministry, so, for those willing to believe, Jesus' works were an authentication of his ministry.

The third and final passage is Luke 11:29–32:

> When the crowds were increasing, he began to say, 'This generation is an evil generation; it seeks a sign, but no sign shall be given to it except the sign of Jonah. For as Jonah became a sign to the men of Nineveh, so will the Son of man be to this generation. The queen of the South will arise at the judgment with the men of this generation and condemn them; for she came from the ends of the earth to hear the wisdom of Solomon, and behold, something greater than Solomon is here. The men of Nineveh will arise at the judgment with this generation and condemn it; for they repented at the preaching of Jonah, and behold, something greater than Jonah is here.'

As Jonah became a sign to Nineveh leading them to repent, so Jesus, who here speaks of himself as 'greater than Jonah', was a sign to his generation, although they failed to repent. The sign which authenticated Jonah's message was that the people of Nineveh recognized God's word to them through the prophet and repented. Jonah was a sign to the Ninevites as a prophet, not as a survivor of drowning. As Stuart argues, in Jonah chapter 3 there is no evidence whatever that anyone in Nineveh knew about the events of chapter 2.[27] What the Ninevites believe in is God, not Jonah. His authority comes from God's word, not his earlier experiences. By contrast, in clamouring for a sign, many of Jesus' contemporaries failed to see that Jesus and his message were the word of God. Ironically, Jonah preached judgment to the Ninevites and the result was mercy; but the One who was greater than Jonah preached mercy and the result for that generation was judgment. As we shall see later, it is perhaps significant that in Luke's account Jesus was on the road to Jerusalem when he spoke these words.[28]

Desmond Alexander makes a further suggestion which helpfully illuminates our understanding of the meaning of the 'sign of Jonah'. Drawing on contemporary Jewish sources,[29] he quotes the writing of Rabbi Jonathan (AD 140):

[27] Stuart, p. 497.
[28] Luke 9:51.
[29] Mekhilta Exodus 12:1.

> The only purpose of Jonah was to bring judgement on himself in the sea, for it is written, 'And he said to them, "Take me and cast me into the sea."' [Jonah 1:12] Similarly you find that many patriarchs and prophets sacrificed themselves for Israel.

Alexander comments: 'Might this understanding of Jonah suggest Jesus' understanding himself as one who would give his life for others?'[30] Indeed, and might this not be an authenticating sign of the servant of the Lord?

Although in considering the 'sign of Jonah' we have drawn some parallels between Jonah and Jesus, it is instructive to see that in several respects the two were very dissimilar. For example, Jonah was disobedient, while Jesus was obedient; Jonah was angered by Nineveh's repentance, while Jesus wept over Jerusalem's refusal to repent; and although Jonah was perhaps more successful in gaining a response to his message than any other prophet in Scripture, the ministry of Jesus to his generation appeared to end in failure.

'This generation'

Jesus says that Jonah is a sign to 'this generation'. In what way was Jonah a sign to Jesus' contemporaries? To help us consider this in a little more depth, we shall look briefly at another contemporary Jewish text[31] which may further enrich our understanding. It is possible to assume from this material that the expression 'the sign of Jonah' was common currency in Jesus' day.

'The Lives of the Prophets', a kind of early Jewish commentary, identifies Jonah with the son of the widow of Zarephath.[32] This may well sound a little odd to us, not least since there is no mention of it in the Hebrew Scripture, but the story offers an insight into a feature of popular thought in Jesus' generation. It focuses on the God who brought new life to Jonah, the widow's son in Zarephath. It goes on to tell how the restored Jonah returned to Jerusalem to foretell its destruction. Here Jonah is an amazing sign of new life, as well as a sign warning the city to repent. In the story, Jonah says that two indicators of the city's imminent destruction would be 'the stones crying out piteously' and 'the city being filled with Gentiles'. The original biblical accounts of Jonah and the widow of Zarephath contain no mention of Jerusalem, but these stories of hope and resurrection

[30] Alexander, p. 94.

[31] 'The Lives of the Prophets', a Jewish text dating from approximately the first century AD; see Hooker, chapter 2.

[32] 1 Kgs. 17:9ff. Also mentioned by Jesus in Luke 4:26. In the NT 'Sarepta'.

were brought together to address the first-century problem of Jerusalem.

Dominated by Herod's great temple and boasting some of the most wealthy and elaborate houses for priestly officials, the magnificent city of Jerusalem in Jesus' day was occupied by the Romans. The city was of central significance to the Jewish faith, yet, while under pagan control, its future remained compromised. The prophet Jonah, in the 'Lives of the Prophets', warned of the city's destruction. Jesus, the One who was greater than Jonah, referred to the 'sign of Jonah' as a sharp reminder of the urgent need for repentance. It may be that in using this phrase, Jesus was saying to the people of his day that the destruction of Jerusalem was imminent. In the same way that Jonah had been a sign of God's judgment and mercy towards Nineveh, so now Jesus was a sign of God's judgment and mercy towards the Jerusalem of his generation. Those of Jesus' generation were under the same judgment as Nineveh. Mercifully, the One who was greater than Jonah was willing to save.

It will never be known whether the repentance of the city might have averted the terrible destruction which befell Jerusalem in AD 70 in the way that the repentance of the Ninevites brought about the deliverance of that great city. In the event, the stones did not cry out piteously for Jerusalem; rather, Jesus wept over her.[33] Ultimately, the resurrection of Christ proved to be the supreme sign of God's mercy and forgiveness. Ironically, it found greater acceptance among the Gentiles than among the Jews.

Guardians of the tradition

In this connection it is clear from the Gospels that many of the ordinary Jewish people of Jesus' generation did in fact turn to him, recognizing in him the work of God. As we have seen from these verses, the greatest opposition appears to have come from the religious leaders, those faithful guardians of the tradition and teaching concerning the nature of God. The influence of religious leaders can be considerable for both good and ill. In their very attempt to remain faithful to their interpretation of the Scriptures several of the leading Pharisees of Jesus' day rejected the One of whom their Scripture spoke. The irony of this is staggering. As those responsible for the spiritual leadership of the community, they felt an anger towards a God who could not be constrained by their systems of faithfulness, but who was free to rule according to what threatened to be a chaotic or uncontrollable law of grace. Yet God's gracious and unreasonable love is the sinner's only hope.

[33] Luke 19:41.

Aware of the ever-present difficulty for those in positions of religious authority, Albert Nolan has suggested that the 'sign of Jonah' is that the scribes and Pharisees, like Jonah, were angry towards Jesus because they did not want God to be merciful to sinners. Such an approach to God as Jesus appeared to be offering would undermine their authority and status in the community and their role in maintaining moral order. In interpreting the reference in Jonah 4:11 to the people of Nineveh as 'ordinary people who cannot tell their right hand from their left in terms of theological sophistication', Nolan writes:

> This is surely what must serve as a sign to the Pharisees. God is once again relenting and feeling compassion for simple people. God has changed and that is why the times have changed. It is a new time, a break with the past; a time which can only be understood in terms of the new eschaton, the new definite future event – the kingdom of the poor and the oppressed.[34]

'The sign of Jonah' – a Gospel theme

Before leaving this point we need to return to the teaching of the Gospels. Here we find that Jesus told many parables which clearly reflect the dominant theme of divine mercy for the penitent. In his stories, this mercy is vividly offset against the stiff-necked attitude of Jonah-type figures. For example, the 'unmerciful servant' who, having been forgiven a great debt, could not forgive his servant a lesser debt portrays a Jonah figure.[35] Again, in the parable of the prodigal son, the elder son, unable to celebrate his father's gracious welcome of the younger son, is a Jonah figure.[36] In the parable of the Pharisee and tax collector at prayer,[37] the Pharisee is acutely aware of his own spiritual stature but is dismissive of the tax collector's humble penitence. The Pharisee is a Jonah figure. Similarly, in the story of the labourers in the vineyard,[38] those who bore the heat of the day and then complained bitterly when they were rewarded at the same rate as those who had spent only a short time at work are akin to Jonah.

In all these stories there is a tension between the 'religious insiders' who believe they are worthy of God's favour and those 'outsiders' who hardly dare imagine that God has anything for them. In

[34] Nolan, p. 80.
[35] Matt. 18:23–35.
[36] Luke 15:11–32. At the end of this parable, Jesus leaves us wondering how the elder son will respond to his father's compassionate generosity. Here is an echo of the inconclusive ending of the story of Jonah.
[37] Luke 18:9–14.
[38] Matt. 20:1–16.

his attitude towards Nineveh, Jonah was showing the same characteristics as the Pharisees of Jesus' day. 'The story of Jonah is the story of the religious 'insider' – whether in post-exilic Judaism, at the time of Jesus, and today in the Synagogue as well as in the Church.'[39]

Here, the 'sign of Jonah' is the way people respond to the call to repent. In the biblical story, Nineveh's repentance infuriated Jonah. Jonah was unwilling to change his ways: the 'sign of Jonah' may be an unwillingness to repent in the presence of God. Looking at it this way, the 'sign of Jonah' signalled God's generosity in the face of human hardness. Penitent sinners, be they debtors or tax collectors, Jew or Gentile, believer or unbeliever, insiders or outsiders, may turn and be saved, despite continued resistance from the stiff-necked 'Jonah' figures.

Yom Kippur

For centuries the book of Jonah has been read on the Day of Atonement. Yom Kippur, or the Day of Atonement, is the most solemn fast day in the Jewish liturgical year. The origins of this major penitential season are traced in the book of Leviticus. The message of Jonah, which is appointed to be read in the afternoon service, underlines so many of the great lessons of Yom Kippur – that it is impossible to run away from God's presence, that God takes pity on all his creatures, and that he is ever willing to accept true repentance. Still today, Yom Kippur marks the time when Jewish people come in penitence before the Lord and seek restoration with the human community, including not only the immediate circle of family, friends and colleagues, but also the wider human community of peoples and nations.

Within the broader spectrum of Jewish theology, the role of God's ancient people Israel *vis-à-vis* the nations of the earth is that they are to be God's chosen means of blessing to the nations. The purpose of their election is first stated in Genesis 12:2–3. We find an echo of this understanding in the early second century AD. Using the imagery of Jonah and the mariners in the great storm, Rabbi Johanon, writing in *c.* 140, suggests:

> The ship is a type of the world which only can find its salvation through the willing martyrdom of the Hebrew, who, although inoffensive in his conduct with his fellow-men of all nationalities, is nevertheless quite willing to allow himself to be doomed to

[39] Knight and Golka, p. 132.

> destruction in order to relieve his fellow-men of the threatened ruin.[40]

Jonah, the Hebrew, is seen here as giving his life in order to save the pagan sailors, his fellow men.

Another Jewish commentator writes from a contrasting perspective about the choice of the book of Jonah for reading at Yom Kippur.

> Jonah, the son of Amittai, revolted against God. He wished to place his own will, and his limited concept of Justice above God's command . . . He suspected God of 'weakness' and a desire to act not according to the strict letter of the law, or of seeking to avert a punishment which He had already decreed upon the people of Nineveh . . . What he forgot was that mercy and forgiveness were in themselves part of a righteous judgement . . . That is why the Book of Jonah fits so well into the Yom Kippur service. The very sense of the Day of Atonement is faith in providence and denial of fate; faith in repentance and its redeeming power, hatred of evil in man and hope that man will ultimately overcome that evil. The moral horizon of Yom Kippur is wide and distinct, limitless and universal, in the perspective of which the barrier between one of the covenant and one of the uncircumcised is obliterated . . . On Yom Kippur prayers are offered for Nineveh, for all the Ninevehs of the world.[41]

It is in confession of our sin, weakness and failure that, as believers in God's mercy, we open ourselves to the possibility of compassion towards others. It is through a recognition that all people are created with a capacity to hear and respond in repentance to God's word that hope of salvation can be nurtured. It is in seeing that our own salvation is contingent on the salvation of others that we can enter the gates of heaven. It is through a realization that God can forgive even the Ninevehs of this world that believers open themselves to the hope of forgiveness.

One of the prayers which may be used in the concluding service of the Day of Atonement is as follows:

> We have grown accustomed to sin, and the fragments of scripture lie shattered in our life; charity has withered with calculation, and the sparks of purity have burnt out. Yet still we come on Yom

[40] Assembly of Rabbis, p. 995.
[41] Ibid., pp. 1018–1019.

Kippur, and God who said, 'I have forgiven' whispers it again to us, and waits for our reply.

> What shall it be? What form will it take?
> Let us repair what can still be repaired.
> Let us give back the gain we earned by injustice.
> Let us make peace with our injured brother.
> Let us restore the person we wronged.
> Let us admit what is false in ourselves.
> Let us put right what is wrong in our family life.
> Let us not sour the joy of living.
>
> May God give us the courage to do these things and help us to rebuild our lives. And when we have finished our tasks, may He permit us to enjoy the light sown for the righteous so that He can delight in us.
> The Gates of His Mercy are still open. Let us enter in.[42]

As the reading draws to an end we find the Lord gently enquiring of his prophet, 'And should I not pity Nineveh?' If Jonah replies 'Yes' then he embarks on the way of repentance and travels to a new place. If he replies 'No' then he is locked into self-righteous anger and immobilized. In the text he remains silent as the Lord God offers him the way to life. I have forgiven, he whispers, and waits patiently for his, and our, reply.

[42] Ibid., p. 653.

1. The literary genre of Jonah

The traditional Christian doctrine has always been that Jesus Christ is the Word of God.[1] Holy Scripture bears witness to Christ as the Word of God. The Scriptures, inspired by the Spirit of God, testify to God's revelation to humanity, a revelation which finds its highest pinnacle in the Lord Jesus Christ, who is *the* Word of God incarnate.

Sacred Scripture is a literary anthology. The pages of the Old Testament in particular offer a wide range of literary styles and forms. As we read its pages we recognize different kinds of writing. Each book of the Bible gives clues which shape our expectations. For example, following the Hebrew text, the Psalms and much of the prophetic literature is set out in modern translations of the Bible in poetic form. By contrast, earlier English translations set out each of these texts as if they were prose. Whether reading poetry or prose, readers adopt an approach to the literature which shapes their expectations of it.

Scripture also uses different literary forms or genres to convey the word of God. No one form is adequate to the task; many forms are needed to witness to the glorious riches of gospel truth. The genres we encounter as we range over Hebrew Scripture include letters (Jer. 29), royal edicts (Ezra 1), songs (Is. 5), sermons (Deut.), court records (2 Sam. 20:23–26), liturgical rubrics (Lev. 6), parables (2 Sam. 12), allusions to Ancient Near Eastern myths (Is. 51:9), genealogies (1 Chr. 1–9), codes of moral teaching (Exod. 20), accounts of battles (2 Kgs. 23), love songs (Song) and much more. We also find examples of historical data, as in Isaiah 1:1, and specific theological interpretation, as in 2 Kings 14:26–28. All the books of Scripture have their own integrity and authenticity. Their theological and spiritual truth is recognized in the way that they correspond to the whole range of human experience. When inspired by the Holy Spirit of God, prayerful reflection on human experience in the presence of God may give birth to what is called 'revealed truth'.

[1] John 1:2–3.

Readers also bring to the text certain expectations of the kind of truth they may encounter. For example, Christians are frequently drawn to the kind of truth expressed in the Psalms. They anticipate the poetry of the Psalms having the capacity to plumb the spiritual depths of human experience. On the other hand, we generally expect the prose of 1 Chronicles to give us clips of information which were considered important within the overall theological conventions of that book. Similarly, we anticipate a different aspect of truth in Genesis 1 from that which we encounter in Ezra 1. Again we find in the Gospel of Mark a different way of communicating the truth about Jesus Christ from that found in the epistle to the Hebrews. All these texts glow endlessly with different facets of incomparable divine truth. All are bearers of God's truth and their genre is necessarily gloriously diverse.

This is not to cast doubt on the fundamental nature of revealed truth in Scripture. Nor is it to deny the indispensable work of God's Holy Spirit in enlivening the truth of God's word in different ways at different times. Rather, it is to recognize that the Word of God in Jesus Christ cannot be contained in any one kind of literary form. The gospel of God breaks through our literary conventions. They are no more than earthen vessels. As we have seen, holy Scripture makes use of many different styles of human literature: poetry, narrative, letter, genealogy, court records, liturgy. Just as there is no one single form of literature to express the rich diversity of human culture, so no one single literary form is adequate to give full expression to God's word. Together these different literary forms testify to the precious spiritual Bread and Water of Life. Even as the heaven of heavens cannot contain him, neither can our different modes of human literature and expression.

Clues concerning the genre of Jonah

What type of literature are we reading when we turn to Jonah? What kinds of truth may we expect to encounter as we read the book? To respond to these questions we must consider the genre of Jonah. A superficial glance at the text shows that chapter 2 is clearly in poetic form. Immediately that simple observation suggests how we might read it. By contrast chapters 1, 3 and 4 are set out in prose. Do we therefore expect them to retell an historical event, or is the story they tell an extended parable? What kinds of truth may we encounter as we follow Jonah on his amazing journey? Are we reading an historical account of the prophet's life written from a theological perspective? Or are we reading theological truth distilled from historical reality but expressed for us here in parable form?

Scholars have argued for various possibilities such as that Jonah is a humorous treatise against Jewish exclusivism in the post-exilic era, or that the text reflects a general loss of confidence in the prophets in Israel following the restoration from exile in Babylon. What clues are available to help us understand what we are reading in these four short chapters?

History is the beginning but not the end

While the very existence of the Bible is clear testimony to significant historical realities and facts, it is plain to see that the Bible itself is much more than an ancient historical narrative spanning a period of over two thousand years. Events of history recounted in the Bible are, like all human history, mediated through the perspective of interpreters. Even inspired theological interpreters sometimes give the same historical events different significance. The significance they attribute to an event will depend on their perspective and their underlying purpose in recounting the history. For example, when telling the history of Israel and Judah the writers of 1 and 2 Kings offer a different perspective from that found in 1 and 2 Chronicles. Sometimes the storyline itself has curious differences; a notable example of this is found in their respective accounts of King Manasseh.[2]

It cannot be doubted that the text of the Bible is shaped by events in human history. However, the meaning of those events, for example the exodus, is disclosed by the word of God to his people, Israel. These theological disclosures lead to a writing of history in a way which transcends the actual events. Thus we see in the Scriptures theological truth being expressed in images and motifs which give flesh to abstractions and propositions. A biblical scholar has correctly said that the Bible speaks

> ... largely in images ... The stories, the parables, the sermons of the prophets, the reflections of the wise men, the pictures of the age to come, the interpetations of past events all tend to be expressed in images which arise out of experience. They do not often arise out of abstract technical language.[3]

For example, the transformative story of the Israelites crossing the Red Sea is infused throughout the literature of the Old Testament.

[2] Compare 2 Kgs. 21 and 2 Chr. 33.

[3] J. A. Fischer, *How to Read the Bible* (Englewood Cliffs, N.J.: Prentice Hall, 1981), p. 39, quoted in Ryken, Wilhoit, Longman III (eds.), *Dictionary of Biblical Imagery*.

It was the key event by which the Lord God brought his people, Israel, into existence. It portrayed her as the Lord's 'firstborn', as a 'priceless jewel' in his crown, as the wife of the Lord. All manner of images were deployed as a way of expressing the Lord's unique covenant relationship with Israel. An event, grounded in an actual human experience, became the window through which God's chosen people came to understand and interpret their entire history. The exodus transcended history; it became a fundamental article of faith, a reality by which the history of God's people came to be judged. It was the key to understanding the identity and calling of Israel. It came to be expressed by means of powerful and vibrant images which resonate with the human condition. Images such as slaves being freed to worship and serve the King of kings, slaves being the chosen people, a kingdom of priests, the ones to inherit the Promised Land, abound in this story. Such images resonate deeply with the human calling to identify the purpose and meaning of life lived in relationship to a creating and redeeming Lord.

Translating all this in terms of how we might read the book of Jonah, we need, first, to notice that the two books, Exodus and Jonah, are different. The first sets out the theological and historical framework in which God's people come to exist, while the second paints a picture of how God's people sometimes behave towards God and others. Concerning Jonah, we could say that the four chapters describe an historical event. Thus everything described, his attitude towards God, the sailors, the great fish, Nineveh's repentance, the worm and the castor oil plant, are all factually necessary to the divine revelation. This approach is well attested from antiquity and is still followed by some commentators.[4] Alternatively, we could say that in this short book the meaning of the prophet's personal experience is being interpreted to us theologically by means of a parable.[5] As an equally well-attested means of divine revelation, the parable makes use of powerful and humorous imagery in disclosing a rather unpalatable truth about God's people. The historical reality of Jonah's attitudes towards the Lord and Nineveh are not in doubt; the divine disclosure of God's mercy towards Nineveh is not in doubt. It is the way these truths come to be expressed which gives them a wider and more enduring application. The concern is no longer with the historical Jonah, with what he said and did and

[4] For example, Alexander, *Jonah*. Readers will find a helpful résumé of key points in this debate.

[5] See also article entitled 'Jonah, Book of' in Ryken, Wilhoit, and Longman III (eds.). The entry describes the book of Jonah as 'a satire – the exposure of human vice through ridicule. In fact the book is a handbook on how *not* to be a prophet' (p. 458).

when, but with the universal motifs of human disobedience in the face of God's call.

In particular, the book of Jonah draws out themes of the sovereign grace of the Lord God in the face of human evil. These theological truths are the glory of the book. They are not grounded in a wishful imagination, nor do they inhabit the minds of the deluded; they are grounded in the ongoing and experienced ways of the Lord God with his people through the millennia. In a sense, the book of Jonah is a little like a testimony. The nature of the profound truth conveyed concerns the relationship between the Lord God of Israel and Jonah son of Amittai. The story is told not simply as a historical memoir of a disobedient man, but as a significant way of challenging those who claim to know and love the Lord to consider all his ways. Whether we take the book as 'history with a moral' or as 'parable grounded in experience', there is no doubt about its overriding message.

In the three Gospel accounts of his allusions to Jonah, Jesus draws attention to himself as being a 'sign' to this 'evil generation' just as Jonah was a sign to Nineveh.[6] He also says, 'As Jonah was three days and three nights in the belly of the whale, so will the Son of man be three days and three nights in the heart of the earth.'[7] Here Jesus makes use of popular Jewish thinking in which the disobedient Jonah of the biblical text had come to be linked with a miracle of resurrection.[8] Referring to both Jonah and himself suffering death, Jesus implies that it is the Son of man who will actually and literally be raised from the dead. He argues that Someone greater than Jonah is standing in the midst, yet those seeing and hearing him are blind to what they see and deaf to what they hear. Here it must be acknowledged that, for some readers, the historicity of Jesus' resurrection implies the historicity of Jonah. For others, Jesus is making a statement about himself, the One who is greater than Jonah. Drawing on language and imagery which was familiar to his audience, he was drawing attention to himself and away from the disobedient prophet. In the event, the historicity of Jesus' resurrection does not depend on the historicity of Jonah's incarceration in and eventual expulsion from the belly of the great fish. It depends on the uniqueness of the Lord Jesus Christ, the extent of New Testament testimony, the consequent transformation of hundreds of thousands of human lives and the ongoing witness of the Christian church throughout the world.

[6] Luke 11:29–30.

[7] Matt. 12:40. It should be noted that too literal an approach to these words raises the problem of why, according to the Gospel accounts, Jesus was not in the tomb for three days and three nights.

[8] See Introduction, pp. 33–39.

That Jonah was called by God is beyond doubt, but the book in which the call of Jonah is worked out is a prophetic oracle in parable form. It is an historical fact that God's people were called to serve him and were often guilty of disobedience to his call. This stance does not underestimate the evidently historical dimensions of Scripture. Rather, it reflects a judgment being made on the literary genre of Jonah having a greater affinity with the art of parable than with historical writing.

Set in parable style, Jonah's stance in regard to his call is sketched against the background of the giantesque. With the exception of his call, everything to Jonah was larger than life. His task was bigger than that of other prophets; this dove-like man was called to go alone to preach God's judgment to the aggressive, powerful, distant and huge city of Nineveh. His brief, eight-word sermon provokes a thoroughgoing repentance of this city from top to bottom. The fish which swallows Jonah is of monstrous size. Over against all these giants looming on Jonah's little horizon is the lavish, immeasurable and unfathomable grace and mercy of the Lord God. But this he cannot see; Jonah is too caught up with great things.

Whether we regard the story of Jonah as history or as something else, it cannot be doubted that we have in these forty-eight verses an incomparable story. While of itself it may fascinate and intrigue, it is the magnificent articulation and portrayal of the character of God, so consonant with the teaching of the Lord Jesus Christ, which grips and absorbs us. To express these truths in the form of a parable is no diminishment of its meaning, any more than the truth offered by Jesus in his story of the prodigal son or Dives and Lazarus is lessened by their literary genre.

In searching the text for clues to the genre of Jonah we might consider evidence from the following sources.

The canon of Scripture

Ecclesiasticus 49:10 refers to 'the twelve prophets'.[9] From this we can deduce that by the early first century BC Jonah was reckoned among this prophetic collection. However, this is only marginally helpful in our search for clues concerning the genre of Jonah. Even a casual reading of just two of 'the twelve' prophetic texts, such as Jonah and Nahum, shows striking differences between them. In one, the reader is driven by the pace of a narrative story, and in the other pounded by a series of awful oracles of judgment against Nineveh.

[9] Hosea, Joel, Amos, Obadiah, Jonah, Micah, Nahum, Habakkuk, Zephaniah, Haggai, Zechariah, Malachi.

If we were to read all 'the twelve' we would discover that, in terms of literary style, Jonah is the odd one out. There is no implication here that Jonah was not a prophet; by its very inclusion the text was clearly regarded as prophetic. The case here is simply that the prophetic text of Jonah is most unusual when compared with the other eleven texts in which it is set.

Prophecy

This leads us to ask how prophecy was understood. Both Jonah and, for example, Nahum were included in the prophetic collection, so we are forced to see that two very different kinds of texts were reckoned as prophecy. We discover that this is in keeping with a very broad view of prophecy in the Hebrew Scripture generally. For example, the books we know as 1 and 2 Samuel and 1 and 2 Kings were known from ancient times as the 'former prophets'. In other words, they were conceived primarily as prophetic texts and not historical texts in the modern sense of the word 'history'. They comprise narratives written from a theological stance – that is, the narratives are interpreted from a prophetic perspective. The prophets discern the work and word of God in the events that are related in these texts. The book of Jonah is likely to be the work of a prophet discerning God's word as he interprets the experience of the people of Israel.

Historical

The Bible reader is first introduced to the historical Jonah in the 'former prophets'. In 2 Kings 14:25 we are given specific information concerning his home town, family origins and the name of the Israelite king with whose reign he was historically associated.[10] Following an account of Jonah's work, we are given a prophetic interpretation which sets his work in a particular theological context.[11]

> For the LORD saw that the affliction of Israel was very bitter, for there was none left, bond or free, and there was none to help Israel. But the LORD had not said that he would blot out the name of Israel from under heaven, so he saved them by the hand of Jeroboam the son of Joash.

[10] Whether or not Jonah and Jeroboam II were contemporaries is unknown, but 2 Kings 14:25 states that the word of the Lord through Jonah was fulfilled in the days of Jeroboam II.

[11] 2 Kgs. 14:26–28.

> Now the rest of the acts of Jeroboam, and all that he did, and his might, how he fought, and how he recovered for Israel Damascus and Hamath, which had belonged to Judah, are they not written in the Book of the Chronicles of the Kings of Israel?

God's grace towards his people was associated with Jonah's prophecy. This might be an important clue in discerning the genre of the book of Jonah. Israel is described as having 'none to help' her. Through the words of Jonah the Lord is her 'helper'. Could it also be that the Lord, who had created all the nations of the earth, might be a helper to other nations in their distress? The answer to that question would depend on how Jonah, or Israel, viewed the people of Nineveh.

Absence of historical interest

For some reason, the book of Jonah lacks the kind of historical data found in 2 Kings 14. No dates are given. No mention is made of Jeroboam II or even the name of the king of Nineveh, reflecting a lack of interest with historical data such as characterizes other prophetic texts. Any expectations we may have of a clear historical context are simply not fulfilled by the text. In most other prophetic texts there are indications of a historical period, given either by reference to a date or to the reign of a king.[12] Since this is a common feature elsewhere in Scripture, we may infer that its absence in the book of Jonah is a clue suggesting that a specific historical context is not essential to understanding the book's message. This could suggest that the book has a primarily theological interest generated by a range of historical events. For example, although many psalms echo historical events, detailed references to them have been omitted since the point of the psalm is no longer the events themselves, but the theology which has emerged from them. In this way fundamental theological principles have gained a wider application.

The book of Jonah and 2 Kings 14

It is possible that a further clue to the genre of Jonah may be found in the opening phrase of Jonah 1:1. Characteristically, the first Hebrew word of the text, *wayᵉhî*, which may be rendered 'And it happened that...' or 'Now it was that...', heralds the start of a story. The absence of this word at the opening of the other prophetic books points to its use here as peculiar to Jonah. The expression is,

[12] Jer. 1:1–3; Ezek. 1:2; Hos. 1:1; Amos 1:1; Mic. 1:1; Zeph. 1:1, etc.

however, frequently found in narrative literature,[13] and with two exceptions (1 Sam 1:1 speaking of Elkanah, and 1 Kings 16:1 speaking of Jehu) refers to individuals who have already been mentioned in the text. Thus, here in Jonah, some previous knowledge of the prophet is being assumed. This clue underlines the prophet's actual existence; the story in the book of Jonah may focus on a feature of the man's relationship to the Lord.

It is very likely that we are intended to see historical continuity between 2 Kings 14:25–26 and Jonah. Although there remain obvious differences in literary style between them, the reference to God's mercy suggests there is undoubtedly some theological affinity between the two texts. Might this suggest that the book of Jonah is an exploration of the significant theological themes of 2 Kings 14:25–26? In both texts Jonah is associated with the Lord's goodness and mercy in the face of evil. While 2 Kings speaks of the Lord's compassion towards Israel despite the wickedness of her king, Jeroboam II, Jonah 4 speaks of the Lord's compassion towards Nineveh despite her wickedness. The text also highlights the Lord's mercy towards the prophet himself despite his callous obstinacy. In both texts the prophet Jonah is associated with the grace of God. While in 2 Kings this appears to enhance his standing, in the book of Jonah the prophet experiences the costly pain of the grace of God. He struggles, unsuccessfully, to reconcile the justice and mercy of God in relation to Nineveh, whereas in 2 Kings he may have presumed on that same justice and mercy in relation to Israel.

A prophetic oracle or a story about a prophet?

The book of Jonah is evidently a story about a prophet and in sharp contrast to other books which bear the name of a prophet, it contains only one brief oracle (3:4). In other collections brief stories about the prophet sometimes serve to give clues to the historical context into which the prophet is called to speak the word of the Lord. For example, both Isaiah 20:1 and Jeremiah 36 are passages which paint the background to the oracle. By contrast, the book of Jonah paints a unique and fascinating picture of the prophet, his character and the adventures which befall him. The pretext of his all-too-brief oracle in 3:4 is simply the 'wickedness of Nineveh'. The narrator is concerned to give more attention to the character of Jonah than to the wickedness of Nineveh. Curiously, he reveals much more about the nature of Jonah's rebellion against God's word than about Nineveh's rebellion.

[13] Eg. Josh. 1:1; Judg 1:1; Ruth 1:1; 1 Sam. 1:1, etc.

By contrast with the precision we find in the passages of Isaiah and Jeremiah already referred to, the 'wickedness of Nineveh' lacks any comparable sense of historical precision. The focus and emphasis of this short text remains firmly on the prophet's unparalleled response to God's call. Corresponding to the unheard-of horror of his response, the story leads the reader through unknown territory. Striking literary artistry shapes the brief narrative featuring the Creator God speaking to a great fish, the wind, a plant and a worm. Astoundingly, the wicked Nineveh, the oldest and greatest city in the world, demonstrates wholesale repentance on hearing the eight-word oracle of a foreign prophet. Even more amazingly, the story leaves Jonah, surely the patron saint of evangelists, unrepentant. The focus is on Jonah. The story of the prophet is itself the prophetic oracle.

Jonah as a theological text

Not all books have an obvious historical provenance, but it is fair to say that in all biblical books there is a grappling with the revealed nature of the God of Israel. As the people of Israel reflected on their experience in prayer, debate, joy and tragedy, their prayerful struggling raised questions: 'Who is God?' and 'Where is God?' in all their experience. Such questions opened their hearts and minds to fresh revelations of his nature. Such struggles are frequently found on the lips of the psalmists.[14]

Here it is crucial to remind ourselves that the Scriptures are not a systematic theology of God but an ongoing pilgrimage with God who is the great Shepherd of the sheep. Fundamental questions concerning evil, suffering and death have teased and tormented the minds and hearts of women and men for generations. Texts from different parts of the Ancient Near East also reflect this struggle, showing attempts to understand and explain unanswerable questions which remain even into the third millennium of the Christian era.

The book of Jonah shows an interest in the nature and meaning of Israel's vocation, in repentance, election, justice and mercy. There were periods in the history of both Israel and Judah when these issues were pressing. For example, did defeat and exile mean that God had deserted his people or that he was unable, through some lack of power, wisdom or love, to save them? In such circumstances were they left to their own devices and, if so, what did that say about the nature of a God they believed to be faithful to his covenant with them? While it might be asserted on moral grounds

[14]Eg. Pss. 44, 74, 88.

that some individuals deserved punishment, what could be asserted on moral grounds concerning those who remained faithful to God but who nevertheless suffered the same tortures as the wicked? And what could be said of the wicked who appeared not to suffer at all? Or what of the nations who followed other gods and prospered, apparently enjoying great blessings? What had the Lord God got to do with that? Closer to home, what could be said of the apostate Israelite king, Jeroboam II, whose reign was blessed with much longed-for peace and prosperity?

Jonah's interest in these big theological themes is set within an overall context of a journey or pilgrimage. As he goes he discovers that God goes with him. He cannot shake God off. He cannot hide, lose himself or put himself in such bad odour with God that he is deserted by him. This is one of the most significant themes penetrating the whole of this brief text. It suggests a searingly honest appraisal by a prophet of the ubiquitous human desire and inclination to do one's own thing instead of journeying through life's wilderness with God. Worthy of equal note is the absence on the prophet's part of any sense of penitence or act of repentance. The impression given is of a self-righteous person who has little awareness of his own need of divine mercy. So deeply embedded are these expressions of human arrogance and sin in the prophet's attitude and psyche that God's faithful commitment to remain with him, if only as a constant irritant in his life, is seen as a profound act of divine humility and sheer love. This is indeed 'a gracious and merciful God, slow to anger, and abounding in steadfast love, and ready to relent from punishment'.[15]

Does the writer set out to describe a religious experience?

Whatever its historical provenance, the book portrays a familiar spiritual struggle. Different images are used to speak of the inner conflict experienced by the prophet. He hides himself away, yet cannot escape God's presence. In seeking almost to become a nonentity, he is swallowed by something greater than himself and is forced to recognize that life is bigger than his own horizons. Even in his disobedience to God's call he discovers God still revealing himself to those who had not looked for him. He discovers that God's work is not hindered by his rebellion; rather, his rebellion is made all the more painful to bear in the presence of this unstoppable God. He longs for God to be God, yet fights against a God who

[15] Jonah 4:2, and many other parts of the Old Testament. See also chapter 8, pp. 185–189.

insists on being himself; he longs to escape from God, yet yearns to be rescued by God. He experiences inner turbulence and is inconsistent, going from extreme anger to almost delirious joy before collapsing into a death wish. These feelings remain unresolved as the book closes, for Jonah is unable to accept that the compassion of his God is wholly free. Moreover, he cannot see that he himself is the object of God's saving compassion.

The text lends itself to reflection on inner religious experience. The book of Jeremiah contains passages which describe the inner feelings of the prophet in the face of his call.[16] They express Jeremiah's anger, fear and yearning. Called in the most extreme circumstances to be God's witness at a time when Jerusalem and the temple would fall to the forces of King Nebuchadnezzar, Jeremiah does not duck the call of God – but, unlike any other prophet, he reveals the personal cost involved. The book of Jonah reflects the struggle of a prophet in the face of his call. His call is equally difficult, but his response is to flee from it. We witness throughout Scripture human beings struggling with the call of God. In Jonah this complexity is presented in narrative terms. In somewhat different vein, the book of Job depicts a man's theological and spiritual struggle to come to terms with the nature of God; a struggle which has loud echoes of the struggle of the righteous in Israel and Judah who suffered the horrors and deprivations of exile.

There is much humour in Jonah. Hyperbole, irony, satire and the central roles played by pagans, a fish and a worm suggest that the self-importance of Jonah, and of whoever aligned themselves with his approach, was being critiqued. As in many of Jesus' parables, humour is a significant tool in pricking pomposity and exposing hidden truth. Jesus drew on a strong tradition in his use of parables. Their value in conveying spiritual and moral truth was well known in ancient Israel. As a tool for God's Spirit of truth they were almost unparalleled. We find parables on the lips of prophets,[17] would-be rulers[18] and wise men.[19]

The profound truth of God's ways illustrated in the four chapters of Jonah prefigures the gospel truth incarnated in the Lord Jesus Christ no less than the glorious statements concerning the Messiah which appear in the books of Isaiah and Zechariah. The kind of truth we encounter in Jonah concerns the human tendency to rebel against the call or the word of God. Such rebellion in the human heart is

[16] Jer. 11:18 – 12:6; 15:10–21; 17:14–18; 18:18–23; 20:7–12 and 14–18. See Introduction, pp. 27–28.

[17] 2 Sam. 12; Is. 5.

[18] Judg. 9:8ff.

[19] Eccles. 9:13ff.

self-evident. We only need to look around and within us for evidence. Furthermore, this ubiquitous human instinct is most especially strong when believers are being challenged to adjust their thinking of God. Or, to put it another way, to let the God we proclaim in our creeds be the God we say he is, is often very hard to do. Jesus' address to the religious leaders of his day embodies this very challenge. We glimpse this, for example, in the Gospels.[20]

In terms of the book of Jonah, there is no doubt that historical events gave rise to this particular expression of truth. These events, frequently reflected in the writings of the prophets, concern God's dealings with Israel, Judah and the nations somewhere during the period 750–550 BC. The complexity of those events for the self-understanding of God's chosen people not only exposed the narrowness of Israel's actual beliefs compared with her professed beliefs,[21] they also showed that God was free to reveal his saving compassion when and where he chose. Ironically, the freedom of God exposes the bondage of his people. Perhaps this lies very close to the surface of the story of Jonah.

In responding to a range of historical circumstances evidenced in the Old Testament as a whole, the prophetic author of the book of Jonah uses a style of writing which corresponds to the word of the Lord to his generation and ours. Its profoundly theological emphasis reverberates throughout the life and teaching of Jesus of Nazareth.

[20] Matt. 23; Mark 2:16–17; John 8:58–59, etc.
[21] Jonah 4:2; cf. Exod. 34:6; Ps. 86:5, 15; Joel 2:13, etc.

1:1–3

2. A prophet protests

God calls Jonah (1:1–2)

> Now the word of the LORD came to Jonah the son of Amittai. (v. 1)

How might we read these words? Is this opening phrase a typical introduction to a prophetic text, or does it signal to the reader something else? We have already seen that prophetic texts vary considerably in form. For example, narrative prophecies in 1 and 2 Kings give accounts of a number of prophetic figures, most notably Elijah and Elisha. Their dramatic adventures are recorded in a series of memorable stories. By contrast, the so-called 'latter prophets'[1] lean very heavily towards an interest in the content of the word of the Lord rather than narratives about the prophets' lives.

The appearance of the word *wayᵉhî* at the beginning of a passage points to the start of a narrative.[2] Translated in the RSV as 'now', and elsewhere as 'and it happened that . . .' or, 'Now it was that . . .', this little word as it appears in verse 1 signals to the reader the beginning of a narrative prophecy.[3] The nuance of this Hebrew verb leans more towards 'a happening' than towards 'an absolute statement'. In other words, it lends itself to the telling of a story through which the word of the Lord was made known, rather than to a presentation of prophetic oracles.

Overall, these simple words contain a mystery. How does the word of the Lord come to the prophet Jonah? Does it come through a vision, a dream, someone speaking to him, a letter, a circumstance,

[1] Isaiah, Jeremiah and Ezekiel as well as 'the twelve' listed earlier.

[2] Although present, the RSV translation of Ezek. 1:1 does not reflect *wayᵉhî*. The Hebrew of 1:1 opens with Ezekiel's own account in the first person of the vision he was granted. It continues in 1:4 after the insertion of historical data.

[3] The same formula is used at the beginning of other narrative books: cf. Josh. 1:1; Judg. 1:1; Ruth 1:1; 1 Sam.1:1; Est. 1:1.

an adventure? Is there a voice from heaven which only Jonah hears? No answer is given to these questions either here or in the rest of the Old Testament. It is only Jonah's response which indicates in the clearest possible way that God's word to him was indeed powerfully real. Jonah was called. He was deeply disturbed by this and, as we shall see, unable to accept it.

Jonah the son of Amittai

The word of the Lord comes to Jonah son of Amittai. In 2 Kings 14:23–29 we are told that Jonah son of Amittai came from Gath-hepher, a little place in the territory of Zebulun.

> In the fifteenth year of Amaziah the son of Joash, king of Judah, Jeroboam the son of Joash, king of Israel, began to reign in Samaria, and he reigned forty-one years. And he did what was evil in the sight of the LORD; he did not depart from all the sins of Jeroboam the son of Nebat, which he made Israel to sin. He restored the border of Israel from the entrance of Hamath as far as the Sea of the Arabah, according to the word of the LORD, the God of Israel, which he spoke by his servant Jonah the son of Amittai, the prophet, who was from Gath-hepher. For the LORD saw that the affliction of Israel was very bitter, for there was none left, bond or free, and there was none to help Israel. But the LORD had not said that he would blot out the name of Israel from under heaven, so he saved them by the hand of Jeroboam the son of Joash.

It is fair to assume from this account that the prophet Jonah either pre-dated or was contemporary with King Jeroboam II. The king's forty-one-year reign in Israel is summarized in 2 Kings 14:25: 'And he did what was evil in the sight of the LORD.' Yet, by the word of the Lord through Jonah, Jeroboam secured the frontier towns and borders of the land. As we read 2 Kings, we see that the reason for Jeroboam's strategic and military success lay in the divine compassion for his suffering people, Israel. Their distress was very great (v. 26); they endured such severe incursions from warring neighbours that their very existence was threatened. It was in fulfilment of his promise that the Lord saved Israel. Interestingly, these verses illustrate a belief that the Lord is king over his people *even* when they are subject to 'evil' rulers; that it is the word of the Lord, not the rule of kings, which is powerful and effective on behalf of his people, and that the one through whom the Lord's word is given occupies an unenviable and ambiguous place in the life of the nation. This passage shows that *despite* the habitual wickedness of the king,[4] God's desire to help and save his people is unquenchable. In his mercy God is free to save. He does not override the wicked king, but rather uses the king's personal ambition to bring deliverance for his people.

We cannot know the nature of the relationship between the prophet and the king in this particular instance. Even so, we can look to see how, for example, Nathan challenged David, Jehu challenged Baasha, and Elijah challenged King Ahab and Queen Jezebel. Amos, Isaiah and Jeremiah were also in the forefront of opposition against the 'evil' rulers of their day. Elisha, the great prophet whose death is described in 2 Kings 13, was consulted by rulers of Israel and Judah concerning the outcome of battles they were about to undertake. In the face of many threats to their borders, particularly from Syria in the north and Moab to the east, the people of Israel survived because 'the LORD was gracious to them and had compassion on them, and he turned toward them, because of his covenant with Abraham, Isaac, and Jacob, and would not destroy them'.[5] The key words to the prophet Elijah are a fundamental clue in focusing the purposes of God towards his people: 'Yet I will leave seven thousand in Israel, all the knees that have not bowed to Baal, and every mouth that has not kissed him.'[6]

Set within this broader context of continuous conflict outlined for us in 1 and 2 Kings, the Israelite king Jeroboam II[7] was asserting his power in the face of external threat and internal weakness by strengthening Israel's national borders. Israel stood alone, bitterly afflicted and without a helper. The willingness of a compassionate God 'to save Israel' by restoring her borders, despite the habitual wickedness of King Jeroboam II, shines through in the story in 2 Kings 14. Israel is delivered by the word of the Lord through the hand of Jonah and by the hand of Jeroboam.

The text is not concerned to tell us how Jeroboam heard the word of the Lord through Jonah, or whether Jonah's message was viewed by the king as an encouragement to his nationalistic aspirations. Jonah may be seen as a nationalistic prophet in so far as the burden of his words concerned the securing of Israelite territory. The fundamental connections between land and human community are profound. That God gives land to his people as part of his covenant cannot be denied. A healthy nationalism can serve a number of higher loyalties, such as faith in God. Such a nationalism in Israel was epitomized by many prophets, including Elisha and Jonah. Where a

[4] 2 Kgs. 14:24f.
[5] 2 Kgs. 13:23.
[6] 1 Kgs. 19:18.
[7] Jeroboam II was sole regent in the Northern territory of Israel from 781 to 746 BC; 2 Kings 14:23 refers to his accession to the throne.

healthy nationalism inspired by the Creator and Ruler of all breaks down, ugly demagogues appear whose words are shaped not by faith in the King of kings but by fear. The nature of King Jeroboam II's nationalism is unknown, but it was used for the good of his people and his own glory by the Lord.

In referring to the same landmarks, Amos 6:14 points to the ultimate ineffectiveness of Jeroboam's strategy. It was not reinforced borders that Israel needed but a return to the Lord, her true protector. Without that, Amos saw little hope for the future of Israel. The prophetic words of Amos and Hosea address the spiritual and moral plight of Israel during the reign of Jeroboam II. The king appears not to have addressed this spiritual and moral lack, devoting his strategies instead to consolidating the national and material grandeur of Israel. For Amos and Hosea, this target of his leadership was misdirected. If the prophet Jonah were roughly contemporary with Amos and Hosea, there may have been sharp differences between them. Given their contrasting stance, it is interesting to imagine the kind of debate which may have occurred.[8] The texts are inconclusive on the matter, and to this extent Jonah's reputation as a prophet hangs on various ambiguities.

It is against this kind of background that we might imagine a storyteller enticing his first listeners: 'Now, it happened that the word of the LORD came to [*wait for it . . .*] Jonah [*and, just to add to the suspense, it was . . .*], Jonah the son of Amittai . . .' Maybe the very first recipients of this narrative would have heard stories about Jonah giving words of encouragement to that terrible King Jeroboam II! They might have heard rumours of a conflict between Jonah and his contemporaries, Amos and Hosea. Maybe his very name posed an ambiguity; he was 'son of Amittai'.[9] Jonah is the son of 'faithfulness', and maybe the narrator is inviting his listeners to tune into a key question, 'Faithfulness to what?' There is a touch of irony here. As the story progresses, the actual focus of Jonah's faithfulness becomes increasingly unclear.

The call

To Jonah came a command which required him to extend his boundaries. God said to him,

[8] Prophetic conflict is evidenced in Scripture. Both 1 Kings 18, 22 and Jeremiah 28 illustrate the reality of conflict between true and false prophets. Jeremiah 26:16–19 illustrates how the words of earlier prophets were remembered and how, in this instance, they helped save Jeremiah's life. However, his words threatening the destruction of Jerusalem fell on stony ground in part because his predecessor, Isaiah, had spoken of the Lord protecting Jerusalem: Is. 32:5; 37:35, etc.

[9] The word *'ᵃmittay* is derived from the Hebrew word meaning 'faithfulness'.

> 'Arise, go to Nineveh, that great city, and cry against it; for their wickedness has come up before me.' (v. 2)

The book opens with a command to 'get up and go'. Jonah was being called to do something other than maintain the status quo. As we shall see, however, proclaiming the word of the Lord concerning the restoration of Israel's boundaries was one thing; proclaiming God's word to the wicked city of Nineveh was another. It was totally inconceivable. Cooperating with God in the salvation of his own people was a privilege; cooperating with God in the salvation of his people's enemies was anathema. This call, and the prophet's response to it, is at the heart of the way Jonah is remembered.

Boundaries

From the snapshot of Jonah provided in 2 Kings,[10] we see a prophet who, to some extent at least, came to be associated with Israel's national boundaries.

> He [Jeroboam II] restored the border of Israel from the entrance of Hamath as far as the Sea of the Arabah, according to the word of the LORD, the God of Israel, which he spoke by his servant Jonah the son of Amittai, the prophet, who was from Gath-hepher.

Boundaries are, of course, important. The Lord's words through Jonah encouraged the restoration of Israel's ancient borders, thus giving hope to God's suffering, war-torn people. The re-establishment of their national boundaries would, we may assume, have heralded a period of peace and security. Israel welcomed the restoration of her ancient borders as a sign of God's blessing and a harbinger of the prosperity which peace often brings.

Boundaries are concerned with identity. Through the ages the people of God have rightly been concerned with boundaries, not simply geographical but doctrinal, moral, social and political. Frequently such concerns have featured on the agendas of synods and councils as questions of belief and practice, authority and morality. With questions of identity resolved through clarification of boundaries, the exercise of authority becomes clearer. Boundaries are therefore also concerned with the exercise of authority.

Nonetheless, while drawing lines to create definition and identity is a necessary and vital task to enable life to flourish, there is always

[10] 2 Kgs. 14:25.

the risk that defining boundaries too rigidly may lead to diminishment. For example, for God's people to live with the fundamental assumption that 'we alone are the chosen ones' will result in their diminishment. To draw boundaries between peoples which exclude groups from each other, whether on the basis of age, race, social class, gender or religion, is to impose limits on the One who created humankind in his own image. This then imposes a limit on the people of God themselves. By ruling people out we also rule out growth in our knowledge of God.

Human concern with identity is also a reflection of God's concern. For example, where the traditional theological and moral boundaries of the day serve to impoverish God's people, we see God's readiness to break through them. God's freedom to be God is not compromised by our moral or political correctness. He is not bound by human notions of the moral symmetry of just deserts or theological stances. Indeed, Jonah 4:2 suggests that the prophet knew that God was free to save whoever he chose. A fierce mercy lies at the heart of God's nature, such that no man-made boundary, be it moral or geographical, may exclude the glory of that most exquisite quality from the human arena.

In the New Testament we find that, to the profound disquiet of the scribes and Pharisees, Jesus frequently broke through the conventional social, geographical and moral boundaries of his day. He spoke publicly with women,[11] socialized with sinners,[12] touched lepers,[13] rescued the Samaritan,[14] and challenged the law of the Sabbath in the interests of human well-being.[15]

Even more significantly, the Christian gospel speaks of the incarnation: of God becoming human. It speaks of the Giver of Life suffering death by crucifixion. It speaks of God breaking down the boundaries between death and life for all time in the resurrection. At the heart of the gospel is an awe-inspiring breaking down of conventional boundaries, extending the reign of God to the furthest bounds of heaven and earth so that 'God may be all in all'.[16] Human security resides in God alone, not in the conventional boundaries we create.

Nineveh

We know that Nineveh, whose origins may reach back to the sixth millennium BC, was a very significant city in the ancient world. By

[11] John 4 and John 8.
[12] Mark 2:15.
[13] Luke 5:12.
[14] John 4.
[15] Luke 6:6.
[16] 1 Cor. 15:28 AV.

the reign of Tiglath-Pileser I (1114–1076 BC), it was established as an alternative royal residence to the ancient cities of Assur and Calah for Assyrian kings. Both Ashurnasipal II (883–859 BC) and Sargon II (722–705 BC) had palaces in Nineveh.

During a period of decline, such events as internal dissension and defeat in war, a total solar eclipse[17] in 763 BC, followed by flooding and famine, could well have been interpreted by the Ninevites as a divine judgment. In the face of this, the king of Nineveh at this time[18] may have stepped down and the Ninevites repented. Although the eclipse was a notable event in the Assyrian calendar, no mention of it is made in Jonah. On the other hand, the only known reference to Nineveh's repentance is made in Jonah.

Later, the city was revived by Tiglath-Pileser III (745–727 BC) and Sargon II (722–705 BC). She became the capital city of Sennacherib (704–681 BC) and remained the chief city of the most powerful empire of the biblical world until her final destruction at the hands of a coalition of Medes, Babylonians and Scythians in August 612 BC. The heap of ruins was never rebuilt. In 401 BC Xenophon passed that way with his army and described it as 'a great stronghold, deserted and lying in ruins'. Today the ruins of Nineveh can be found across the Tigris river from the modern-day city of Mosul in Iraq, 250 miles north of Baghdad.[19]

References to the city of Nineveh in Scripture are surprisingly few. Of the eighteen mentions, nine are from the book of Jonah. The most extensive condemnation is found in the vision of Nahum the Elkoshite (626–612 BC). He foresees only fierce judgment befalling Nineveh, as does his contemporary, Zephaniah (639–609 BC).[20] But Nineveh was only a great city of an even greater Assyrian empire. Assyria was at the height of her power between the eighth and seventh centuries BC. Her mighty armies were known for their ruthless cruelty. In this period of her ascendancy, Assyrian imperialistic ambitions knew no bounds. All the surrounding nations were threatened by her power. It is in the face of this threat, frequently depicted in Scripture, that the prophets urged Israel to repent and trust the Lord. Isaiah's vivid imagery conveys the awful power of hostile forces:

[17] Considered a 'sign of ill omen'.

[18] Possibly Ashur-dan III.

[19] Excavations beginning in the 1840s revealed a walled city with a perimeter of approximately 7.5 miles, and 25,000 tablets containing the library collection of Ashurbanipal were discovered. Two mounds remain at the site. One, known as Nebi Yunus, meaning 'the prophet Jonah', stands by a mosque marking the place where the prophet is supposedly buried.

[20] Zeph. 2:13.

Therefore the anger of the LORD was kindled against his people,
and he stretched out his hand against them and smote them,
and the mountains quaked;
and their corpses were as refuse
in the midst of the streets.
For all this his anger is not turned away
and his hand is stretched out still.
He will raise a signal for a nation afar off,
and whistle for it from the ends of the earth;
and lo, swiftly, speedily it comes!
None is weary, none stumbles,
none slumbers or sleeps,
not a waistcloth is loose,
not a sandal-thong broken;
their arrows are sharp,
all their bows bent,
their horses' hoofs seem like flint,
and their wheels like the whirlwind.
Their roaring is like a lion,
like young lions they roar;
they growl and seize their prey,
they carry it off, and none can rescue.
They will growl over it on that day,
like the roaring of the sea.
And if one look to the land,
behold, darkness and distress;
and the light is darkened by its clouds.[21]

This imagery may have been inspired by the fearsome approach of cruel Assyrian armies. No names are given, however, and so the text itself has lost the specificity which would have locked it into this particular context. The effect is to enhance the scope of the text so that its power becomes effective to other generations. The terror described here by Isaiah would resonate with the terror of other powerful enemies as their war machines encroached on Israel's borders. Scripture does not allow itself to be read as an historical source book. Rather, through its pages the Spirit of God addresses the human heart in all generations and contexts.

Much can be known of Nineveh through extra-biblical texts and archaeological excavation. Much more remains unknown. Yet the nine references to Nineveh in Jonah add little to our historical knowledge of the city. Rather, it is used as a foil to the prophet. More

[21] Is. 5:25–30.

is revealed about the rebellion of Jonah than about Nineveh's sin. Still more is revealed about God's grace and mercy.

This might lead us to ask what the reader is intended to understand by 'Nineveh'. As we have already seen, the long history of the city embraces both high points and low points. Commentators vary in their understanding. Some see Nineveh as the 'wicked Nineveh' destroyed by a coalition of Medes, Babylonians and Scythians in 612 BC. Historically it was this city which was remembered subsequently in Greek and Jewish history as 'wicked'. Others go for the Nineveh of the mid-eighth century BC, which experienced a temporary downturn in her fortunes prior to reaching her zenith as chief city in the Assyrian empire, before cruelly adding Israel to her conquered territories in 721 BC.

It is quite possible that we are meant to understand Nineveh as that which constitutes the very opposite of everything that Israel held dear. This view is vividly spelt out by the Jewish writer Hayyim Lewis:

> The Assyrians were the Nazi storm-troopers of the ancient world. They were the pitiless power-crazed foe. They showed no quarter in battle, uprooting entire peoples in their fury for conquest. They extinguished the Northern Kingdom of Israel . . . For Jonah, Nineveh, then, was no ordinary city; it carried doom-laden, tragic memories, it stood as a symbol of evil incarnate.[22]

For centuries its name remained a well-known allegory for evil. The prophecies of Nahum[23] and Zephaniah[24] provide us with clear examples of this sentiment. LaCocque and Lacocque add, 'To go to Nineveh means, for Jonah, to go to hell.'[25]

Political correctness

God's call to go against the flow is frequent in Scripture. Elijah[26] is called to the Gentile town of Zarephath in Sidon to help a widow; Balaam[27] is sent to Moab from where, greatly to the chagrin of the king of Moab, he blesses Israel! Abram[28] was called to leave his homeland in Mesopotamia in order to find a new land of blessing,

[22] Assembly of Rabbis, p. 987.
[23] Nah. 3:1–7.
[24] Zeph. 2:13–15.
[25] LaCocque and Lacocque, p. 73.
[26] 1 Kgs. 17:9. Only Elijah and Jonah are sent specifically to Gentile nations.
[27] Num. 22:20–21.
[28] Gen. 12:1ff.

while Moses[29] was called to lead Israel out of Egypt to the Promised Land. Noah, Joshua, Deborah, Ruth, David, Amos and Jeremiah all turn their back on the established norms and enter into new ways of living. Jesus[30] was called to turn his back on the itinerant life of teaching and healing to set his face towards Jerusalem. Going against the flow, or rejection of the status quo, however, is never portrayed as serving personal self-interest. As several of the examples suggest, few who were called responded with alacrity. For many the call frequently involved misunderstanding, the break-up of families, ridicule, searing self-doubt and death.

Jonah was called to cry against the great city of Nineveh concerning her 'wickedness'. 'Arise, and go to Nineveh, that great city, and cry against it; for their wickedness has come up before me' (v. 2). The Hebrew word translated 'wickedness' is *rāʿâ*, a little word that has many meanings. Its ambience swings from a nasty taste on the one hand to the furthest reaches of moral evil on the other. The meaning of words with such a wide range must be decided by their context rather than etymologically. If the historical context of Jonah is set in the eighth century, then the word *rāʿâ* may suggest 'calamity' or 'affliction', for, as we have seen, there are indications that during that period Nineveh was suffering the effects of various disasters. If, on the other hand, the story is set at a later time, moral 'wickedness' would be the more likely meaning, since the Assyrian empire would by then have devoured and destroyed Israel. The text (3:8–9) suggests that the 'great city' was under a threat of destruction which the Ninevites themselves interpreted as a punishment for sin. Jonah's prescience (4:2) that the Lord might relent from punishing Nineveh, combined with the Lord's reference to the people's ignorance (4:11), could suggest a case of calamity rather than wickedness.

In sharp contrast, Nahum denounced the city in no uncertain terms. Some time before its fall in 612 BC he cries against Nineveh,

> Woe to the bloody city,
>   all full of lies and booty –
>   no end to the plunder!
> The crack of whip, and rumble of wheel,
>   galloping horse and bounding chariot!
> Horsemen charging,
>   flashing sword and glittering spear,
> hosts of slain,
>   heaps of corpses,

[29] Exod. 3.
[30] Luke 9:51f.

dead bodies without end –
they stumble over the bodies!
And all for the countless harlotries of the harlot,
graceful and of deadly charms,
who betrays nations with her harlotries,
and peoples with her charms.
Behold, I am against you,
says the LORD of hosts,
and will lift up your skirts over your face;
and I will let nations look on your nakedness
and kingdoms on your shame.
I will throw filth at you
and treat you with contempt,
and make you a gazingstock.
And all who look on you will shrink from you and say,
Wasted is Nineveh; who will bemoan her?
whence shall I seek comforters for her?[31]

Nahum's terrifying oracle reflects an attitude towards the city of Nineveh commonly found in Scripture. Probably dated between 663 and 612 BC, the oracle may have encouraged Manasseh, king of Judah 652–648 BC, to rebel against Assyria. In 2 Chronicles 33 we read of Manasseh's captivity and imprisonment by Assyria as well as his eventual release (v. 13). With this he was granted a new understanding of God, the outworking of which resulted in religious reform. He took away the strange – that is, the Assyrian – gods and idols from Jerusalem and replaced them with worship of the great God of Israel. Such a reform would have represented a rebellion against Assyria, but by this time the great empire was unable to react. The death of Ashurbanipal around 630 BC added to Assyrian weakness. The Assyrian empire had created many enemies among the peoples of the Ancient Near East and her final demise was now only a matter of time.

Although at first glance the two prophecies are very different, similarities between Nahum and Jonah do, in fact, exist. In both, Nineveh is the enemy which inspires dread in the hearts and minds of God's people. Two possible fates await such enemies: either destruction was inevitable if they persisted in their arrogance (Nahum), or, in the providence of God, even the deadliest enemy could repent and receive mercy (Jonah). The book of Jonah explores the implications for God's people of this second possibility. Both books refer to a core theological theme, even quoting the same

[31] Nah. 3:1–7.

passage from Exodus 34: 'Thou art a gracious God and merciful, slow to anger, and abounding in steadfast love' (Jonah 4:2), and, 'The LORD is slow to anger and of great might, and the LORD will by no means clear the guilty' (Nah. 1:3). Finally, both books conclude with a question, the only two books in the entire Bible to do so.

To denounce Nineveh in Israel would have guaranteed Jonah popularity, but to be called to go and denounce Nineveh to the Ninevites was unthinkable. In calling Jonah to go to Nineveh, God was calling him not only to face the unknown, the opprobrium of his own people, ridicule, humiliation and the relinquishing of his world view, but also to venture alone into a most feared and hated place in order to show God's concern for his enemy. It was tantamount to facing death. The command was utterly and plainly absurd. In Jonah 4:2 we see the prophet pleading that he might die. The depth of his anger was such that he could conceive of no other way of assuaging it than by death. Ironically, it was death to his own narrow notions of God's grace that was being required of him by the God of all grace and compassion.

Jonah's response (1:3a)

> But Jonah rose to flee to Tarshish from the presence of the LORD. (v. 3a)

The normal expectation on hearing the words 'Jonah rose' would be for them to be followed by the words 'and went to Nineveh'. This is what we find in 3:3, but at the opening of the book the reader is shocked to discover that the prophet gets up to flee to Tarshish. The sense of urgency in the Lord's command now fills Jonah's heart. Perhaps not surprisingly from a human perspective, perversity in the presence of this call drives him away from the Lord. Here is the first hint that, when called to do something difficult, the human soul prefers to flee away. To run away appears to be the easier option.

Tarshish

The precise location of Tarshish is unknown. In several biblical references Tarshish is associated with maritime trade.[32] This might suggest it was a common name for any large trading port.[33] Most

[32] 1 Kgs. 10:22, 22:48; 2 Chr. 20:36–37; Pss. 48:7; 72:10; Is. 2:16; 23:1, 14; 60:9; 66:19; Ezek. 27:25.
[33] Stuart, p. 451.

commentators, however, have attempted to identify Tarshish with a particular geographical location. Josephus, the first-century AD Jewish commentator, identified it as Tarsus in Asia Minor. Some have suggested the southern tip of India, while others favour Tartessos on the southern tip of the Iberian Peninsula.

In Scripture, Tarshish was identified by its associations. Ships of Tarshish,[34] built for heavy voyages, crossed great distances laden with silver and ore. It was a place rich in natural resources, frequently spoken of in the context of trading. Travel to Tarshish necessitated long sea crossings; it was like journeying to the ends of the earth. Locating biblical Tarshish is not a new problem. In his 'Lectures', Luther follows an early Jewish Targum (or interpretation) which simply deletes the name 'Tarshish', replacing it by 'the sea'.[35] Sasson observes, 'Although it was certainly not an invented place (as are Eldorado or Shangrila), Tarshish seems always to lie just beyond the geographic knowledge of those who try to pinpoint its location.'[36]

Was Jonah heading for a geographical destination now lost to us, or was he going 'to the ends of the earth', that is, to a place where he would escape the presence of God? Did Tarshish represent for him a pleasant place of security that bordered on non-existence?

Either way it was a place, ironically like Nineveh, where Yahweh was unknown. Jonah believed a journey to Tarshish would be less hazardous than a journey to Nineveh. Or was it that he did not care about the hazards of the journey providing he escaped the hazards of God's call? Sheldon H. Blank, rabbi and biblical scholar, comments, 'What is Tarshish? . . . In the story it is anywhere – anywhere but the right place; it is the opposite direction, the direction a person takes when he turns his back on his destiny . . . it is the excuse we give – our rationalisations.'[37]

Refusing the call to Nineveh and potential exile from his own community with its acceptable lifestyle and familiar norms, Jonah is forced to seek exile in Tarshish. What an irony. He was desperate to get away from the presence of this demanding God. The Jewish exegete Ibn Ezra[38] reminds us of the imagery of the servants of the

[34] Is. 23:1f.; Ezek. 27:25ff.

[35] Luther, *Luther's Works*, 19, p. 9, noted in Bolin, p. 76.

[36] Sasson, p. 79, noted in Bolin, ibid., p. 76.

[37] Assembly of Rabbis, p. 988.

[38] Abraham ibn Ezra lived in Spain, AD 1089–1140. He wrote commentaries on most of the Old Testament and strengthened the Jewish shift away from scholasticism (which tended to bypass the biblical languages of Hebrew and Greek in interpreting Scripture and perpetuated a multi-sense interpretation of the Bible while reinforcing the traditions of the church).

Lord standing in his presence, waiting to take directives. Elijah introduces himself as the prophet of the Lord 'before whom I stand'.[39] Jonah was no longer prepared to stand and wait for an opportunity to serve the Lord. Therefore the phrase can equally mean, 'He fled from the service of the Lord,' since this is indeed the implication of Jonah's action. Following this view, Alexander writes, 'By fleeing from the Lord's presence Jonah announces emphatically his unwillingness to serve God. His action is nothing less than open rebellion against God's sovereignty.'[40] Here is something unprecedented: a prophet of Israel in rebellion against God. While Moses, Amos and Jeremiah had been unable to resist the word and service of God, Jonah takes decisive steps to avoid it. But with what consequences?

Jonah's flight from the presence of the Lord

Such instantaneous action arises out of fear not freedom. Examples of others who resorted to such flight were Moses and David. After killing an Egyptian, Moses fled from Pharaoh.[41] He was rightly afraid of the consequences. In fear of civil war, David fled from Absalom.[42] In the prophetic tradition, however, Jonah stands alone in 'fleeing the presence of the Lord'.

The 'presence of the Lord' is an expression derived from ordinary phrases such as being in 'the presence of the king' or 'in the presence of the people'. It has the sense of directness as when one is face to face with another. It sometimes conveys a significant event, conversation or agreement. To be in the presence of the Lord was something the psalmist longed after.[43] To be excluded from God's presence was to be without the gift of joy or a generous and true spirit.[44] In the way that a small child is secure and so fully alive in the presence of his mother, but anxious and listless in her absence, so the presence of the Lord is life-giving, a source of joy and blessing. Martin Buber crystallized the idea when he wrote, 'The I is created in the presence of the Thou.'

In other words, human identity is dependent on the presence of Another. The phrase 'the presence of the Lord' makes its first appearance in the Bible in Genesis 3 and 4. In the first instance,

[39] 1 Kgs. 17:1; 18:15.
[40] Alexander, p. 101.
[41] Exod. 2:15.
[42] 2 Sam. 15:14.
[43] Ps. 16:11.
[44] Ps. 51:10–12.

Adam and Eve 'hid themselves from the presence of the LORD'.[45] They deprived themselves of the joy and blessing characteristic of God-given life. In the second instance, 'Cain went away from the presence of the LORD, and dwelt in the land of Nod.'[46]

In these early chapters of Genesis men and women are shown as doubting the goodness and wisdom of God, suspecting him of withholding from them something good. Instead of standing in his presence to serve him, their doubts led them to hide themselves from his presence. Whereas Adam and Eve doubted God, their descendants came to doubt one another. In this instructive sequence, the consequence of casting doubt on God is to cast doubt on his creatures. Failure in the first principle causes failure in the second. Adam disregards God and Cain murders his brother. He is condemned by his own actions to be a fugitive and a wanderer in the land of Nod.[47] For this reason Jesus can summarize the Ten Commandments: 'You shall love the Lord your God with all your heart, and with all your soul, and with all your mind, and with all your strength . . . You shall love your neighbour as yourself.'[48]

The 'land of Nod' is the 'place of wandering' where people live who, like Cain, have turned their backs on God's goodness. It is a place where those who have separated themselves from their Creator live without blessing or joy. Those who cut themselves off from their Life-giver make themselves homeless. They are exiles. They wander in 'No Place'. Those who reject the order of God's word live in chaos. Is this what Jesus refers to when he speaks of the 'outer darkness' where there is 'weeping and gnashing of teeth'?[49]

After murdering Abel,[50] Cain went away from the presence of the Lord. When he flees God's presence, Jonah admits to the same inner turmoil as Cain. Adam *hid himself* from God's presence, Cain *went out* from God's presence, and Jonah *fled*. These are images of human beings afraid of their calling, the fear being triggered by humanity's tendency to doubt God's goodness. God does not send Jonah away; rather, fearful of the consequences of God's goodness, he runs away.

While psalmists longed to be in God's presence, we might be thankful for this compelling honesty in a prophet who flees believing that he cannot live in the presence of this God's goodness. Mercifully, we discover here a matching openness in God. He is not constrained by a law of vindictiveness, but by a law of gracious love. When human

[45] Gen. 3:8.
[46] Gen. 4:16.
[47] The Hebrew word *nôḏ* is translated 'wandering'.
[48] Mark 12:30; Luke 10:27.
[49] Matt. 8:12.
[50] Gen. 4:16.

beings turn away from God, he does not turn away from them. When Jonah flees from his presence, God does not leave him. Cain entered a place of restless 'wandering', while Jonah embarked on a stormy journey. But in both stories we are shown a God who protects those who have turned their backs on him. Such is God's love for and commitment to human beings, he neither deserts nor condemns them. Rather, in grace and mercy he sustains them even in their fear and defiance. God's response to their rejection of his call becomes a source of hope for all who have travelled this way. This God will not allow rebellion and evil to have the last word.

The language and imagery stress the energy Jonah expends on his flight. We see him being pursued by the call of God – that is, by the word of God – in the shape of the great storm (1:4, 11, 12, 13, 15), the great fish (1:17), God's second call (3:1) and his own burning anger (4:1). The story-teller speaks of God 'appointing' the great fish (1:17), then the plant (4:6) and the worm (4:7) and a sultry east wind (4:8) as fellow workers in bringing Jonah to his senses. Everything is expressive of God's compassion towards the prophet. He pursues him with loving kindness.[51] Even Nineveh itself becomes a means whereby God can goad his most reluctant servant to repent and return. All that he encounters reminds him of God's call. It proves inescapable. All that ensues following his flight conspires to create in the prophet a willingness to serve God. God was indefatigable.

As far as Nineveh was concerned, her repentance was met by God turning from 'the evil which he had said he would do to them' (3:10). As far as Jonah was concerned, however, God could not change his mind. Indeed, in his love for Jonah, God would not let him go. The great storm, in which the ship is almost wrecked and Jonah cast into the sea, is a mirror image of the prophet's inner storm. His turbulence, excitement and remorse, his whirlwind of passion and guilt, are occasioned by the word of God. Miraculously, the great pagan city of Nineveh repents in response to God's word through Jonah. Equally mysteriously, Jonah remains unrepentant despite God's best efforts.

The reader is drawn into identifying with Jonah because he typifies the human condition. Jonah is a relatively inconspicuous person, not like a David or a Moses. Those heroes of the faith, known to us through their great exploits, contrast with Jonah whose evasion of his inconceivable vocation enlists our sympathy. It is not that Moses and David are stained-glass-window saints. Rather, in contrast to Jonah, they give themselves, albeit with reluctance, to God's call. Jonah has standing in the tradition mainly because of his ongoing resistance to God's call. He opposed God. The story-teller shows

[51] Ps. 23:6.

that Jonah's response leads to chaos, storm, death, compromise, hypocrisy, self-regard and logical but irresolvable anger. Only the continuing presence of the Lord could restore to Jonah the peace and joy he had lost by running away from God.

LaCocque describes Jonah as one who is '"loaded" with the cowardice and the treason of all'.[52] He is no longer simply a figure of ancient history. Rather, Jonah's descent into the netherworld is a sign of the condemnation of human failure to comply with the divine entreaty. In running away from God's call, Jonah runs away from life itself. He follows the way signposted 'Death' along with all who flee the call of God to serve him with responsibility and authenticity. The narrative pursues Jonah in his fall, granting a renewed insight into the nature of God's commitment even towards the fearful and disobedient. The Lord is as good as his word (4:2).

We often make judgments about something on the basis of 'what it will mean for me'. In general elections and at budget time we are often encouraged to evaluate our response to the chancellor's plans for the nation in the context of 'what it means for me'. If his revised taxation proposals mean that I will pay more tax and have less disposable income for myself, I may well feel aggrieved. If, on the other hand, he makes allowances which mean that I will benefit from an increase, then I may well reckon it to be a good budget. The chancellor's first responsibility, however, is the good of the nation as a whole, not the benefit of individuals. When he sets out his overall strategy we may fairly assume that he is not aiming to please or hurt particular individuals, but to create a more just distribution of well-being across the nation. Nonetheless, the good he is working for the whole may have some undesirable side effects for individuals. We might believe passionately in more money being put into improving the national health service, but when it is taken out of our pocket we are aggrieved. God's overall concern is for all the nations of the earth. In implementing the redemptive process, some individuals may feel unfairly treated. The prophets of Israel were sometimes reluctant servants, because their calling often brought with it as much public humiliation as recognition and honour. In God's economy, one of the consequences of his goodness to Nineveh was the cause of Jonah's grievance against him. In 4:2 Jonah admits as much.

Vocation

Already we can see that the book of Jonah suggests that 'vocation' or 'calling' is a dialogue between God and the one called. On this point Leon Roth comments,

[52] LaCocque and Lacocque, p. 90.

> It has become fashionable to talk of the relationship between God and man as that of a dialogue. That is as may be; but it should at least be noted that the dialogue involved is not a tea-table conversation. It is rather a call, even a calling to account; and it is curious to observe from the record of how some of those called upon found in it terror and suffering and how some, for varying reasons, tried to evade it.[53]

Since the future of God's creation is Christ-shaped, sacred Scripture posits that the calling to be human involves a lifelong process of growing up into Christ. Human beings are invited by their Creator to enter into this fullness of life, for it is their birthright. It is a gradual process of growth and change for most people. Those who accept the invitation set the inner compass of their lives towards Christ. The journey involves an ongoing dialogue with the Source of all life, namely, the Lord God. Because the eternal God is who he is, the dialogue is lifelong and the process of growing up into what he intends us to be is continuous. To sustain a lifelong journey involves a discipline of mind and habit by which the pilgrim lends himself or herself to the good influences of God through praise, prayer, Scripture and service. Commitment to a certain quality of life and faithfulness to God's call are characteristic of true believers. The journey is not easy. In the Psalm 23 we discover a fellow pilgrim putting into words his or her own perception of the journey. Those who so lend themselves to this pilgrim God are not simply called to be custodians of divine truth, but to be humble pilgrims who walk with God because they love the truthful way by which he leads them. Vocation, or the ongoing process of being called, is the experience of everyone, for humankind is created in the image of this God. By the design of its Creator, humankind has a God-given capacity to hear and respond to God's call. The book of Jonah depicts a unique conversation between God and humankind in which human resistance is met by God's unfailing commitment to the healing of the struggling sinner.

The dialogue has a particular twist to it within Scripture, for Jonah hears the call and responds to it in a singularly unexpected, albeit understandable, way. Rather than enter into his God-given inheritance, the prophet longs to remain undisturbed. He does not want to be like the God who has created him in his likeness. He is critical of God's ways. Avoiding God's call and running away from his vocation, he courts disaster by seeking his own way to fulfilment instead of engaging with God's way. However virtuous and well intentioned a person might be, virtue alone is insufficient to prove their vocation.

[53] Assembly of Rabbis, p. 988.

Being in the presence of God presupposes taking part in the work of God. This does not always mean doing something dramatic such as going to Nineveh. It means expressing or reflecting God's way of being in the world. Jonah was called to express God's active concern for Nineveh, but being in the presence of a God who loved his enemies was unbearable for Jonah. In this respect alone, Jesus certainly proved to be 'greater than Jonah'.

The Jonah syndrome

Abraham Maslow recognized in the story of Jonah a feature of human behaviour which he described as the 'Jonah syndrome'. He speaks of it as the fear of standing alone. To be called or appointed to a particular task brings not only the joy of recognition but also the obligation of responsibility. It usually involves a level of costly commitment in terms of time and energy. Such a call inevitably involves challenge and pain as well as reward and fulfilment. For Maslow, the Jonah syndrome is an unwillingness to face the necessary obstacles on the way to fulfilment. Here we need to understand 'fulfilment' as equivalent to 'vocation'. He writes,

> To discover in oneself a great talent can certainly bring exhilaration but it also brings a fear of the dangers, responsibilities and duties of being a leader and of being alone. Responsibility can be seen as a heavy burden and evaded as long as possible.[54]

The prophet Jeremiah was initially unwilling to accept God's call. He argued with God: 'I do not know how to speak, for I am only a youth.'[55] He may also have had an inkling of the personal cost of obeying such a call. For Jeremiah it would involve a period of around forty years during which he had to sustain a heavy burden of lonely ministry in which he discovered neither popularity nor success. No wonder he wanted to evade the call.

Some are attracted by the limelight; contemporary society fosters the notion that unless we are in the spotlight we are nobody, or unless we have an opinion about everything we do not count. The constant headline-grabbing antics of stars, sports heroes and politicians not only tends to devalue the lives of ordinary folk; it can also create the sense that 'that is how life should be'. Yet two of the most influential images for the Christian are of salt and yeast. Far from being 'limelight ministry', the working of salt and yeast is 'hidden

[54] Cited in LaCocque and Lacocque, p. 70.
[55] Jer. 1:6.

ministry'. In a real sense it is this hidden ministry which most accurately reflects the ministry of God. The power of these otherwise unnoticed ingredients in everyday life is immeasurable. Christians are called to be salt and yeast in society, and most of us need to gain a good deal of sustained experience of this before we are ready for something more demanding. Many, when called to something more demanding, have taken years before they are reconciled to God's call. As with Jeremiah and Jonah, the call was both unmistakable and unwanted.

The call to go beyond the boundaries of his world and to enter into enemy territory was a call too far for poor Jonah. He feared that God would grant him success in his mission (4:2), but knew the cost of it to his own belief system as well as, ultimately, to his own sense of identity, which was dependent on his world view.

In so far as a person seeks to go beyond themselves to love their enemy, and to break through the boundaries of their safe existence, they may experience a justified fear of loss of control. For some, the 'Jonah syndrome' is a fear of their self-identity being torn apart by such an experience, of being shattered and disintegrated, even destroyed by it.

Jonah's choice was to avoid such disintegration by avoiding Nineveh. But it was also a choice to run away from the Lord who called him. To obey the call would have brought life. To disobey was to choose not to live as far as God's call was concerned. How Jonah must have longed that God had not spoken! But since God is the source of life, his word to us brings life. It is the lack of his word, or deafness or disobedience towards it, that leads to death. It is in engagement with our Creator that we are brought to life and freedom. Maimoniades wrote, 'Man has not been created free; he has received the commandment [call] to be free.' In other words, our true freedom comes through obedience to God's call. God's word is his call. Paul elaborates the theme when he writes, 'I was once alive apart from the law, but when the commandment came, sin revived and I died; the very commandment which promised life proved to be death to me.'[56]

Without God's word (teaching) we live in a state of ignorance, but when we hear God's word our natural inclination is to resist it. This resistance is sin and leads to spiritual death. If God did not call us we would be like those 'who do not know their right hand from their left' (4:11). Our naturally sinful inclinations are revealed by God's call. Jonah's resistance to the ongoing call of God can readily be rationalized in human terms. After all, it was a crazy call! But, as

[56] Romans 7:9–10.

Isaiah puts it, God's thoughts are higher than our thoughts, and his ways higher than our ways.[57]

In resisting God's word, Jonah was also passing judgment on God's attitude towards Nineveh. Our disobedience not only sets us on the road to spiritual death, it is also an expression of our judgment on God's ways. It is this which is the source of human guilt before God. Martin Buber puts it like this: 'True guilt does not reside in the human person but in his failure to respond to the legitimate claims and address of the world.'[58]

True guilt emerges when God's legitimate concerns as Creator of the world are rationalized away by those of us who, claiming to know God, deny his compassion and concern. Such guilt arises in our failure to respond appropriately to human need. Yet in God's gracious mercy, such guilt can have the good effect of leading a person towards growth and the actualization of God's calling. Even guilt can be the spur to fullness of life.[59]

Called to freedom

God's call to Jonah is to go beyond the boundaries of his world view and to transcend himself. He is called to freedom. Afraid of being different, however, Jonah was unwilling to face the freedom of life in all its fullness. Such a challenge would rob him of the security of the familiar. Fear robbed him of true freedom.

Freedom is understood in the Scriptures as freedom to worship and serve God. The classic instance of this is the story of the exodus from Egypt. God calls his people out of slavery in order that they might be free to worship him.[60] He calls an oppressed rabble to become his kingdom of priests, slaves in bondage to be his witnesses in the world. Jonah received the same call. He may have been a slave to a religious system, oppressed by social expectations, or in bondage to boundaries of identity and definition. Such was his position that he took flight and evaded God's call. He wanted to remain in 'Egypt', the safe and secure place of bondage. He was not free either to 'serve' or 'worship' the Lord 'with gladness'.[61]

Although taken from a different context, the words of Democritus are an apt description of Jonah's choice: 'This is not really living poorly, it is dying slowly.'[62] At birth a baby leaves the womb. For

[57] See Is. 55:8–9.
[58] LaCocque and Lacocque, p. 72.
[59] cf. 2 Cor. 7:9–10.
[60] e.g. Exod. 10:24, to 'serve' is to 'worship'.
[61] Ps. 100:2.
[62] Democritus, Greek philosopher 460–370 BC.

nine months it has enjoyed the safe and secure environment which has nourished it, enabling it to grow to the point when it is ready to leave the life of the womb and enter a new life. Were the baby able to choose to remain in the comfort of the womb, it would die. Eventually the safety of the womb would prove to be no safety at all. To refuse to be born is to choose to die. Yet the fundamental security of the womb remains attractive, and we can try to recreate it in our lives.

Could it be that the ideal of the Western world for wealth, comfort, security and peace is, in some respect, an attempt at re-creating a womb-like environment? Although attractive and fundamentally appealing to many, it is a blinkered ideal, for it denies the reality of the world in which we are actually called to live. In particular, this ideal has an unrealistic understanding of evil, human selfishness and death. Only by creating wealth, comfort, security and peace for *all* the nations of the world can this ideal be worthwhile. Without that universal dimension, our divisions and fears will remain. One result of this ideal is that we may become dwellers in either 'gated' or 'ghettoed' accommodation. Much of the newer prestigious housing in Britain today boasts security as a key attractive feature of the accommodation. Rumour has it that those who threaten the security of the wealthy live in the ghettoized housing of the poor. Although this portrayal is an oversimplification, it contains elements of truth which serve to illustrate that, even in Britain, we live in a divided society. The dream ideal is not for everyone after all: it is the rich who have a particular interest in recreating the safety of the womb. Psalm 73 hints at the arrogance of the wealthy. They forget what it is like to be poor, and behave as though wealth is the divine norm. But security gates speak of threat, not freedom. By remaining captive to a false ideal, we imprison ourselves and close down to other possibilities. Might this be an illustration of 'not really living poorly, but dying slowly'?

Sadly, churches can also be infected by the 'spirit of the age'. They can be driven by ideals which have little to do with the Spirit of Christ. While the Saviour calls us to 'go and preach the gospel to all the nations', we can prefer the comfort of our own pew, with the familiar words and cadences which offer a measure of security in an insecure world. As Christians, we know that our ultimate security is in Christ alone; we know that 'here we have no continuing city, that we seek one to come', and yet we can become content with, and even fond of, the way things are. After all, we cannot continually be tinkering with the church. Institutions offer us ways of being together, of identity and belonging. Most importantly, they help shape us but they should not control us. Institutions intended originally to guard the precious truth can sometimes forget that foundational truth and instead focus their life on preserving themselves intact. They may be tempted to seek power and the wealth, comfort, security and influence it brings, in place of the power inherent in forgiveness, the comfort which prayer offers, the security which truth and justice bring and the peace of reconciliation. Where the church thinks of itself as an institution which must be preserved, it may be in danger of allowing itself to be corrupted with an alien spirit; not simply living poorly, particularly in the light of its glorious gospel, but dying slowly.

Joppa (1:3b)

> He went down to Joppa and found a ship going to Tarshish; so he paid the fare, and went on board, to go with them to Tarshish, away from the presence of the LORD. (v. 3b)

To reach Tarshish, Jonah went down to Joppa, an ancient sea port nowadays known as Jaffa in the district of the modern Israeli city Tel Aviv.

In the days of Jeroboam II (781–746 BC) Joppa was in the control of the Philistines. In 701 BC Sennacherib, king of Assyria, captured Joppa and other Philistine cities, a success recorded in the 'Annals of Sennacherib'.[63] Thus it is possible that this Mediterranean port may not have been easily accessible to Israelites before 701 BC. Prior to this time, ships to Tarshish sailed from the more northerly port of Tyre.

Interestingly, and perhaps not surprisingly given its location, stories of great sea monsters were told in Joppa. In later times the Greek legend of Perseus and Andromeda was set in the sea at Jaffa. The port dates back to at least 1500 BC and is first mentioned in the Bible as being in the territory of Dan.[64] It comes to particular prominence as the port where cedarwood from Lebanon was delivered for the temple at Jerusalem.[65] In the New Testament Peter is called to

[63]The Annals of Sennacherib (691–689 BC) are inscribed on a six-sided clay prism. They describe the first eight military campaigns of Sennacherib, king of Assyria 704–681 BC. The prism was found at Nebi Yunus in the ruins of Nineveh in 1830 and is sometimes referred to as the Taylor prism after the man who found it. It can be seen in the Writing Room of the British Museum, London.

[64]Josh. 19:46.

[65]Ezra 3:7; 2 Chr. 2:15. Although historical evidence suggests that, under Philistine control, Joppa would not have been readily accessible during the reign of Jeroboam II, archaeological evidence suggests that the port enjoyed an economic revival in the post-exilic period and wide trading connections across the Mediterranean at this time.

Joppa, where 'a disciple named Tabitha' was raised to life. It is said that he 'stayed in Joppa for many days with one Simon, a tanner'.[66]

More importantly for our story, God's call to 'rise up' is contrasted with Jonah's response to 'go down'. Not only does Jonah go west instead of east, but he goes down instead of up! The road to Joppa would certainly have taken the prophet downhill to the coast. But, as we shall see, the story-teller repeats the phrase (1:3, 5; 2:6), suggesting there was more to Jonah's flight than meets the eye. He was on a downward course. The narrator depicts Jonah's flight from the presence of the Lord as a descent. He is taking the path that leads to death as he seeks to avoid the road to Nineveh. He boards a ship and pays either his own fare or that of the whole ship – the text is ambiguous, but clear enough to show the irony of Jonah paying heavily to escape from the presence of the Lord.

In his poem 'The Burden of Nineveh', Laurence Housman (1865–1959) introduces a friend who reflects on Jonah's decision to go to Joppa and from there to Tarshish. He affirms Jonah in a journey which would take him further away from Nineveh, but reminds him that, even from Tarshish, 'you'll hear the cry of Nineveh, Jonah'.[67]

Reluctant prophet

To a certain extent Jonah follows in an authentic tradition when he expresses his reluctance to accept the call of Yahweh. Moses was most reluctant to do what God asked of him and Jeremiah, too, found a good reason why God should ask somebody else. In a Midrashic commentary on the book of Exodus we find the following observation:

> Jonah tried so hard to escape the mission of God – but had to go against his own will. Jeremiah tried so hard to escape the mission of God – but had to go against his own will. Moses tried so hard to escape the mission of God – but had to go against his own will.[68]

Jonah does not wait to debate the matter. His silence is striking. Imagine the impact of the bride responding with complete silence after the question, 'Will you take this man to be your lawfully wedded husband?' It is unthinkable that when the bride hears the minister addressing these

[66] Acts 9:36–43.
[67] L. Housman, *Collected Poems* (1939).
[68] Assembly of Rabbis, p. 989.

words to her, her response should be silence. We expect the words, 'I will.' Jonah's silence in the face of God's call is shocking.

At least Jeremiah and Moses entered into conversation; they even argued with God about their reasons and fears. In each case God assured them of his help and his presence. Thanks to Moses' hesitancy we have God's promise, 'My presence will go with you, and I will give you rest.'[69] Uniquely Jonah is silent. He makes no answer to God. His silence suggests either disdain or shock. His body language is decisive. Far from being assured by God's presence, Jonah cannot get away quickly enough.

Thinking the unthinkable

The prophet believes it to be impossible that the Lord God should send him to Nineveh. His response to this impossible request is to flee from God. Yet he denies the possibility of such a step. Ironically, he embarks on a course of action, namely to flee from God, which he believes to be impossible. Instead of bringing him wholeness, God's call to Jonah has brought internal division.

Jonah protests at a God who can make such a logically unreasonable demand. It is inconceivable. He votes with his feet. He flees as quickly as possible in the name of sanity. Surely any sensible person would endorse his response? Jonah the son of faithfulness remained faithful to his understanding of God, but, in the process, became faithless to the God who was calling him. What was the prophet avoiding? Following Ibn Ezra, Hayyim Lewis writes, 'Jonah is not escaping from God, for there can be no flight from his presence – he is "the God of heaven who has made the sea and dry land". If anything Jonah is fleeing from himself."[70] On hearing God's call, his instinct for self-preservation took over. He set out on an uncertain sea, hoping that in Tarshish he could become a nobody.

A rabbinic view

It is important to consider at this point some rabbinic thought which has suggested that Jonah was right to protest against God's call. After all, Abram had protested against God's plan to destroy Sodom and Gomorrah.[71] Even though the two cities of the plain were eventually destroyed, Abram's challenge to God had ensured that some people had been saved from destruction. Following a rabbinic belief, the

[69] Exod. 33:14. See also Jer. 1:7–9.
[70] Assembly of Rabbis, p. 988.
[71] Gen. 18.

suggestion is that as the patriarch was concerned with God's people, so the prophet's concern was with Israel, God's covenant people. Thus, in Jonah's view, God should be focusing his chief concerns on his own people and not on the ungodly Ninevites. In refusing to go to Nineveh Jonah was challenging God to show his care for his own people, Israel. By sailing to Tarshish he showed that he was not afraid of undertaking a long and dangerous journey. Indeed, his flight to the sea, a place of chaos and threat for the ancients,[72] shows Jonah being ready even to die for his beliefs, a readiness soon to be tested.

Underlying this view was a belief that God's call to Jonah was unethical. After all, God's own people strove to keep his teaching and laws, to keep themselves pure and devote themselves to God's service. It was only right and just that the enemies of God's people should get what they deserved. That God should show concern for them was an offence to their sense of fair play.

Some evidence suggests that this approach underlies various New Testament attitudes. Jesus, for example, appears to restrict his message to the lost sheep of the house of Israel. Whether he is speaking of his own work,[73] or the commission of the disciples,[74] it is clear that his focus is on Israel. While Jesus' early mission appears to reflect an exclusive focus on the Jewish people, however, other strands in the Gospels point to a widening of this focus to include the Gentiles. For example, Matthew 8:11–12 and John 8:56 build on ancient prophetic hopes which envisage all peoples being invited to the great messianic banquet. These different emphases may reflect struggles within the early church at what was a climactic moment for the mission of God. The conflict between these different approaches is focused in Acts 16. It was resolved when Paul, whose Jewish credentials were impeccable, was called to be the apostle to the Gentiles. But neither Paul nor Jesus himself made the world Christian. Jesus died on the cross and was raised on the third day, but the heart of his message, resounding in all his sayings about the Gentiles, is confidence in the present reality of God and the vastness of his mercy.[75]

Prophetic dilemma

Supposing Jonah obeyed God's command and Nineveh repented, what might be the consequences for Israel? Let us imagine Jonah as

[72] Gen. 1:2; Pss. 48:8; 88:7; 1 Kgs. 10:22.
[73] Matt. 15:24.
[74] Matt. 10:5.
[75] Jeremias, p. 74.

a faithful Israelite, striving each day to live in covenant relationship with God. Maybe he was one of the great and the good, being faithful, devout and careful in setting an example for the younger generation, proud of his achievements and sought out by seekers after God. Now imagine the sense of horror which would fill such faithful guardians of sacred truth if one of their members went to preach God's word to their enemies.[76] And imagine their reaction if it were claimed to be in response to God's call. Imagine, too, the seismic shock that would shake these good folk if the people of Nineveh repented and became, in God's eyes, like Israel! This theme is picked up in the ministry of Jesus. It was virtually impossible for a Pharisee or teacher of Torah to conceive the notion of tax collectors and prostitutes entering the kingdom of God before them.[77]

Now imagine a different scenario. There were many prophets in Israel and Judah who were faithful in proclaiming God's word to his people but who experienced rejection. When the prophets urged God's people to repent they were ignored or abused.[78] The failure of God's people to respond to God's word was a major problem for the prophets of Israel. We see from Isaiah 6 that the call of Isaiah is set within a context where Israel had heard the word of God but had neither understood it nor responded to it. On this Motyer comments,

> Isaiah faced the preacher's dilemma: if hearers are resistant to the truth, the only recourse is to tell them the truth yet again, more clearly than before. But to do this is to expose them to the risk of rejecting the truth yet again and, therefore, of increased hardness of heart. It could even be that the next rejection will prove to be the point at which the heart is hardened beyond recovery.[79]

If notorious Nineveh were to understand and respond to God's word, and were to witness to that by repenting in sackcloth and ashes and displaying a change of life, how would Israel look when so much evidence pointed to her failure to repent? Nineveh's repentance could only expose Israel's lack of repentance.

Both scenarios, Israel's unwillingness to countenance Nineveh's repentance and Israel's unwillingness to acknowledge her own need

[76] While both Elijah and Elisha had dealings with the Gentiles, it is the magnitude of Jonah's call to go to Nineveh which shocks even the prophet. He cannot have been alone in such a reaction.

[77] See e.g. Matt. 5:20; 21:23–32.

[78] A classic example of this is found in Jeremiah 36. The king of Jerusalem destroys the word of the Lord through the prophet Jeremiah.

[79] Motyer, p. 79.

of repentance, depend on a sense of order in which the chosen people remain central to God's concern. It is an egocentric sense of order designed to maintain a status quo based on self-interest. While self-interest may characterize human institutions in general, it is when such self-interest is 'baptized' with a sense of divine approval, admitting no change except on its own terms, that it becomes a source of wickedness akin to idolatry.

Only in accepting grace as fundamental to God's dealing with humankind is it possible to avoid the sterility which characterizes the status quo enshrined by legalism. As a closed system, such legalism as this excludes life. An open system grounded in the grace of God excludes death. The poet William Cowper captures this sentiment in his poem 'Self-acquaintance'.

> Legality holds out a bribe
> To purchase life from thee;
> And discontent would fain prescribe
> How thou shalt deal with me.
>
> While unbelief withstands thy grace,
> And puts thy mercy by,
> Presumption, with a brow of brass,
> Says, 'Give me, or I die.'[80]

We may reckon it easy, sometimes even comfortable, to live in God's presence, but to live in his service is difficult. Most of us, like Jonah, seek to evade it.

[80] William Cowper (1731–1800) in D. R. Etchells, *Praying with the English Poets* (London: SPCK, 1990).

1:4–8

3. Storm at sea

God's response (1:4)

The tensions which have been created in the first three verses now begin to be played out. God has called, the prophet has remained silent. Called to 'get up', Jonah 'went down'. Called to go east, he went west. From standing in the presence of the Lord, he sets out to flee God's presence. Those listening to the story are now on tenter-hooks. What will happen next? 'But the LORD . . .' Something new is about to happen. The rapidity of Jonah's response is matched by the speed of Yahweh's reply. In the space of a few words the Lord initiates the great storm:

> But the LORD hurled a great wind upon the sea, and there was a mighty tempest on the sea, so that the ship threatened to break up. (v. 4)

At first sight this suggests a God who behaves like an angry deity, indiscriminately causing havoc. Although it is not said that he is angry, the use of the word 'hurl' conjures up a violent image of God. His action is matched later by the mariners who, in order to save the vessel and their own lives, first hurl the ship's cargo overboard (v. 5) before they finally, and as the last resort, hurl Jonah himself overboard (v. 15). In the same way that their action was intended to save them, God's hurling of the wind and tempest also had a salvific purpose. Divine control is not limited to stilling the storm. The storm itself was also an agent of the divine will. God's response is not that of a vengeful deity: rather the great wind is an extension of his word to Jonah concerning Nineveh. The prophet fled to escape God, but he could not evade the turmoil thus created. The great wind and tempest now afflict the sailors, and, if the prophet had any sensitivity at all, we may fairly assume that it mirrors a storm within him. External and internal turbulence, occasioned by God's word, now threaten other people.

Storm

Israelite faith asserted that God was in control of the storm's chaotic forces. Yahweh's control of the wind and sea is a frequent theme in Scripture.[1] But storm imagery itself, like the reality it depicts, cannot be stilled.

In the Old Testament the image of the storm often gives expression to an inner reality of the hero. Notable instances include God speaking to Job 'out of the whirlwind'[2] of his experience of suffering and injustice. God's instruction to Elijah to 'stand upon the mount before the LORD'[3] is another example. From this vantage point the prophet witnesses God's great storm corroborating his own inner turmoil. Here was a man being called to serve God in politically and religiously stormy times as far as the kingdom of Israel was concerned.

As if to underline the stormy role of prophecy, Jeremiah speaks of 'the storm of the LORD'[4] breaking on the heads of the false prophets. Speaking of the false prophets as those who had not heard God's word but who yet spoke 'peace' to God's people, Jeremiah said that the divine storm was about to break on their heads. By proclaiming peace they had deceived the people, and in the process had themselves become the wicked who opposed God.[5]

In the book of Jonah we see God initiating a storm to halt the prophet's flight. God's violent hurling of the great wind in Jonah 1:4 resonates with primeval images of the creation event. Many ancient stories portray the creation at the hands of a God wresting it from the power of the sea, itself a symbol of darkness, violence and deathly power. The writer of Jonah echoes this mythological imagery as a way of conveying to his readers the unheard-of horror of the situation. It is as though the word of God has brought chaos and darkness to his people, the very opposite of what it brings in the creation stories. There all things respond in a glorious harmony of obedience to the word of the Creator who calls them into being,[6] but in the book of Jonah God's word is met by a man who refused to be brought into being. It is the prophet's response which causes the great wind, bringing storm and tempest into the lives of the mariners.

[1] See, e.g., Exod. 10:13–19; Num. 11:31; Job 26:12; Pss. 81:9; 107:25, 29; 135:7; Is. 50:2; Jer. 49:32–36; Amos 4:13; Nah. 1:4; Mark 4:37–39.

[2] Job 38:1f.

[3] 1 Kgs. 19:11f.

[4] Jer. 23:19f.

[5] Jer. 23:18–22.

[6] Gen. 1.

In all these instances God was in the storm. It was a means whereby God spoke to people. It was seen as a way through which God revealed himself to his people.[7]

Just to add to the drama, Jonah's destination was in the west, popularly regarded as a place of darkness and death. It was towards the west that the sun died. Jonah's flight to the west may carry with it the implication of his flight into darkness. This kind of imagery is probably the origin of the euphemism 'to go west', a phrase used to denote the demise of something.

Wind and tempest

In so many ways the simple words and images used in the book of Jonah are redolent with depth and association. Here, for example, 'wind' translates the Hebrew word *rûaḥ.* It is a characteristic of the Hebrew language that a word can bear many meanings, and this in part accounts for its delight and power in conveying subtle nuances. Prophetic writers especially exploit the language, employing various literary devices such as puns to articulate the word of God. *Rûaḥ,* one of the Hebrew words better known to the English reader, may also be translated 'breath' and 'spirit'. In Genesis 1:2 'the *rûah* of God was moving over the face of the waters'. In Ezekiel 37:5 the Lord says to the dry bones in the valley, 'Behold, I will cause *rûaḥ* to enter you.' In Isaiah 11:4 the longed-for Messiah 'with the *rûaḥ* of his lips . . . shall slay the wicked'. In all these examples the *rûaḥ* of God is associated with bringing order out of chaos, life out of death and justice in place of wickedness. It speaks of an agitated yearning in the heart of God for the perfect completion in goodness of creation. Until such harmony and well-being appear, the 'Spirit of God', fluttering like a mother bird over her chicks, is at work in creation. *Rûaḥ,* denoting 'wind', is spoken of by the psalmist as an agent of God.[8] In his work of creation and redemption God uses *rûaḥ* to bring Jonah to his senses.

The Hebrew word translated 'tempest', or 'storm', in v. 4 is *sāʿar.* It possesses the characteristic of onomatopoeia, hinting at the sound of the wind as it shrieks through the ship's rigging. Those who heard the story told in its original tongue would not have missed that nuance. As in English, the word 'storm' can be either a noun or a verb, so the word carries with it the possibility that God both sent a storm or tempest, and that he 'stormed' on the sea. The picture conjured up is of a giant blowing hard onto the sea and then wading in and wreaking havoc. Indeed, 'the ship threatened to break up', or,

[7] As in Job 40:6; Jer. 30:23; Ezek. 1:4; Zech. 9:14.
[8] Pss. 104:4; 135:7.

even more literally, 'the ship surely thought that it would result in being broken'. The colours in the language are wildly vivid. That Yahweh was the source of the tempest was confirmed when, finally, Jonah was hurled out of the ship into the sea. At that point, when the prophet gave himself up in order to save the lives of the mariners (v. 15), the storm was satisfied. In an instant the sea was stilled.

Gentile response (1:5–8)

> Then the mariners were afraid, and each cried to his god; and they threw the wares that were in the ship into the sea, to lighten it for them. But Jonah had gone down into the inner part of the ship and had lain down, and was fast asleep. (v. 5)

Confronted with the storm, the sailors do all that they humanly can to save their vessel and their very lives. They pray to their gods and hurl the cargo overboard. And, since we must assume they would not have set sail on such a dangerous voyage had there been any hint of bad weather, they set about investigating the cause of the storm. They had done their job well and were without blame – but the runaway, down in the lowest part of the ship, was fast asleep. He had put himself as far away as possible from life on board; he had achieved oblivion.

Deep and distant places

The word translated 'inner part' or 'lowest part' carries with it the idea of the 'furthest recesses' or 'depths'. Examples of its use in other parts of Scripture add to the flavour of the word. David hid himself from Saul in the 'innermost parts' of the cave.[9] The king of Babylon, who had set himself high among the nations, was humiliated and brought down to the 'depths' of *Sheol*.[10] To Jeremiah, the image of a great tempest, stirring itself on the margins or 'farthest parts' of society, was a hopeful symbol of the Lord's judgment in the face of international evil.[11] The image is extended in Jeremiah 31:8, where the Saviour God comes in triumph, gathering his people from the 'farthest parts of the earth' to restore them to their homeland. No remote scrap of land, no isolated tribe, no outcast, no dreg of the human species is beyond God's knowledge and care. It was through the least

[9] 1 Sam. 24:3.
[10] Is. 14:15.
[11] Jer. 25:32.

likely, the marginal, that he would bring his truth to bear in his work of redemption.

Curiously, in relation to Jonah, we discover that the location of Zebulun, the tribe in whose territory the prophet's home town was situated, is described as being 'at the shore', on the very edge of the sea.[12] Is there a hint here that Jonah was a man most at home on the margins of life? Being thrust into the centre of international affairs was not his métier. He preferred anonymity. He did not court publicity, preferring instead a quiet life. He would rather be a nobody in Tarshish than a somebody involved in God's mission in Nineveh. So at home was he in the inner recesses that, amid the fury of the storm, Jonah slept. But even if Jonah's personal preference was to lie low, he claimed allegiance to a God who called human beings to be involved in his work of redemption in the world. Declaring God's saving presence to be everywhere, the prophet Jeremiah puts it like this:

> Am I a God at hand, says the LORD, and not a God afar off? Can a man hide himself in secret places so that I cannot see him? says the LORD. Do I not fill heaven and earth? says the LORD.[13]

The unusual Hebrew phrase *yarkᵉṯê hasᵉp̄înâ*, translated 'the inner part of the ship', could also be a wordplay on the phrase *yarkᵉṯê ṣāp̄ôn*, referring to Mount Zion in Psalm 48:2. In the psalm Mount Zion is seen as 'the city of the great King' and a place of sure defence or refuge. In using this phrase, is the narrator tickling the ears of his listeners with sounds which remind them that Jonah's only secure refuge is his God? Jonah was taking drastic steps to escape and hide from this great God, and to find his security in what he imagined was God's absence. Despite all this, and equally humorously as we shall see, he was the means of the sailors coming to understand God in a new way.

Deep sleep

We might ask how it can be that a man overtaken by such a storm in himself could possibly fall asleep so deeply. It is not unusual, however, for people in profound denial of the situation in which they find themselves to seek out ways of avoiding its implications. Sleep, drink or drugs offer respite from inner turmoil. Jonah's sleep was a way of escaping the implications of his call, as well as the additional implications of his response.

[12] Gen. 49:13.
[13] Jer. 23:23.

The prophet's sleep was not a sign of faith and serenity in the way it was when Jesus was asleep in the boat.[14] The word *tardēmâ* is translated 'fast asleep'. At certain times God is spoken of as causing a particularly deep sleep to fall on someone. For example, God caused *tardēmâ* to fall on Adam before the creation of woman.[15] Later God discloses his everlasting commitment to his people in a dream after *tardēmâ* has fallen on Abram.[16] Jael[17] is enabled to slay Sisera, the enemy of God's people, because he was in *tardēmâ*. And when in conflict with Saul, king of Israel, David was preserved from death by *tardēmâ* which the Lord caused to fall on Saul's bodyguards.[18] In this way God may disable his people's enemies,[19] and even pour out *tardēmâ* on prophets, rendering them incapable of prophesying![20] In these examples God is at work creating and saving, unhelped and unhindered by a disabled humankind. While sleep gives Jonah a temporary way of escape, might it also be a hint that God is about to do a new thing with the man? Or was his deep sleep a sign that he was dead to the needs of the world? Either way, it is perfectly clear that Jonah was playing no active part in God's work. The contrast between the mariners' response to the storm and that of the prophet is striking. The key features of verse 5 can be set out in the following way, highlighting the logic of the contrast:

> Then the mariners were afraid,
> and each cried to his god;
> and they threw the wares that were in the ship into the sea . . .
> But Jonah had gone down into the inner part of the ship
> and had lain down,
> and was fast asleep.
>
> So the captain came and said to him, 'What do you mean, you sleeper? Arise, call upon your god! Perhaps the god will give a thought to us, that we do not perish.' (v. 6)

The Israelite who had fled from the centre of all things is now presented as paralysed in the heart of an endangered universe. Jonah is surrounded by pagans seeking deliverance. As they awaken him, the word of God addresses him once more, but this time on the lips of a

[14] Luke 8:22f.
[15] Gen. 2:21.
[16] Gen. 15:12.
[17] Judg. 4:21.
[18] 1 Sam. 26:12.
[19] See also Ps. 76:6.
[20] Is. 29:10.

heathen mariner. The captain urges him to wake up and pray to his god. The captain uses the same words to address Jonah as God used in verse 2: 'Arise . . .' God does not always address us through saints; he is just as free to use sinners as vehicles of his call. Surely Jonah must have been stung into remembrance? But even now, with certain disaster – including his own destruction – pending, there is no indication of the prophet calling on God. He remains silent. Jonah's lack of concern in this situation is as incredible as God's call to him in the first place! Is the man of God only comfortable so long as he is in control of when and to whom he preaches?

Is it sometimes the case that we Christians lie low through complacency or fear when surrounded by dire need? It is certainly the case that we do not often have answers when tragedy strikes, even though we have confidence in the Creator of all things. Our presence, prayer and solidarity with those in trouble witness to our God's concern with and involvement in all the different kinds of suffering with which human beings are afflicted.

Where is Jonah when disaster strikes? What does he mean? Religion apart, the natural response of anyone looking disaster in the face is to do something, anything, which might avert the tragedy or provide some form of damage limitation. Even the musicians on the deck of the *Titanic* did what they could in a hopeless situation. But Jonah remains silent. The man who fled from his evangelistic calling finds himself in the middle of an evangelistic situation. Is it that his initial disobedience jams his mouth shut? In asking 'How can you sleep?' the ship's captain was surely asking more than he knew. There is an unconcealed irony in this question. In an hour of danger to so many people of diverse beliefs, Jonah, the messenger of the Lord God, the Creator of heaven and earth, is asleep. We are reminded of Isaiah's complaint, 'Who is blind but my servant, or deaf as my messenger whom I send?'[21] Here a heathen shipmaster admonishes a prophet to pray, being apparently more aware of the power and efficacy of prayer than the fleeing prophet.

Tensions

We noted earlier how the writer set up tensions in the first three verses. Here we have further tensions emerging. We see an evident contrast between the frantic mariners struggling to save themselves and the prophet of God in a deep sleep; between the heathen praying for salvation and Jonah remaining silent. From the perspective of the ordinary believer, these things ought not to be. From the perspective

[21] Is. 42:19.

of the agnostic observer, they are intolerable. The Gentile sailors are more awake than Jonah. They are doing naturally what he has been called to do; they seek deliverance while he seeks oblivion. In this event we see a foreshadowing of what is yet to come. The people of Nineveh, whose wickedness had come up before God, turn out to be more responsive to God's word than Jonah, the prophet of the Lord. These tensions were the very stuff of the storm.

The actions of the sailors may have been driven by fear and panic. They were also practical expressions of their faith. Their gods may have been false, their beliefs may have been misguided, but their actions were thoroughly correct. They knew they were dependent on something greater than themselves; they knew how to express that dependence. Jonah's God was the true God, his belief was well founded, but his actions were wrong. His beliefs and his actions were uncoordinated. He was 'all at sea'. Right belief is no better than wrong belief if it is not corroborated by right actions.

In the New Testament James writes to Christians who have difficulties in this matter. He says:

> But be doers of the word, and not hearers only, deceiving yourselves. For if any one is a hearer of the word and not a doer, he is like a man who observes his natural face in a mirror; for he observes himself and goes away and at once forgets what he was like.[22]

Later he adds:

> What does it profit . . . if a man says he has faith but has not works? Can his faith save him? If a brother or sister is ill-clad and in lack of daily food, and one of you says to them, 'Go in peace, be warmed and filled,' without giving them the things needed for the body, what does it profit? So faith by itself, if it has no works, is dead.[23]

The tensions between faith and action remain unresolved throughout the book. They lie close to the heart of the story.

Faith asleep

Ellul sees in Jonah's sleep the sleep of the church at a time when those outside are struggling for salvation.[24] Or the sleep of high-minded Christians who are principled and embracing high ideals of acceptance,

[22] Jas. 1:22.
[23] Jas. 2:14–17.
[24] Ellul, p. 30.

justice, truth and love, who yet harbour racism, classism, sexism, prejudice and inequality in their very lifestyles. Being fast asleep to all but our own self-interest, we church people can sometimes be blind and deaf to the cries of many whose lives are no more than a grim struggle for survival. We may complacently espouse high moral and spiritual ideals without ever realizing our own human solidarity with others who struggle. We may even, from a comfortable distance, blame others for not being good, or diligent, or intelligent enough to seek these ideals. We may even believe ourselves to be in a tiny minority of good, faithful people, tempted to say 'I, even I only am left', being all but blind to the thousands of folk who call on God in their need. Some, unlike the Jonahs in the church, thankfully do expose themselves to God's uncomfortable countercultural call, even taking their families to live and work in difficult, inner-city 'problem estates'.

The lot fell on Jonah

> And they said to one another, 'Come, let us cast lots, that we may know on whose account this evil has come upon us.' So they cast lots and the lot fell upon Jonah. (v. 7)

In the face of Jonah's continued silence, the mariners pursued the only way they knew to save themselves. Their heathen insights were not far off the mark. They believed that someone was aboard ship who had displeased their god. This accounted for the storm which imperilled all their lives. Is the story-teller dropping a hint here that Jonah's silence resulted in the sailors' presumption that Yahweh was like one of their gods?

In order to discover who the culprit might be, they cast lots and the lot fell on Jonah. Some Jewish interpreters have suggested here that, despite the peril they were in, the sailors were not content with the outcome of just one lot. No, they cast lots. They needed a corroboration of lots in order to be absolutely certain that they had identified the right person. The divine response was decisive. The lot fell on Jonah. He was the cause of the storm. In evading his responsibility before God, Jonah was responsible for the peril of the pagans.

The casting of lots was a normal procedure when discernment was needed. Proverbs 16:33 refers to the belief that the Lord makes his will known in the casting of the lot. Before the establishment of a hereditary monarchy, for example, lots were cast in choosing a king.[25] The practice continued into the New Testament period: the Roman soldiers cast lots for the clothes of Jesus, whom they had

[25] 1 Sam. 10:21.

crucified.[26] When the disciples were seeking a replacement for Judas Iscariot, the lot fell on Matthias.[27]

With regard to the pagan practice of casting lots as a way of discerning the will of the gods, it has been said:

> The drawing of lots 'works' – for magic is indeed the technology of ancient heathendom just as technology is the magic of modern heathendom. Both, practically speaking, are equally effective in their respective sphere of action: the lot is cast to determine 'for whose cause this evil is upon us', and it falls on Jonah.[28]

Evil

The Hebrew word, *raʿ*, meaning bad or evil, pervades the narrative.[29] In the first eight verses of chapter 1 there are three occurrences of this little Hebrew word with a big meaning. It is first used in verse 2 where God, speaking of Nineveh, says, 'Their *raʿ* has come up before me.' Here *raʿ* is normally translated in such a way as to convey a sense of moral judgment. Thus the RV, RSV, NIV and NRSV translate it 'wickedness'. However, when *raʿ* appears for the second and third time in verses 7 and 8, the NIV and NRSV translate it 'calamity', while the RV and RSV use 'evil'. Popular imagery of Nineveh requires that we attribute a moral quality to the word in verse 2, but can the same moral nuance be intended in verses 7 and 8?

Raʿ has many shades of meaning. Fundamentally, 'evil' is an action or a state of being which is detrimental to life in its fullness. Whether in the physical, moral or spiritual realm, evil is a departure from that which is ideal and desired for the full flourishing and enjoyment of life as God intends it. In the same way that our experience of physical or moral darkness presupposes our experience of light, so evil presupposes goodness. In biblical thought, goodness and evil are not purely abstract concepts; they are moral and practical attitudes, actions and ways of living.

Raʿ is frequently used, for example, to speak of people who are wicked. The lethal combination of their attitudes, thoughts, words and actions result in the destructive hurt of others. The grim consequences which accumulate in the face of this human evil are illustrated in Ezekiel 6:11: 'Thus says the Lord GOD: "Clap your hands, and stamp your foot, and say, Alas! because of all the evil

[26] Mark 15:14.
[27] Acts 1:26.
[28] Assembly of Rabbis, p. 993.
[29] See Jonah 1:2, 7, 8; 3:8, 10; 4:2. The feminine form is *rāʿâ*.

abominations of the house of Israel; for they shall fall by the sword, by famine, and by pestilence."'

Ra' may also mean 'bad' or 'unpleasant' in the sense of giving pain or causing unhappiness, as in Proverbs 15:10, where *ra'* is translated 'severe': 'There is severe discipline for him who forsakes the way; he who hates reproof will die.'

Ra' may also denote fierceness or wildness, as in Genesis 37:20 and 33: 'Come now, let us kill him and throw him into one of the pits; then we shall say that a wild beast has devoured him, and we shall see what will become of his dreams.'

Ra' can also refer to something of poor or inferior quality, such as in Jeremiah 24:2: 'One basket had very good figs, like first-ripe figs, but the other basket had very bad figs, so bad that they could not be eaten.'[30]

In Isaiah 45:7 the Lord describes his actions by saying,

> I form light and create darkness,
> I make weal and create woe,
> I am the LORD, who do all these things.

The RSV rightly uses 'woe', meaning calamity or disaster, to translate *ra'* here. 'Weal' is used, perhaps less felicitously but nevertheless poetically, to translate the Hebrew term *šālôm*. In other words, Isaiah does not assert that the Lord creates moral evil. Rather, he affirms that as absolute sovereign the Lord creates a universe governed by a moral order. Calamity or woe will surely ensue from the wickedness of the ungodly. In the divine mercy it becomes a means of recreating *šālôm*.

Thus, in a world where meteorological storms were believed to be influenced by the gods, the sailors were naturally anxious to know why the 'calamity' (*ra'*) of the storm had come upon them. They believed the storm was a sign of divine displeasure occasioned by wickedness. Today we are unlikely to use a word with moral overtones such as 'evil' when speaking of a meteorological event, but we might want to speak of the human suffering, affliction, misfortune or adversity caused by natural events such as typhoons, floods or earthquakes.

For the people of Nineveh, Jonah and the mariners, *ra'* brought disaster and suffering. None was at peace, not even Jonah, despite his slumbers. The moral wickedness of Nineveh, the spiritual disobedience of Jonah and the physical power of the storm which hit the mariners created 'woe', 'calamity' or 'evil'. The mariners were

[30] AV translates *ra'* here as 'naughty': '. . . very naughty figs . . .'

innocent sufferers. The people of Nineveh may or may not have been innocent, but the man Jonah, by turning away from God, was guilty of evil. By his disobedience he not only deprived Nineveh of an opportunity to repent, he also brought disaster on the poor mariners on whom he depended for his great escape. He was avoiding involvement in the work of God by avoiding God's call to address the legitimate claims of God's world.

When the lot fell on Jonah he was identified as the cause of the 'evil'. In his state of disobedience, Jonah could not be separated from his *ra'*. In the absence of penitence on his part, his very presence was the affliction. He had to go. We shall return to the word *ra'* in chapters 3 and 4, where it has further significance in the story.

Who are you?

> Then they said to him, 'Tell us on whose account this evil has come upon us. What is your occupation? And whence do you come? What is your country? And of what people are you?' (v. 8)

In their desperate struggle to discern the cause of the storm which threatened all they had, the mariners put four questions to Jonah.

> They first asked him about his work ... for perhaps he was a magician or sorcerer and had caused this storm by sorcery. Then they enquired as to his route ... perhaps he was a messenger for such evil men. Next they asked about his country – perhaps he came from a bad country or from an area that they hated. Finally they enquired as to his people ... perhaps he came from an evil-doing people.[31]

Here Abraham bar Hiyya captures in his final comment the irony of the situation. How could a good man be the cause of such calamity or *ra'*? All the evidence pointed to Jonah's guilt. How could he alone be the cause of such terror? Surely he must be associated in some way with an 'evil-doing people'?

Identity of God's people

The form of the Hebrew emphasizes the force of the question, 'And of what people are you?' This is the ultimate question, the climax of several concerning Jonah's identity. What kind of person could this

[31] Assembly of Rabbis, p. 993.

be who does not pray for deliverance from the storm? What kind of thing can he have done to cause this evil? What kind of people shelters such a man as this? Underlying these questions is the key one: 'What kind of God do you serve?' What kind of God would unleash a wind of such ferocity? What kind of behaviour could provoke such a disaster? To what kind of God was Jonah bearing witness?

In the stricken ship the prophet shares solidarity with the pagans. All are under the threat of destruction. He knows the reason for the storm and must now choose whether to keep quiet or to confess his guilt. All look to him. In admitting responsibility he may yet save the ship; in remaining silent all will be lost.

In his sleeping Jonah had spoken volumes! He did not want anyone to know who he was. The strength of his desire to remain unknown was greater than his willingness to show solidarity with the suffering of others. The sailors' questions were critical in leading to Jonah's identity being made known. In challenging him, the sailors also aided his own self-recognition. At last Jonah is on the road to acknowledging his identity, of owning who he is. In this acknowledgment he can begin to accept responsibility; he learns that what he does, as well as what he does not do, affects the well-being of others.

In remaining hidden among the crowd, we can, like Jonah, hide from responsibility and escape self-knowledge. In recent years statistics have suggested that fewer people make the effort to vote in local and general elections than used to be the case. While a weariness with politics may be one reason for this, another must be the unwillingness in potential voters to accept responsibility. It is easier to be one of the faceless people who are generally dissatisfied than to stand up and share responsibility for the situation. To stand up and do something is often difficult. We risk rejection and disgrace. It is easier to avoid the legitimate claims of the world, to hide, to take the line of least resistance, than to risk humiliation. Today we can hide in leisure pursuits, academia, fashion, wealth accumulation or even organized religion, all the while believing we are pursuing a good life. But as long as we are consumed or driven by these pursuits, we will be in danger of remaining faceless to each other and ourselves. The good life is to be found in working for the well-being of others in response to God's commitment, shown in Jesus Christ, to our wholeness and well-being. We human beings are driven not by stars and planets but by the forces of gods, such as greed, which we are sometimes loath to own, or of which we are ignorant. In being unable or unwilling to own our God, we become unable to know or own our lives and identities. In seeking our security and identity in the crowd, we lose our own souls. 'Conformity and the impulse to remain one of the crowd is the great destroyer of selfhood.'[32]

Yet we might imagine that Jonah was well known, even admired, among his own group or congregation. There would be no question about his identity in that context. But such was his commitment to his own group that he had lost touch with others outside it. He not only lost touch, he also lost the language common to humanity. He did not know who he was in relation to others outside his own group, and had lost the means of finding out. He had forgotten that his God was no sectarian deity. He was the Lord of heaven and earth. Questions on the lips of the heathen outsiders were crucial for Jonah to regain his identity, and it is in this context that he names his God (v. 9). In the same way that the pagan sailors did great service to the prophet, so the world can be God's instrument in addressing the Christian churches and enabling them to recognize themselves afresh.

The nations and Israel

The relationship of God's chosen people to the world is a question which has to be faced by each generation of believers. Broadly speaking, the question is this: are the chosen ones to assimilate and live in equal relationship to the rest of humankind, or are they to stand apart from the world in order to maintain their distinctive calling?

Those seeking guidance from the Scriptures on this question will find some passages indicating that God's people are a distinct and holy people called out from the midst of a sinful world.[33] Other passages challenge the easy assumption of God's people who, while failing to fulfil the moral obligations of their calling, still claim exclusive rights to being God's chosen ones.[34] The burden of Amos here is that the Lord has close dealings with all the nations, yet it is to Israel alone that the knowledge of salvation has been revealed. As recipients of this revelation, God's people are expected to live as lights shining in the world, not as arrogant people boasting of their good fortune in having been chosen by God. In espousing such a proud attitude, Israel's light was in grave danger of being extinguished. Yet other passages assume that God calls and empowers both individuals and nations who do not know him in order to bring about his salvation.[35]

[32] LaCocque and Lacocque, p. 86.
[33] Ezra 10:11.
[34] Amos 9:7.
[35] Both Ezra 1:1ff. and Isaiah 45:1ff. speak of the Lord choosing Cyrus, the Persian king.

Generally speaking, it is a commonly held belief in the Old Testament that the Gentile nations can be a means of Israel's salvation as well as being co-inheritors with her of the blessings of the Creator Redeemer God.[36] Isaiah 44:28 – 45:1 refers to the great Persian ruler Cyrus as the Lord's anointed, that is, his messiah. The passage goes on to say that Cyrus does not know the Lord who calls him by name. Maybe this great king, whose reign and character are well attested in ancient literature outside the pages of Scripture, never knew the Lord God who so named him and used him as a means of deliverance and blessing for his people.

In the New Testament Jesus says that those who are his disciples *are* different.[37] Not that this means they should keep themselves separate from everyone else. Rather, he teaches them that they are salt and light; their saltiness and their quality of light are strikingly recognized in the context of food which needs salt and darkness which needs light. In similar vein, the holiness of our Lord Jesus Christ did not drive him to remain apart from sinners. It drove him to be born in Bethlehem, to mix with collaborators and other sinners, and to die the death of a criminal in the company of thieves. There is something world-affirming about the gospel of Jesus Christ. 'For God so loved the world that he gave his only Son, that whoever believes in him should not perish but have eternal life.'[38] The world is *worth* saving. It is capable of being transformed through the compassionate love of the Lord who values it so much that he gave his life for its life.

Paul teaches that deliverance will be complete only when both Israel and the nations are brought to the knowledge of God. This will be the occasion of the cosmic celebration, the messianic banquet. Paul argues that without the Jews the Gentiles cannot fully enjoy God's salvation.[39] In the same way God's work of salvation is incomplete without the Gentiles.

The distinctiveness of God's chosen people

Among the nations of the world, Israel was chosen to receive the sacred revelation we now have in Scripture. The theological and literary heritage of that tiny nation is incomparable on any scale. Through the wealth of this heritage the souls of nations have been nourished to this day. Her ancient Scriptures have been a light to the

[36] See, e.g., Is. 19:25; 45:20, 22; 51:5; 57:6; 60:11; Zech. 8:23.
[37] Matt. 5:13–16.
[38] John 3:16.
[39] Rom. 11:12, 28–36.

nations. Who would have imagined the words of Genesis 1 being read from the surface of the moon by the first men to set foot there?[40] But most especially it is in their witness to the Lord Jesus Christ that the full significance of the Scriptures lie.

In the book of Deuteronomy,[41] the 'chosen ones' are reminded that they are not chosen for any special quality in themselves; they are chosen because the Lord loves them. The reasons for his love are not disclosed. In the same way, the reason why God loves the world is not disclosed in John's Gospel. He loves because he chooses to love and because it is his nature to love. His committed and passionate love is shown in the inexhaustible way he stays with his people. The story of God's love affair with the world and its people began at creation and continues unabated today. Sadly, the 'chosen ones' are often subject to the most insidious temptation to consider themselves to be a cut above the rest, a temptation about which Paul warns Christians in the most severe way.[42]

Christians are not called to be a cut above the rest

Christ's followers are called to go into all the world and make disciples. The Lord Jesus gives us a responsibility which is international in scope because he is the Lord of all creation. He does not call us to set up international organizations, but to make disciples. In the Gospels Christ gives us a pattern to follow.[43] When sending out the disciples he instructs them to offer the greeting, 'Peace be to this house.' They go in his name, at his call and share his peace with those to whom they go. It is the peace ushered in by the kingdom of God which they are to offer. It is not merely a cosy feeling which is experienced between some people but not others. It is the equivalent of a divine amnesty in which the Lord God no longer remembers the sins and debts of his people. He has made up his mind to forgive us; he does not need us to persuade him. He comes to us in peace. Our risen Lord is the evidence of this. His followers are to tell others by their lips and their lives that the divine King comes in peace. This offer of wholeness is made to everyone.

God's peace is contingent on only one thing: that we actively receive it. No demand is made, for example, to give up smoking, covetousness or greed *before* we can receive God's peace. The grace of God always precedes ethics. It is as we receive the gracious gift of God's peace in

[40] Neil Armstrong and Edwin Aldrin in July 1969.
[41] Deut. 7:6–8.
[42] Rom. 11:21.
[43] See, e.g., Matt. 9:5–38; 10:1–14; Mark 6:8–11; Luke 10:1–10.

Christ that our lives gradually become subject to his just and gentle rule. The sharing of peace brings stability as we live patiently with each other, gradually being changed from glory to glory.

The world to which we are sent, however, proliferates with rampant self-interest. Everyone is affected by it. God's peace is to be offered to people where they are. The peace of the kingdom may be rejected, for it shows up self-interest in sharp relief. Whatever clothes of respectability it wears, self-interest is revealed in our neglect of people, our readiness to use others for our own ends, the exploitation of children and the vulnerable by big business, the creation of addictive cultures which consume our souls, the poisonous, unforgiving, punitive and manipulative strategies we adopt to undermine others.

In the face of all this, it is the distinctive calling of the Lord's own people to bring the peace of the kingdom of God to the world. The Lord Jesus himself offers us the clearest pattern for our calling: his disciples are not greater than their master. They will find themselves on the edge of established structures. They will be misunderstood and humiliated and their goodness abused. Far from gathering his frightened little flock into the safety of the fold, Matthew tells us that the Good Shepherd sends them out as sheep among wolves.[44] They will suffer for his sake.

Christian distinctiveness has sometimes been sought in well-intentioned but restrictive and isolationist ways. It was understood as a call to be separate from the world, to disavow and repudiate the theatre, literature, sport, fashion, make-up and dancing. This valiant attempt to assuage the tides of evil certainly had the effect of marking Christians out. But such a negative approach, while rightly condemning certain attractive features of human society, failed to communicate the glorious peace of the kingdom of God. It suggested that Christ came to restrict human life rather than bring it to its fullness. Christian distinctiveness does not lie in sectarianism, perfectionism or social isolationism. It lies in the call of Christ to go and make disciples of all nations. They go knowing all too well their own frailties and failures, but trusting in the transforming grace of God's peace.

The popular image of the crusader going to frighten and force people to convert to Christ does great injustice to Christ's teaching and call. Rather, the image of one beggar leading another beggar to the place where he or she will find bread captures the spirit of Christian distinctiveness. Jonah was as much in need of the Lord's grace and mercy as the mariners and the Ninevites. Moreover, it was not the prophet who brought them to new life; it was the word of a gracious God.

[44]Matt. 10:16.

1:9–16

4. The prophet speaks

> And he said to them, 'I am a Hebrew; and I fear the LORD, the God of heaven, who made the sea and the dry land.' (v. 9)

Jonah's silence is broken. At last he speaks. The narrator highlights his first utterance by putting it at the centre of the narrative. It is as though a word has been sought from the prophet since he fled. The reader has looked for an explanation of his action. The narrative builds up to this point when the prophet's word is finally uttered. The rest of the story flows from here. This can be demonstrated by an arrangement of the main elements of the story in chapter 1:

A Introduction – Jonah flees the Lord (1:3)
  B The Lord hurls the storm (1:4)
    C Sailors pray and act (1:5b)
      D Jonah acts (1:5c)
        E Sailors question Jonah (1:6–8)
          F *Jonah speaks* (1:9)
        E1 Sailors question Jonah (1:10–11)
      D1 Jonah responds (1:12)
    C1 Sailors act (1:13–14)
  B1 Sailors hurl Jonah, the storm ends (1:15)
A1 Conclusion – sailors fear the Lord (1:16)[1]

As if to suggest matters being resolved, the events leading up to Jonah's first speech (F in the diagram above) are mirrored as the first part of the story comes to a conclusion. By setting out the chapter in this way, we can see that A, B, C, D and E reach their climax in F. Similarly, E1, D1, C1, B1 and A1 show a corresponding progression towards the end of this first section.

[1] Limburg, p. 47.

'I am a Hebrew' (1:9)

In one sense the prophet ignores the question concerning his occupation. He does not say that God has given him the task of going to Nineveh; he is escaping still from his vocation. Yet in another sense he has stated it by saying that he 'fears the Lord'. In one sense he does fear the Lord, for he is an Israelite, one of God's covenant people. Yet again he does not fear the Lord, for he is running away from him. He also overlooks the question about where he is from; only the reader listening in at this point knows that he comes from the presence of the Lord.

His words 'I am a Hebrew' are unique in the Bible. The more usual expression would have been 'I am an Israelite', or 'I am a prophet in Israel'. Why might the narrator have put the unusual word 'Hebrew' on his lips?

One possibility is that 'Hebrew' was better understood by foreigners than 'Israelite'. If this is the case, and evidence suggests this usage elsewhere,[2] then Jonah was shown as someone sensitive to this convention.

Another possibility is that the narrator introduces the word 'Hebrew' because the audience he was addressing would be better able to identify with that description. In this case the word 'Israelite' was avoided because it carried connotations of the covenant, with its overtones of nationalism or exclusivism. Explicit references to the covenant theme are noticeably absent from Jonah. Moreover, in a text concerned with Israel's relationship to other nations, this could have been appropriate.

Alternatively, 'Hebrew' may be used with the specific purpose of Jonah marking himself off from the pagans. It may have been equivalent to him saying 'I am a Christian'. In this case he speaks plainly and unambiguously to strangers, even if it offends them.

Or maybe there is a humorous attempt here to contrast themes from Genesis. For example, Abram 'the Hebrew'[3] responded obediently to God's call to leave home in search of the Promised Land. Jonah the Hebrew, on the other hand, set out to find his own promised land!

In the New Testament, Paul, setting out his curriculum vitae, speaks of himself as a 'Hebrew born of Hebrews'.[4] This probably refers to his retention of the Hebrew or Aramaic language and culture in the midst of the Hellenism of his day, and this despite

[2] Gen. 39:14, 17; 41:12; 43:32; 1 Sam. 4:6, 9; 13:19.
[3] Gen. 14:13.
[4] Phil. 3:6ff.

being an apostle to the Gentiles. He is saying to the Philippian disciples, undermined by Jewish believers who asserted the need for circumcision and the fulfilment of Jewish law, that he himself was a genuine Jew – a Hebrew. As such his credentials were impeccable and his teaching, even though it contradicted that of the Jewish believers on this point, was to be trusted.

Since Jonah's first words are set at the centre of the narrative, we expect them to have special significance. Jonah himself interprets for his interrogators the meaning of being a Hebrew by adding, 'and I fear the LORD, the God of heaven, who made the sea and the dry land'. He confesses his allegiance to Yahweh, the supreme God of heaven, adding that he is the creator of the sea (and no doubt the storm) and the dry land, a phrase which must have had particular poignancy to those who heard it. Ironically, it is his claim to fear Yahweh, a claim blatantly at odds with his response to God's call, which the narrator considers most significant.

In confessing that he is a Hebrew who fears the Lord, the God of heaven, Jonah emerges from his hiding place, and in so doing becomes who he is. His recognition by the sailors aids his own self-recognition. At last he is on the road to acknowledging his own identity, of owning who he is.

Jonah's flight is stopped by the questions from the heathen crewmen. He hears them, and in so doing shows the first indication of overcoming the human impulse to hide. He is no longer simply one of the crowd. Jonah's hopes for anonymity were dashed by the hopes of the sailors to identify the cause of the storm.

Now his claim is open to being challenged by the pagans. They were in no doubt that the gods were capable of rescuing them if only they could find the right key, that is, the right god, and the cause of the storm. In putting Jonah on the spot, the pagan sailors were putting his God on the spot. It is they who force the issue. Jonah appears to have been happy to let the storm do its worst, but the pagans will not accept this and Jonah, in extremis, is forced to declare himself as one who 'fears' the Lord. His claim will now be put to the test.

Words used when referring to the Deity

Before proceeding further, we should also notice that Jonah speaks to the sailors of 'the LORD, the God of heaven . . .' Different words are used in the Hebrew Scriptures when speaking of the Deity. In the book of Jonah we find two words being used. Both terms, 'LORD' and 'God', derive from different Hebrew words and both are used here in verse 9. With the exception of the Jerusalem Bible, the

English versions use 'LORD' as a representation of the Hebrew word *yhwh* (usually rendered in English as YHWH). The Jerusalem Bible uses these four Hebrew letters, adding the vowels to give 'Yahweh', instead of using 'LORD'.

The use of 'LORD' derives from ancient Jewish practice. The divine name, YHWH, was regarded with the greatest reverence and not spoken. Whenever the Hebrew word *yhwh* occurred in the text, the word *'ᵃḏōnāy*, meaning 'My great Lord', would be read instead. The vowel sounds of the Hebrew word *'ᵃḏōnāy* were combined with the consonants of *yhwh* in order to remind readers to use the word *'ᵃḏōnāy*.[5]

The four Hebrew letters, known technically as the tetragrammaton, lack any vowel sounds, making it impossible to know just how the name should be pronounced. The divine name revealed by the Lord to Moses in Exodus 3:13–15 is linked, possibly by the sound of the phrase, to *ehyeh*, meaning 'I am'. The emphasis of the word leans much more towards 'I am present' than towards 'I exist'. It refers to the unique nature of the covenant God of Israel. YHWH is 'I AM', the God who is present, who has been and who will be present for his people. Further reference is made to God's name in Exodus 33:19 and 34:6–7, where it focuses particularly on the merciful, compassionate and redemptive aspects of God's nature.

The second word, 'God', translates the Hebrew *'ᵉlōhîm*. This word is plural and just occasionally means 'gods', as in Exodus 20:3. Most usually, however, it is a plural of majesty used in referring to Israel's God. In English we normally indicate the plural, meaning more than one, by adding 's' at the end of the word. In Hebrew idiom the plural is used not simply to indicate quantity, but also frequently to indicate quality. Thus *'ᵉlōhîm* does not mean 'a number of gods'; it means a particular quality of godness or godhood. The plural word intensifies and amplifies the idea of god: *'ᵉlōhîm* is more godlike than any god. It refers to the supreme Deity, that is, the God of gods. This supreme God reveals his name to his own people as YHWH. To the nations who do not know the name and covenant character of God, the supreme God is known as *'ᵉlōhîm*. In speaking of 'the LORD, the God of heaven' Jonah is confessing his fear of YHWH, the name of the God who has brought Israel into being, and affirming his knowledge that YHWH is the supreme God of all creation, that is, *'ᵉlōhîm*. Thus YHWH is God of the Gentile nations too.

[5]The incorrect term 'Jehovah' arose from Christian misunderstanding of the Hebrew idiom in the late Middle Ages.

In forty-eight verses there is a total of thirty-nine references to the Deity: *yhwh* is mentioned twenty-two times, *'elōhîm* thirteen times and *yhwh 'elōhîm* four times. This high frequency of references to the Deity underlines the theological character of the book and contrasts with some other biblical texts where little[6] or no[7] reference is made to God.

A question might be asked about whether there is any special significance in the way the narrator uses these terms in Jonah. Scholars vary in their views.[8] The Jewish scholar Magonet argues strongly that the significance of the usage of the two words lies in the two aspects of God's nature, his compassion revealed in YHWH and his severity revealed in *'elōhîm*. God's people are those who experience and live by YHWH's compassion. Others, such as the mariners and the Ninevites, live by his severity until such time as they experience his compassion. Jonah's instinct to sever his links with the compassionate God rebounds on his own head. He is delivered only by the compassionate YHWH.

Whether or not the narrator deliberately weights the two words with subtle meaning, the text is plain. On the lips of the Gentiles, 'For thou, O LORD, hast done as it pleased thee' (1:14), and on the lips of Jonah, 'Deliverance belongs to the LORD!' (2:9). It is the Lord God who is sovereign, bringing both disaster and deliverance. Now in what way does Jonah 'fear' this God?

Fear (1:9–16)

'Fear' is a recurrent theme in these verses and, in part, the book is an exploration of its meaning. Different nuances of 'fear' are suggested. For example, when Jonah says he 'fears God' he acknowledges that he himself is a creature, finite and limited in every way. He recognizes his capacity to be in relationship with his Creator. For this reason he claims to 'fear' (RSV) or 'worship' (NIV) the Lord as Creator of everything, including the storm and the pagans who press upon him. On the other hand, his 'fear' causes him to run away from this Creator. It is because of this fear that he has been hiding in the bowels of the ship.

Martin Buber makes the following helpful comment:

[6] The narrator of the book of Ruth refers only twice to God. Similarly, in the narratives of 2 Samuel 8–11 only one reference is made to the Lord (11:27).

[7] Such as in the story of Esther.

[8] Sasson, p. 18, sees no patterns, and Stuart, p. 438, considers the usage 'not easily explained'. Magonet (1983), p. 38, argues a case for the names pointing to two theological systems being at work.

> 'Fear of God' . . . never means to the Jews that they ought to be afraid of God, but that, trembling, they ought to be aware of His incomprehensibility . . . It is the dark gate through which man must pass if he is to enter into the love of God. He who wishes to avoid passing through this gate, he who begins to provide for himself a comprehensible God, constructed thus and not otherwise, runs the risk of having to despair of God in view of the actualities of history and life, or of falling into inner falsehood. Only through the fear of God does man enter so deep into the love of God that he cannot again be cast out of it.[9]

The 'fear' of the sailors (v. 5) compelled them to pray to their gods and to lighten the ship's cargo. As the storm rages, experienced mariners struggle to save the ship, its passenger and crew. By contrast, Jonah's fear of God led him to hide. In fleeing the Lord's presence we see that his 'fear' energized him to save himself in an emergency. Cocooned from realizing the consequences of his action, he is careless in the midst of a suffering world. His 'fear of the Lord' is distinctly ambiguous. Real 'fear of the Lord' is shown in humble obedience reflected in the worship and service of God. Complacency creeps into the human heart as the fear of the Lord diminishes.

Ironically, the pagans were more committed to their faith than Jonah was to his; at least they prayed and sought divine assistance. By Israelite standards theirs was an inadequate faith, one which deprived the mariners of the fullness of blessing. By contrast, Jonah, who enjoyed all the blessings of knowing Yahweh, epitomized the privatization of faith. In other words, his faith was a private matter, unconnected to the world around him. But God will have none of this. He will forever call his people out for their own sake as well as for the sake of the world. This is not to say that God constantly calls believers to incredible and heroic acts of faith. It means simply that, daily, Christians are called to 'follow Christ' in whatever way he leads them. At times this may be something extraordinary, such as leaving home, family and career to serve Christ in an alien culture. For most of us it involves daily taking up a cross and living a life which witnesses to a frequently countercultural gospel. In these verses we see God, through the distress cries of the pagans, calling Jonah to get up and do something. This illustrates the dialectic between the world and the believer, the implication of which is that God uses pagans to rouse believers. The unsung sacrifice made by many dedicated and unbelieving international aid workers is a challenge to comfortable Christians who may prefer only to sing about God's love.

[9] Assembly of Rabbis, p. 627.

Standing or walking?

It is often easier to stand by credal statements than to walk by them. The role of the world is to challenge believers to identify themselves as witnesses to the Lord God and to walk or live by the beliefs by which they stand. Such a call is hard for believers when privatization and conformity are the prevailing values in society. To a degree some Christian thinking has undergirded, if not actually shaped, these values with its stress on individual salvation over corporate responsibility. When, for example, through the media or through personal experience a general belief that the world is evil prevails, it is hard to affirm God's love. It is well nigh impossible, if we concede to the view that God makes no difference to everyday lives, to proclaim God's peace in the person of Jesus Christ. Today it is very easy to be shaped by good pagans who believe themselves wise in the ways of the world and who, cynically, do not believe the Lord Jesus Christ has any relevance to today's world. Was Jonah shaped by some conformism which made him unable to respond to an alien culture? Or did the prevailing belief in the wickedness of Nineveh lead him to think that God should write off the city? Or was he tempted to believe that God really could not make any difference to the people of Nineveh? In fleeing his presence Jonah was setting out to ensure that God made no changes in his life!

Multifaith culture

It might be worth recalling that the culture in which Jonah was set was no less 'multifaith' than ours today. Jonah was being challenged by God to venture out in a way unheard of in a polytheistic culture. Surely the Ninevites, and the mariners, had their own gods to help them? 'No,' says the Lord, Creator of heaven and earth, the sea and the dry land. Jonah must go, for the religious instincts which God has created in the human heart are fulfilled by his love alone.

It is easy to imagine when reading the Hebrew Scriptures that the chief concern of the prophets was with the moral and spiritual integrity of Israel. To a large extent this is true, but it is also true that frequent mention is made of God's concern for the other nations. In some passages the prophets pronounce judgment on pagan nations for their crimes.[10] In other places Israel herself is condemned for her behaviour because, by her social complacency, injustice and wickedness, she brought God's character into disrepute.[11] In

[10] Is. 13 – 23; Jer. 46 – 50; Amos 1 – 2; Nahum, etc.
[11] Is. 1; 2:6 – 4:1; Jer. 7; Ezek. 20 – 22, etc.

misrepresenting him to the pagans she dishonoured him. YHWH was not a God to collude with his people in wickedness. He had called them to be a means of blessing to the nations; they were to be a light to the nations, a witness to God's excellent teaching. A frequent image of 'utopia' in Scripture is when the nations flock to Jerusalem to learn about the glory of Israel's Lord and God.[12] Only in YHWH could their hearts' needs be fulfilled.

How might this speak to a society in which different faith groups more or less coexist? For many today Christian belief, which was formerly regarded as absolute, has become relative. In a country where the national religion of Christianity has long been unchallenged, we Christians may have come to rest on our laurels. Christianity brought in its wake great blessings: a moral code, a literary heritage, great reformers and a zeal for Christ which inspired thousands of men and women to travel the globe to introduce the Christian gospel to other cultures. Ironically, in a country which has such a prestigious Christian history, many have become uneducated in the real nature of the Christian faith. Christianity and the Lord Jesus Christ have become just one faith among many from which to pick and choose. It is in this context that the devout seriousness of some adherents to other faiths, such as Islam, has become a challenge to Christians and pagans alike.

In contrast to a pagan culture, however, Christians, Muslims and Jews have much in common: a belief in one God, and a merciful God at that; a high regard for sacred Scripture,[13] moral values and the centrality of family and community life as the forum in which responsible human living takes place. All this contrasts sharply with the rather haphazard view of many pagans that 'god' exists, that Scripture is ancient and irrelevant, that moral values are relative and that a general hedonism is the only way in which individuals and their families can survive the myriad choices and problems of life which face them.

The Christian battle was once believed to be against these different monotheistic faith communities. Indeed, to our deep shame, Christian history is littered with atrocities against Jews and Muslims performed in the name of Christ. But maybe the Christ of these Christians was too small. Just as Isaiah claims the incomparability of YHWH,[14] so also Christians claim the incomparability of Christ.[15] It is his gracious

[12] Is. 2:1–4; 56:6–9; Mic. 4:1–3, etc.

[13] All three monotheistic faiths share some aspects of Scripture in common. The New Testament witnessing to the uniqueness of the Lord Jesus Christ, as risen from the dead as the Son of God, is distinctively Christian. This claim is a stumbling block to many.

[14] Is. 40:18, 25.

[15] John 14:6; Acts 4:12, etc.

beauty and glory which will draw all people to himself, not the punitive, physical or verbal violence of his followers. Christians do not need to fear other faith communities. They simply need to fear the Lord, by entering more deeply into knowing and then following this fearless Christ. Maybe, in the same way that Jonah was called to show his 'fear of the Lord' by his love and obedience, Christians too need to fear the Lord Jesus Christ by their love and obedience. Standing by creeds must be expressed by walking with the Lord God. Perhaps the greatest need in Britain today is twofold: first, for the gracious and compassionate love of God in Christ Jesus to be revealed afresh in contemporary mode through the lives of his followers, and second, for Christians to live by a love and faith which is countercultural and challenging of contemporary values and norms. By such witness Christ will draw all people to himself.

Across the pages of the New Testament we see many instances where Jesus and his followers find ways of engaging creatively with the religious and cultural diversity of their day. Whether it was Jesus in conversation with the Samaritan woman, the Roman centurion or the Syro-Phoenician woman, Peter and Cornelius, or Paul witnessing in the great Greek city centres of Athens, Corinth and Ephesus, we see from the earliest times an ability to share with people, whatever their religious and cultural heritage, the treasures of the good news of God's peace through Christ.

I recall some years ago being in a party of Christians climbing Mount Sinai. A small group of young Muslims straggled up the rocky path with us. As dawn broke we reached the summit. While we stared around, fascinated by what we saw and eagerly absorbing what our senses offered, our Muslim friends fell to the ground in worship. Both Christians and Muslims regard the mountain as significant, but it seemed to me that our Muslim friends were pilgrims while we Christians were tourists.

Pressure mounts

> Then the men were exceedingly afraid . . . (v. 10a)

The sailors were 'afraid' – the word's third appearance in the story so far. Now its force is intensified by Jonah's confession. Literally, verse 10 reads, 'And the men were afraid – greatly afraid.'

The pagans recognized the awfulness of Jonah's flight more clearly than he did. They saw a human being challenging his god! What's more, his flight from God was impacting on their lives in the dark roar of the storm. The fear of the sailors forced Jonah to face the social implication of his flight from the presence of Yahweh. In other words, his flight from God's presence affected the people around him. They say to him:

> 'What is this that you have done!' For the men knew that he was fleeing from the presence of the LORD, because he had told them. (v. 10b)

Though the author does not give us the words Jonah used when telling the mariners that he was fleeing from the Lord, they only added to the sailors' anxiety. Reflecting on the unspoken feelings of the mariners after having heard Jonah's confession, Matthew Henry offers the following comment: 'If a prophet of the Lord be thus severely punished for one offence, what will become of us that have been guilty of so many great, and heinous offences?'[16]

'What is this that you have done?' they ask. This question is identical to that posed by the Lord God to Adam in the Garden of Eden.[17] Is the writer hinting here at some comparability between Adam and Eve and Jonah? Certainly, in both stories the culprits seek to hide from God, and it is becoming plain that Jonah's game of hide-and-seek with God is having serious repercussions on the lives of others. The terror underlying the mariners' question is intensified when they learn of his flight from God. Whatever the nature of their religious belief, it was characterized by a certain seriousness. They were clear that the storm which threatened their lives was related to a fearful lack of seriousness in Jonah's religious belief.

> Then they said to him, 'What shall we do to you, that the sea may quiet down for us?' For the sea grew more and more tempestuous. (v. 11)

Again the sailors take the initiative. Again they force Jonah to take responsibility. Recognizing that the prophet is the cause of the storm which threatens them all, they ask him what they should do.

This is the seventh question addressed to Jonah since his flight: 'What do you mean, you sleeper?' (v. 6); 'Tell us on whose account this evil has come upon us. What is your occupation? And whence do you come? What is your country? And of what people are you?' (v. 8); 'What is this that you have done?' (v. 10); 'What shall we do to you?' (v. 11). All the questions in verses 8–11 concern Jonah's identity and responsibility. The intensity of the questioning parallels the heightening of the storm. Jonah's failure to conform his life to his

[16] Henry, p. 1143.
[17] Gen. 3:13

professed faith in Yahweh led to this external threat, both for himself and for those around him. As the English poet John Donne has it, 'No man is an island, entire of itself.'

Imagine for a moment how you might feel in Jonah's shoes. The text itself remains silent on his inner state, but are we to believe that he was calm and placid in the face of God's call (v. 2), his sudden flight (v. 3), the great storm (v. 4), the urgent request of the captain (v. 6), the barrage of questions from the crew (v. 8) and his own, unrecorded, disclosure to the sailors concerning his responsibility for the calamity?

The silence of the text on Jonah's inner state is not unusual in biblical writing. The focus of interest normally lies with God's concerns. In the narrative Jonah is a significant character. The writer may intend that he represents no-one but himself. Alternatively, Jonah may be representing Israel, or God's people in any age. He may be a means by which the Lord can speak in many situations. The silence of the text at this point, underlined by the prophet's own silence, invites our interest in the man. What was he going through? Was he unfeeling and unaware, insensitive to and untouched by these events? Or was he susceptible to the fears, feelings, doubts and prejudices which characterize most people? For most human beings these experiences would be accompanied by a great deal of inner turmoil.

He found God's call to be disagreeable. Instead of being armed for fight, his adrenalin equipped him for flight. And who, aboard a wooden sailing ship suddenly caught in the middle of a great storm while out at sea, would not feel afraid? To know that the responsibility for the terrible tempest and all that it threatened rested on their shoulders alone would be a fearful burden for anyone to bear. To be a passenger forced to face a barrage of pointed questions from frightened and accusing foreign crewmen may have proved to be the least of Jonah's problems. Because of their fear he began to share his response to God with others. In this lies the beginning of the storm's end.

Now, the focus of their questioning shifts away from Jonah. The sailors ask him, 'What shall *we* do to you, that the sea may quiet down for *us*?' The literary balance shows the tension in their minds. For their own sake they had to do something about Jonah. Jonah's flight from God imperilled their lives. They were caught up in a conflict which was not of their making. By avoiding his responsibility Jonah forced responsibility on others. In avoiding his vocation he burdened others. But the sailors, motivated by their fear of God, wanted to do the right thing. They certainly did not want to incur further trouble by their actions. Their fear prompted them to find favour with God. Jonah's fear had prompted him to flee. Their attitude towards God was diametrically opposed to his.

They were impelled by the storm to act, and they had two options. They could imitate Jonah's response to crisis by trying to flee from the urgency of God's call; they could ignore the calamity, allow Jonah to go back to sleep, and rid themselves of all responsibility. In doing so they would, of course, suffer the full consequences of the storm: they would all drown. Alternatively, they could kill him in the hope that his death would appease what they understood to be an angry deity. Jonah, knowing that obedience to God's call would entail the disintegration of his world view, was painfully aware that a form of death for him was inevitable. His flight from the presence of God (1:3ff.) was in fact the start of his journey to death. Yet, rather than die to his theological world view and be transformed into God's likeness, he opted for death by drowning. Indeed, he reckoned it was better for him to die than to endure the consequences of a fuller understanding of Yahweh's ways with his people. And now, at this point in his flight from Yahweh's presence, his death would at least have the added virtue of saving the lives of the pagan mariners.

Jonah's willingness to die so that the sailors might be saved appears to have a certain altruism about it. In chapter 4, however, we discover that the prophet's desire for death has something of the flavour of escapism. Confronted on the one hand by God's mercy (4:2–3) and on the other by God's judgment (4:7–8), Jonah's longing to die suggests that his personal and theological world view has been so undermined that he sees death as the only route to security and relief.

In some instances ambivalence, such as swithering between altruism and escapism, reflects a depressed state of mind. On the one hand, Jonah's death would be the means of others being saved. On the other hand, his deepest and most cherished beliefs were being undermined and found wanting. Under such pressure, death may be seen as the only way out of the impasse.

The behaviour of the pagans towards Jonah was exemplary; they feared killing a man even when their own lives were in danger. Does the writer suggest that it is god-fearing people such as these whom Jonah wishes to exclude from the mercy of God?

A way of escape

Jonah's second utterance (v. 12), like so much else we have seen of him already, is full of ambiguity, surely reflecting his inner turmoil.

> **A** Take me up and throw me into the sea;
>> **B** then the sea will quiet down for you;
>
> **A1** for I know it is because of me
>> **B1** that this great tempest has come upon you.

The beautiful symmetry of this phrase is matched by a hidden ambivalence. Jonah urges the sailors to treat him like some excess baggage and hurl him into the sea. This would not simply save the ship; most importantly, it would still the storm. There is a whiff of ironic humour here, since Jonah should not have been on the ship in the first place! He admits that he is the cause of the storm, but hidden in this command is a certain awkwardness. For some reason he puts the responsibility for his death onto the poor, distraught sailors who were quite clearly reluctant to throw him overboard. What hindered him from jumping overboard and drowning himself? Having embarked on the way down to death, Jonah now appears to shy at the final hurdle. A certain ambivalence hovers in the air: do we see here an act of heroic self-sacrifice on Jonah's part, or an act of assisted suicide? Why was it that, if Jonah had it in his power to save the ship's crew, it was to them that he gave the awful responsibility of throwing him overboard? Both Jonah and the sailors knew that their deliverance would cost him his life.

Was it that Jonah needed their help? Through their questions they had helped him to acknowledge who he was. His identity had begun to emerge. Now, more is revealed. It was his disobedience which had brought them to the jaws of death. Their costly obedience would save them. Commanding them to hurl him overboard, Jonah helped them recognize God's response to their obedience. It was God, not Jonah, who was the source of their deliverance. Although reluctant, the sailors were obedient to Jonah's command, a response which contrasts with his earlier disobedience. By taking the difficult decision to act in this way, they helped resolve Jonah's dilemma and were on the way leading to life.

By choosing to run away from God's call, Jonah chose the way to death and despair for himself and others. In accepting his part in bringing all this upon others, Jonah, through an act of self-offering rather than suicide, finally opts for the lives of others rather than his own.

On this passage, Jerome speaks of Jonah as one who 'slew thee [Death] for he surrendered his dear life into the hands of those who sought it'. Jerome here overstates matters. In his desire to see Jonah as a prototype of Jesus Christ, he implies that the sailors had sought Jonah's death. The text as we have it, however, clearly shows that the mariners did not want the prophet's death; they struggled to save his life. As we shall see, they fought heroically to save him.

> Nevertheless the men rowed hard to bring the ship back to land, but they could not, for the sea grew more and more tempestuous against them. (v. 13)

Even if the sailors believed in scapegoating Jonah, they went out of their way to avoid throwing him overboard. They rowed desperately to get the ship back to land. They literally 'dug into the water', but the harder they rowed the more ferocious the storm became, rendering their best efforts futile. As far as God was concerned, Jonah was not yet ready to reach land. His deliverance was being stored up until the Lord commanded the fish to vomit him out 'upon the dry land' (2:10).

An ancient belief

There are several examples in ancient literature of a belief that a storm at sea could be caused by a guilty traveller. In 411 BC the orator Antiphon wrote a defence for a man accused of murdering a companion. As proof of the man's innocence he cited the fact that the accused had subsequently travelled by ship and no harm had befallen it. He wrote,

> I hardly think I need remind you that many a person with unclean hands or some other form of defilement who has embarked on shipboard with the righteous has involved them in his own destruction. Others, while they have escaped death, have had their lives imperilled owing to such polluted wretches.[18]

On his voyage to Rome, Paul was shipwrecked on the island of Malta. As he was gathering brushwood for a fire on the beach, a viper clung to his hand. Some who saw this said to one another, 'No doubt this man is a murderer. Though he has escaped from the sea, justice has not allowed him to live.'[19] Clearly this ancient belief, which informs the attitude of the sailors in the book of Jonah, was still current in the days of the early church.

Urgent prayer

> Therefore they cried to the LORD, 'We beseech thee, O LORD, let us not perish for this man's life, and lay not on us innocent blood; for thou, O LORD, hast done as it pleased thee.' (v. 14)

We should notice that the prophet has not yet called on the God he claimed to fear. Such resistance and bloody-mindedness become a common experience when we are out of step with God. At such

[18] Herodes 82, cited in Bolin, p. 82.
[19] Acts 28:4.

times a kind of spiritual lockjaw sets in, making it grimly hard to reopen the conversation. Jonah prefers death to pleading with God.

Why was he dumb before God? We recall that he had set out to flee from God's presence. He imagined he could be at peace if only he could get away from God. In the horror of the storm he realizes that God has not left him! He is still tormented by this God. His last resort, therefore, is silence.

As we learn from the example of Job, the only way to flee *from* God is to flee *to* God, but the effort of turning round is often immobilizing. The importance of verbalizing prayer is indicated in Psalm 142:1:

> I cry with my voice to the LORD,
> with my voice I make supplication to the LORD.[20]

Words give substance and clarity to thoughts and feelings. Through the spoken word we communicate, not only with others but also with ourselves. Through our words we articulate attitudes, sensitivites and yearnings which might otherwise remain inchoate.

It is truly said that confession is good for the soul. To acknowledge wrongdoing, to accept responsibility in the presence of those offended, brings healing and health. In Psalm 32 the psalmist finds his own inner distress healed. The words of verse 3 give us a graphic account of the physical effects of not being on speaking terms with God: 'When I declared not my sin, my body wasted away . . .' Articulating who we are before God is a crucial step in knowing who we are and being empowered to move on. In this context, the wicked are those who suffer torments *because* they do not confess their sin. In confessing his rebellion to the sailors, Jonah makes the first step along the way to being reckoned as righteous before God. Psalm 32 continues:

> For day and night thy hand was heavy upon me;
> my strength was dried up as by the heat of summer.
> I acknowledged my sin to thee,
> and I did not hide my iniquity;
> I said, 'I will confess my transgressions to the LORD';
> then thou didst forgive the guilt of my sin.
> Therefore let every one who is godly
> offer prayer to thee;
> at a time of distress, in the rush of great waters,
> they shall not reach him.
> Thou art a hiding place for me,
> thou preservest me from trouble;
> thou dost encompass me with deliverance. (vv. 4–7)

[20]The NIV has translated the Hebrew phrase 'with my voice' on the first line as 'aloud'.

The faithful are those who offer prayer to God. The sailors will be saved from the storm, but Jonah, who is not yet on speaking terms with God, will suffer death by drowning. To everyone on board the sinking ship, Jonah's death was inevitable. At a time of 'the rush of great waters', how could Jonah the prayerless possibly be delivered?

Before relating the nature of Jonah's deliverance, the narrator presses on in order to tell us how the mariners were saved. In the book of Jonah we discover that it was the pagans who, in sheer desperation, cried to God for salvation. Their prayer is phrased in the language of the most urgent entreaty – 'We beseech thee . . .' or, 'O please . . .' – language which appears in other life and death situations.[21] As they prepare to hurl Jonah overboard, they pause in recognition of the consequences *for them* of throwing a man to certain death. They seek absolution beforehand: '. . . lay not on us innocent blood.' One man must die for them all, or else all will surely drown. They do not want to be saved from perishing at sea, only to perish for throwing a man to certain death. Their prayer expresses a terrible dilemma. They recognize that they are caught up in a conflict between God and his prophet. They interpret their role in the conflict as being the means whereby the Lord's desire for Jonah's death can be fulfilled. We have been told (v. 4) that it was the Lord, Jonah's God, who had thrown the storm at the ship in the first place. In keeping with the Bible's world view, the mariners placed responsibility for the situation squarely onto the Lord. We find in Psalm 135:6 a general affirmation of this view:

> Whatever the LORD pleases he does,
> in heaven and on earth
> in the seas and all deeps.

They shared a world view in which the Lord was ultimately behind everything. Yahweh, the supreme God, Creator and Redeemer of all, was responsible for everything, blessings and disasters.

Although the disaster experienced by Jonah and the mariners is attributed to the prophet's disobedience, disasters which befall others in Scripture cannot, however, always be so readily accounted for. The narrator of the book of Job, for example, goes to great lengths to describe how Job was 'blameless and upright, one who feared God, and turned away from evil'.[22] In the scheme of things, the disasters which befell this good man were appointed to fall on the wicked. A careful comparison of what befalls Job in chapters 1 and 2

[21] Gen. 50:17; 2 Kgs. 20:3; Ps. 118:25.
[22] Job 1:1.

with what befalls the disobedient in Deuteronomy 28:31–35 implies that Job was afflicted because of his sin. Indeed, Job's friends adopt this conventional interpretation of his sufferings and urge him to repent. In the end, however, they are accused by God: 'After the LORD had spoken these words to Job, the LORD said to Eliphaz the Temanite: "My wrath is kindled against you and against your two friends; for you have not spoken of me what is right, as my servant Job has."'[23] This, combined with the narrator's evaluation of Job in 1:1, strongly suggests that the point being made is that not all the disasters which befall people are the consequence of their disobedience. We have seen that the disaster which befell the mariners was not their disobedience, but Jonah's.

This theme also echoes in the New Testament. Jesus' disciples give voice to the same popular view that a disaster such as human blindness must be the consequence of someone's sin.

> As he passed by, he saw a man blind from his birth. And his disciples asked him, 'Rabbi, who sinned, this man or his parents, that he was born blind?' Jesus answered, 'It was not that this man sinned, or his parents, but that the works of God might be made manifest in him.'[24]

We find another instance of Jesus rejecting this popular view in Luke 13:1–4:

> There were some present at that very time who told him of the Galileans whose blood Pilate had mingled with their sacrifices. And he answered them, 'Do you think that these Galileans were worse sinners than all the other Galileans, because they suffered thus? I tell you, No; but unless you repent you will all likewise perish. Or those eighteen upon whom the tower in Siloam fell and killed them, do you think that they were worse offenders than all the others who dwelt in Jerusalem? I tell you, No; but unless you repent you will all likewise perish.'

The cosmos in general and the human environment in particular are so shot through with the Spirit of Yahweh, its Creator, that for humankind to imagine it even possible to escape this God, to hide away or to live without reference to the Maker and Saviour of all, is illusory. Again, the psalmist puts it well: 'The fool says in his heart, "There is no God."'[25] Jonah's lips had not actually articulated the

[23] Job 42:7.
[24] John 9:1–3.
[25] Pss. 14:1, 53:1–6.

words 'There is no God', but his heart was wanting to make God in his own image. Such a home-made god would be comfortable to live with, but because such a god would share Jonah's own prejudices and moral perspectives, it would be powerless to redeem and re-create Jonah and the rest of humankind. Indeed, a god made in our own image is no God at all. Such an idol would be exclusive, ineffective and ephemeral to the whole created order.

Jonah certainly had a problem with God, but instead of facing up to it, which was what he was called to do, he ran away from it. In the storm his sin rebounded not only on his own head but on others', too. Like Jonah, Job also had a problem with God. He struggled to know why God treated his faithful servant so badly. We discover the psalmist echoing the same question:

> If we had forgotten the name of our God,
> or spread forth our hands to a strange god,
> would not God discover this?
> For he knows the secrets of the heart.
> Nay, for thy sake we are slain all the day long,
> and accounted as sheep for the slaughter.[26]

The psalmist was deeply troubled by the way Yahweh's blessing appeared to fall on the wicked while the good people suffered. Psalm 73 is a particularly vivid depiction of this painful observation. Despairing that all his efforts to walk with God have been a waste of time (v. 13), the psalmist finally draws near to the presence of God (v. 17). It is there, in worship and service, that he relinquishes speculation concerning God's justice in the face of the obvious injustices around him. It is in the submission expressed by worship that his perspective is cleared, and his soul restored.

Fearlessness in the presence of God

From the basis of the same world view, Jonah exemplifies a different approach. Instead of showing his 'fear' by returning to the sanctuary of God's presence in worship and service as the psalmist did, Jonah flees from God's presence. According to verse 4:2, he preferred to speculate on God's justice and moral governance of the earth rather than worship. Why should he go to Nineveh if God was going to forgive the wicked city anyway? The answer was simple: he was called to fear – that is, to worship and serve – his God, Yahweh.

[26] Ps. 44:20–22.

The effect of his response to Yahweh was felt in the lives of other innocent folk.

We cannot fully understand the reasons for Jonah's action. We should not, however, judge him too harshly, for, in the presence of God's call we are all tempted to adopt different approaches which enable us to resist his call and remain intact.

Jonah's unwillingness to go to Nineveh at Yahweh's command (1:2) may suggest that he simply thought it impossible that *he*, Jonah son of Amittai, could make any difference at all to the great, wicked Gentile city. Like others, we sometimes succumb to the belief that, in the face of so much evil in the world, we are insignificant and helpless. The prophet Elijah faced a similar temptation, but he shared it with God and was reminded that he was by no means alone.[27]

Or again, perhaps Jonah took the belief in God's sovereignty just a little too far. Complacency that God is in his heaven and all is well with the world, or even fatalism that God is able to do what needs to be done anyway, can rob us of a sense of responsibility. In 4:2 Jonah says that he ran away from God's call because he knew God was gracious and merciful: God did not really need Jonah in order to save Nineveh. Jonah knew the Lord was sovereign over all. He would do what was right without any need of Jonah. If we are content to rest in this idea, we do not need to be confronted by his impossible demands!

Christians claim to worship the God of heaven and earth, but do we imagine this phrase is shorthand for a static God sitting on his throne? Or do we imagine the Creator God as one whose work of creation never ceases? What kind of God do we worship? Did Jonah have difficulties with a *living* God, one who was continually creating and calling his people to follow into his future? Was it that he simply could not handle an unpredictable and vulnerable God bursting with life, love and hope? It might be a lot easier to settle for a static God.

Sometimes Christians can become a little cynical. We can come to believe that things will never get better and that, if anything, they are getting worse. Indeed, we would not be the first to think that things were getting worse. Those who believe they have seen all there is to see of life may hold out little hope of things ever improving. We might even believe that everything is predetermined, mapped out and unchangeable. At its worst such determinism may lead us to assume that God would do his own thing whatever anyone else did.

In a multicultural society Christians can be divided over how to relate to people of other faiths. Some will value the insights of other faiths and others will reject them. Some will want to learn to live in peace alongside their neighbours of other faiths, believing that such

[27] 1 Kgs. 19:18.

human acceptance mirrors God's acceptance of people in Christ. Others will long to convert people of other faiths to Christianity, believing that only through Jesus Christ can God be known and worshipped. The conviction that God so loved the world that he sent his only begotten Son, so that everyone who believes in him will not perish but have everlasting life, is lived out in different ways by Christians. Through his covenant people the Lord planned to bless all the nations.[28] Was it that Jonah would rather die with his own little idea of God intact than adjust that understanding, and his faith of a lifetime, to accommodate the inclusion of people of another faith?

In all the temptations that assail us when we are called to discipleship, we discover our own need to be willing to grow and face the pain of change. In praying for the kind of reconciling and just peace which characterizes the kingdom of God, the kind of peace for which the church prays weekly, there may be a need for believers to take two steps backwards. Kingdom peace comes on God's terms, not on ours. In responding to God's call to work with him in the world, in hope and anticipation of new things happening, his people must expect that they, too, will be called to change and become new in response to that divine love. The mission of God is about radical change. A new creation is something much more radical than everyone else coming to see things from our own perspective. The chosen people of God must change too.

Answered prayer

> So they took up Jonah and threw him into the sea; and the sea ceased from its raging. (v. 15)

The sailors hurl Jonah into the raging sea, and the fantastic happens: the storm immediately abates, stillness surfaces. They receive their promised reward: 'the sea ceased from its raging.' The situation is transformed by their obedience. The sea loses its power to inflict danger, a loss signalling that the power was never its own but Yahweh's. The obedient response of the sea was instant. Jonah, by his own command, was thrust by the sailors into the very heart of God's storm. His flight from the presence of the Lord led him to the heart of the stormy, unruly God who was intent on changing Jonah's tidy little life.

The Hebrew word rendered 'raging' here is elsewhere used of human anger[29] and of the Lord's anger.[30] To the sailors there must

[28] Gen. 12:3.
[29] 2 Chr. 16:10; 26:19; 28:9; Prov. 19:12.
[30] Is. 30:30.

have been the suggestion that the Lord who sent the storm was appeased, that the offence committed against him had been atoned for.

> Then the men feared the LORD exceedingly, and they offered a sacrifice to the LORD and made vows. (v. 16)

Once again, the word 'fear' appears. Whereas the sailors' fear in verses 5 and 10 referred to their terror of the storm, the same word is used now to express their response of worship towards Yahweh.

As we have already noticed, the writer plays on this word throughout the chapter. 'Fear' may produce paralysis, but it can also galvanize into heroic deeds, as it did the sailors. While it can produce flight, it can also produce fight. Jonah's fear of Yahweh led him to be terrified at the prospect of change, and he fled from God's presence. The sailors' fear resulted in them coming to worship the Lord. They were willing to let their idea of God change. They came to understand him for themselves. Their response to Jonah's confession in verse 9 implies some hearsay knowledge of this God, but now they really knew that he had power over the sea. This created within them a sense of awe, which drew them to acknowledge his greatness in worship. The offering of sacrifices refers to the costly offering of animals.[31] It is improbable, however, that the sailors made burnt offerings on board a stricken wooden vessel which had earlier been emptied of all its cargo! Most probably they offered sacrifices when they returned to dry land, in the same way that Noah and his family made offerings to God when they had been delivered from the great flood.[32] On the other hand, the action of the sailors may simply echo a pattern seen in other shipwreck stories where, after the storm had subsided, those who were saved offered thanks. However, their action here certainly seems to be more than a formality; it points to the mariners having come to a new knowledge of the Lord.

Concerning their vows, we can only guess that the sailors promised to tell others how they had been saved from disaster at sea and, in particular, how Yahweh had answered their prayers. The storm was a wild and terrible chaos which threatened to devour them. Yahweh had rescued them from the very jaws of death. They would not, however, have prayed to him for deliverance without Jonah's intervention, so there is ironic humour in the fact that this maverick prophet was successful in turning people to God, even when he himself was trying to avoid God! The writer's play on such

[31] Exod. 24:5; Lev. 22:29; Deut. 18:3.
[32] Gen. 8:20ff.

a key word as 'fear' suggests not only humour but a concern to raise questions in the minds of his readers. Furthermore, with a twinkle in his eye, the story-teller appears to hint at a certain playfulness in the nature of the Lord, who has arranged affairs in so paradoxical a manner. It is as though the narrator is illustrating, through this vignette, the words of Isaiah:

> I was ready to be sought by those who did not ask for me;
> I was ready to be found by those who did not seek me.[33]

Reflecting in similar vein, Paul muses on Israel's response to God in Christ: 'But of Israel he says, "All day long I have held out my hands to a disobedient and contrary people." '[34] Both Isaiah and Paul could have been writing about the Israel exemplified by Jonah.

It is worth recalling here a parallel with the early chapters of Genesis. Adam and Eve are brought into being by God's word, the breath of life. The command of God brings them into the sphere of self-awareness and relationship with their Creator.[35] Their preference for self-determination, however, brings about their expulsion from Eden. Given so much, humankind is portrayed as blowing it all for the sake of going it alone without their Creator. Jonah responds in a similar way to God's command. He perceives God's call as intrusive on his freedom, putting him in a position he chooses to avoid.

Some of this comes very near to the bone. The irony is that God's people are sometimes so caught up in what they understand to be involved in being God's people that they miss the point completely! Like Jonah, they are overtaken in 'righteousness' by those whom they reckon to be unbelievers. The satire in the story could go no further!

The Jonah mindset

It could be said that the prophetic writer of the book of Jonah expresses the view that pagans had the capacity and willingness to respond to Israel's God. Jonah was called to tell these 'outsiders' of God's concern. As an 'insider', a person well established in his faith and knowledge of Yahweh, Jonah encountered an inner resistance to this call.

[33] Is. 65:1; cf. 1 Kgs. 8.41–43; Is. 2:2–5; 56:6–8.
[34] Rom. 10:21.
[35] Gen. 2:16.

We see instances of a similar response in the New Testament. A kind of spiritual myopia concerning the glorious grace of the God and Father of our Lord Jesus Christ was a characteristic of the religious leaders Jesus encountered. To mention just one example, the leader of the synagogue was more concerned to keep to the letter of the law than to rejoice in a woman made whole by Jesus' word and touch.[36] Another example of the Jonah mindset is found in Peter and the apostles when they were confronted by Paul's calling to be an apostle to the Gentiles.[37]

Instances of the Jonah mindset exist in the church today. Examples might include our presumption that the institutional church rather than the world for which Christ died is at the centre of the Creator's concern, coupled with a sense that this same church is the means by which the world will be saved. Corresponding to this, there is sometimes a blindness on the part of clergy and ministers to forms of Christian witness by ordinary people working in secular professions. Perhaps the church's obsession with orders of ministry and authority has contributed to this? Perhaps it has been in opting for maintenance over mission that this mindset has taken root.

The very early churches appear to have had little concern for sustainable structures and stability. The gospel of Christ cannot be canned, packaged, patented or containerized. In short, the Spirit of God refuses to be institutionalized. Rather, as the Scriptures themselves demonstrate, God uses a range of cultures, contexts and languages through which to visit and bless his people. He is not limited to a particular denomination or church tradition. He transcends all these human cultural contexts and, although he may graciously reveal himself through them, he is not limited by them, contained by them or restrained by them. Any institutional form of religion may, like Jonah, seek to silence the radical call of the living God by maintaining him in their own image. Like any human institution, churches can become more interested in maintaining themselves than in living by the vision and hope of the Holy Spirit of God which created them. Our desire for theological and moral tidiness and our unwillingness to live with the provisionality of faith point to a search for security in something other than our Creator.

Mercifully, the writer also suggests that Jonah's unfaithfulness was no stumbling block to the Creator of heaven and earth. The Lord revealed himself to both the mariners and the Ninevites. Both responded by worshipping the Lord, and demonstrated a change in their knowledge and fear of the supreme God. Yahweh will be

[36] Luke 13:10–17.
[37] Gal. 2.

gracious to whom he will be gracious.[38] Paul and Isaiah say that he will reveal himself to those who do not seek him.

Although beset by many problems, the churches in the New Testament appear not to have been anxious about their own demise. Instead of a settlement or maintenance mentality, they had a pilgrim mindset. In this respect they were more truly children of Abraham, who, in contrast to Lot, chose the less fertile and more risky places west of the River Jordan in which to live. This was the choice of Abraham, through whom God promised to bless all the nations of the world. Living by faith meant moving, living in tents, adopting a lifestyle dependent on God. Lot chose to settle in the prosperous Jordan valley. His interest in the short-term ease of a house in Sodom was a step on the road to spiritual and moral decline. Ultimately his dependence on God for salvation from the destruction of the cities of the plain is reasserted.

Is the greatest enemy of God's people something innocently familiar crouching at the door?[39] In other words, does the church, in any generation, tend to regard itself as chosen by God and proceed to fix God in its own image? Do the belief and practice of the church then become the only orthodoxy? Do its members inevitably become 'insiders' who find it difficult to share their faith with 'outsiders'? Such an agreed way of being the church is comfortable; it is something consoling and innocently familiar, something which an institution may even judge to be essential – but it can become sin crouching at the door. Does the author play with this kind of truth in the humorously powerful tale of the struggling Jonah?

[38] Exod. 33:19.
[39] Gen. 4:7.

1:17 – 2:10

5. Alive or dead?

The second part of the story is contained within a literary frame in which the Lord prepares a 'great fish', first to 'swallow' (1:17) and then to 'vomit out' (2:10) the prophet. The passage 1:17 – 2:10 continues the story of Jonah and includes a psalm on the lips of the runaway prophet. Since the brief, three-verse narrative found in 1:17, 2:1 and 2:10 is virtually complete without the psalm, doubts exist in the minds of some scholars whether or not the psalm was added to the narrative at a later time. Details of the various arguments can be studied in commentaries,[1] but here we shall focus on the meaning of these verses as the received text which, for centuries, has been indisputably one with the biblical book of Jonah.

Both the short narrative and the longer psalm lend themselves to a chiastic arrangement. The story may be set out as follows:

A And the LORD appointed a great fish to swallow up Jonah; (1:17a)

  B and Jonah was in the belly of the fish three days and three nights. (1:17b)

  B1 Then Jonah prayed to the LORD his God from the belly of the fish . . . (2:1)

A1 And the LORD spoke to the fish, and it vomited out Jonah upon the dry land. (2:10)

In this brief narrative we see that Yahweh retains the initiative. Jonah's contest with God is ill-matched. The account illustrates the impossibility of escaping God's presence and the folly of attempting such a thing. It shows Jonah's dependence on God even when he is in a state of rebellion against him.

[1] E.g. Alexander, Knight and Golka, Limburg, Magonet, Stuart, Wolff, etc. See Bibliography for details.

As we shall see, the psalm in 2:1–9 comes between the point at which Jonah addresses the Lord (2:1, B1 opposite) and the Lord's response (2:10, A1 opposite). The section concludes with a humorous touch as the Lord calls the obedient fish (2:10) and not the rebellious prophet!

Into the depths (1:17)

As far as the sailors were concerned, Jonah had drowned. For the narrator, however, it is the drowned man who remains the chief interest. So he leaves the mariners to worship – not their old gods which had proved helpless, but Yahweh, the God of the prophet who had saved them – and turns our attention back to Jonah.

> And the LORD appointed a great fish to swallow up Jonah; and Jonah was in the belly of the fish three days and three nights. (v. 17)

In the same way that human beings designate people for particular tasks,[2] so the Lord is said to 'designate' or 'appoint' a great fish to swallow Jonah. Yahweh as king deploys a creature which obeys him unquestioningly in order to save a rebellious man from drowning. This same word, 'appoint', which could equally be translated 'employ' or 'nominate', is found also in 4:6, referring to the plant, in 4:7, referring to the worm, and in 4:8, referring to the sultry east wind. On each occasion the creature responds obediently to the voice of its Creator. The contrast with Jonah's response is clear, and the irony plain.

Animal obedience

The obedience of animals contrasting with the disobedience of humankind is a theme frequently mentioned in Scripture. The prophet in Isaiah 1:3, for example, contrasts the domestic animals who know their owner with God's people who fail to know him:

> The ox knows its owner,
> and the ass its master's crib;
> but Israel does not know,
> my people does not understand.

In his Gospel Luke reflects early Christian traditions. Building on this verse from Isaiah, the evangelist speaks of Jesus Christ being laid

[2]Dan. 1:11.

in a manger.[3] Christian tradition has it that he was born in the place where ox and ass were kept and fed, for they, at least, knew who he was.

Another example of the creation being obedient to the word of its Creator can be found in Jeremiah 8:7:

> Even the stork in the heavens
> knows her times;
> and the turtledove, swallow and crane
> keep the time of their coming;
> but my people know not
> the ordinance of the LORD.

Even the mighty ocean knows its bounds:

> Do you not fear me? says the LORD;
> Do you not tremble before me?
> I placed the sand as the bound for the sea,
> a perpetual barrier which it cannot pass;
> though the waves toss, they cannot prevail,
> though they roar, they cannot pass over it.

There is a similar passage in Job 38:8–11:

> Or who shut in the sea with doors,
> when it burst forth from the womb;
> when I made clouds its garment,
> and thick darkness its swaddling band,
> and prescribed bounds for it,
> and set bars and doors,
> and said, 'Thus far shall you come, and no farther,
> and here shall your proud waves be stayed'?

In other stories we meet an ass more accustomed to recognizing God's word than a prophet,[4] birds serving as messengers of God,[5] and lions being obedient to the heavenly messenger.[6] In the book of Jonah the story-teller shows us a God who, in appointing the fish, the plant, the worm and the wind, intends to remain in dialogue with his wayward creature, Jonah. In the depths of the fish's belly, the

[3] Luke 2:7, 12.
[4] Num. 22:22–30.
[5] Gen. 8:10–12; 1 Kgs. 17:6.
[6] Dan. 6.

belly of *Sheol*, Jonah is protected from the noise and clamour of all that had threatened him. His safe haven is not unlike the place he sought in the bowels of the ship, a place of refuge far away (he hoped) from the demands of the world and the call of God.

As we shall see, the wriggling prophet is not going to be let off the hook of God's call. But might there be a reason why God chose a great fish to swallow him? Had he been rescued by a heavenly chariot, for example, such as the one in which Elijah had been taken to heaven, the wrong signal would have been given. We can see that Elijah's circumstances at this point were entirely different from Jonah's. The Lord could have appointed a great bird to transport him to dry land; instead he appointed the great fish. The Lord does not usually protect us from the consequences of our own choices and actions. In his faithfulness and graciousness towards us, Yahweh comes with us into the consequences of our choices in order to save us there. Jonah had chosen the sea as his escape route; it is there that the Lord awaits him. The narrator is careful to focus on Jonah's command to be thrown headlong into the sea. His disobedience in the face of God's call was guaranteed to propel him in a downward direction. This time, however, as if to indicate that his descent had been halted, he is not described as going 'down' but as being unceremoniously 'swallowed' by a mysterious fish. Jonah had lost the initiative and God had yet more cards to play. Jonah was to discover for himself the impossibility of escaping God's presence. To learn this he needed to be in the place of human powerlessness, ultimately the place of death. Salvation is not, in the first instance, the Lord God taking us 'out' of our mess, but God meeting us 'within' it. Jonah will find salvation within his watery grave, for there, in the place which eloquently speaks of death, God will meet him.

An attractive rabbinical interpretation of God 'preparing' or 'appointing' a great fish to rescue Jonah is that the fish had been prepared for this moment during the six days of creation. God was preparing, not only to save Jonah's life but also to teach him some of the ultimate secrets of God's ways with his creation. Salvation is his design for all creatures, whether for a nation whose evil had come up before him or a prophet whose evil resulted in his descent from the presence of God.

The great fish

And this is the tragedy of the Book of Jonah, that a Book which is made the means of one of the most sublime revelations of truth in

> the Old Testament should be known to most only for its connection with a whale.[7]

Although the text speaks not of a whale but of a 'great fish' (1:17; 2:1, 10), it is surely the case that Jonah has become one of the best-known characters in the Bible *because* he was swallowed by a great fish which spewed him out after three days and three nights in its belly. In some respects there are similarities between this story and others such as Daniel in the lions' den and Shadrach, Meshach and Abednego being thrown into the fiery furnace.[8] These are all very threatening places to be! From ancient Babylonian sources we know that both incarceration with lions and being thrown into the fiery furnace were forms of punishment used by powerful regimes to enforce their will.

There are, however, no known instances of a person being swallowed by a great fish *and spewed out alive* three days later. It is well known that some fish will eat human flesh, that others are capable of swallowing large objects and that some large fish have swallowed a human being. On such rare occasions when the poor victim has been removed from their fishy grave, they have been either horribly dead or unconscious and near to death. This contrasts sharply with Jonah, who is portrayed throughout his ordeal as fully conscious and coherent, both mentally and emotionally, being able both to recite or compose a penitential psalm and offer thanksgiving in worship of the Lord, before being vomited up by the huge creature.

In ancient folklore the theme of individuals being swallowed by great sea monsters and surviving is commonly found. Those heroes who miraculously escape death gain new status among human beings. Nonetheless, such survival is unparalleled in known human history. Humankind has long yearned for power to overcome death as such folklore testifies. Indeed, Jonah's sojourn in the belly of the fish soon became linked in Jewish thought with the hope of resurrection:

> For as Jonah was three days and three nights in the belly of the whale, so will the Son of man be three days and three nights in the heart of the earth. The men of Nineveh will arise at the judgment with this generation and condemn it; for they repented at the preaching of Jonah, and behold, something greater than Jonah is here.[9]

[7] Smith, p. 492.
[8] Daniel 3 and 6.
[9] Matt. 12:40–41.

When Jesus used this episode from Jonah as an image of his own death and resurrection, it is clearly in the context that he himself was the One 'greater than Jonah'. The whole tenor of Jonah's story is very different from that of Jesus of Nazareth. Jesus came to fulfil the word of God while, as we have seen all too clearly, Jonah seeks to flee from it. Having elected the sea as his escape route, it is the great fish which becomes the place of encounter between Jonah and the God he is afraid of meeting. Ultimately, the prophet's flight becomes a route to discovering that he had set himself an even more impossible task than the one to which he had been called. God pursues him to the very gates of death and beyond, as if to say that by virtue of his presence alone the gates of repentance are always open. In the absence of God repentance is illusory, and without repentance and forgiveness there is no new creation. It is from within the 'belly of *Sheol*', in the depths of the sea, that Jonah first speaks to his Lord. At his weakest point he now discovers that God's presence embraces even death itself. He cannot divest himself of Yahweh, the great 'I AM'.

Remarkable though the story of Jonah is, as with other Old Testament characters it is the Lord's gracious forgiveness of him which leads to his restoration. There are pale reflections in the Scriptures of the One who is to come, but the resurrection of the Lord Jesus Christ is of a wholly different order from the restoration of Jonah.

Was the 'great fish' historical?

Generally speaking, as we read the Bible we may have a sense that what we read is historically reliable. That being said, 'It is safe to say that the ancient world did not regard historical writing in the same way that we view it in the modern era, where history is a largely scientific record of verifiable events, governed by evidence and proof.'[10] This obliges us to dig a little deeper into the kind of history we read in the Bible. In terms of this 'modern' understanding of history, facts and events in themselves are neutral; they have no meaning in themselves. Their meaning is derived from how people perceive and interpret them. How we interpret facts or events depends on our perspective, beliefs and presuppositions. For example, the various ways in which the actual historical events of the Second World War are presented to schoolchildren in England, France, Germany, Israel, Russia, Japan and America will vary. What is more, the interpretation of these events may be challenged within living memory.

[10]See 'History', in Ryken, Wilhoit, Longman III (eds.), p. 385.

Modern 'history' may even be rewritten or denied when a new political regime comes to the fore.

On the other hand, the recording of the history we encounter in the Bible is not motivated by political, economic or social factors, but is always theologically and morally orientated. History is viewed in the Bible as being under God's control. Biblical history is therefore confessional; it acknowledges God's intervention and leads, first, to praise for what he has done and, second, to faith in the God who is revealed in the event. Scripture itself, however, asserts that the Creator God is greater than human history. He engages with it, intervenes in it and reveals himself through it; he shapes it and uses it as an instrument of his saving purposes for individuals and nations. But this God is not limited by human history, for, ultimately, history will end when the creative and redemptive work of the Lord God is complete.[11] The Lord God is the beginning and the end of history, the Alpha and the Omega.[12] This theological statement urges us to see human history as dependent on and relative to the ultimate purposes of the Creator.

It is not the prime purpose of sacred Scripture to provide a modern historical record of events in the Ancient Near East. That Scripture can be a reliable source of historical events is not here in dispute, but, more importantly, its pages witness the hand of God in the things that happen to people and nations. The discernment of this is less connected to a meticulous knowledge of the events in question than it is to the eye of faith. What does the prophetic writer 'see' or perceive of God's hand at work in this or that circumstance? What does the Spirit of God reveal in this or that event? God's call will inform the prophetic writer's perception and shape his understanding. Thus the authority of Scripture derives less from the historicity of all it contains and more from the divinely inspired interpretations of events in which the nature of Yahweh is discerned. 'God is his own interpreter.'

As we have already shown, much has been written concerning the 'great fish'. From the early Christian period there were different views surrounding the nature of this little book. While some scholars such as Origen (AD 185–254) favoured an allegorical approach, others such as Augustine (AD 354–430) favoured a more literal approach. Both approaches are grounded in a profound reverence for sacred Scripture as the Word of God.

Perhaps it is this shared belief in sacred Scripture which can offer us a clue. The infinite, divine word to human beings must be presented in terms which finite human beings of all generations, cultures

[11] 1 John 2:17.

[12] Is. 44:6; 48:12; Rev. 1:8, 11; 21:6; 22:13, etc.

and languages can approach, comprehend and relate to. We may therefore expect it to reflect the gloriously rich diversity of human culture and literary form. In its written form the Word of God is for all people at all times and of all cultures. It does not belong exclusively to one particular social or religious group. While, therefore, the written Word of God will contain, among many other things, both history and allegory, even these two great literary forms are inadequate to the task of revealing the eternal, sacred Word of our Creator. Ultimately Jesus Christ is the Word made flesh.

It is in the face of this greater reality that we hold our magnifying glass over the verses in Jonah which tell us of the great fish. Of the forty-eight verses in this little book, it is the three verses in which the fish is mentioned which have exercised and dominated interpreters' minds for centuries. The division of opinion between the historicists and allegorists can be sharp, each finding evidence to support their case. Nonetheless, in our shared call not only to hear but to obey the word of God, we need, perhaps, to remind ourselves that the book of Jonah does not reach its climax by asking the reader, 'Do you believe that the great fish was historical or allegorical?' Rather, God asks, 'And should not I pity Nineveh, that great city, in which there are more than a hundred and twenty thousand persons who do not know their right hand from their left, and also much cattle?' (4:11). Centuries later Jesus would demonstrate that God's pity for the great city of Jerusalem was the key question for his people.[13]

Canaanite mythology

There is a significant irony in the provision of the 'great fish' which we need to look at before moving on. Canaanite mythology, which was prevalent in Israel in the eighth century BC, contains stories of the god Baal in combat with the great sea monster called Leviathan. The stories speak of a primeval conflict surrounding the creation of the cosmos. There is evidence in Scripture that Isaiah, for example, obviously knew these ancient stories and made use of them in such a way as to link Yahweh's redemptive acts of the exodus event with God's creation of his people Israel.[14]

Images from this familiar mythology were used to speak of the incomparability of Yahweh's supreme creative and redemptive power to save. It is true that the specific Hebrew terms associated with this Ancient Near Eastern mythology, for example the words 'Rahab' and 'Leviathan', are not found in the text of Jonah, but

[13] Luke 19:41ff.
[14] Is. 27:1; 51:9–10.

without doubt the theme of Yahweh's incomparable power is evident throughout. Whereas the pagan mythologies show the forces of the sea, the great sea monsters like Rahab and the power of death threatening not only humankind but even the gods themselves, in Jonah we find God playing with these forces of chaos. In this most incredibly wonderful short story God is not in combat with hostile mythological forces. Neither the sea nor the great fish are hostile to God's will: they are wholly subservient to his call. They are his obedient servants in the struggle to bring the prophet, who in his own person embodied hostility and rebellion towards God, to new birth. The great fish had long since served or worshipped Yahweh. An old rabbinic saying runs like this: 'God spends eight hours administering the universe, eight hours reading the Torah and eight hours playing with Leviathan.'

The sea

The influence of Canaanite mythology concerning the sea is also seen in Scripture.[15] In so far as it was the home of the sea monster, Leviathan, the sea symbolized the threat of the re-emergence of chaos. In biblical terms, that threat of chaos and evil is ultimately hollow. The parting of the Red Sea, allowing God's people an escape route out of slavery in Egypt, demonstrates God's ultimate authority over the power of evil and chaos to oppose his will. The great fish in the book of Jonah was not Leviathan. Ironically, the one who was hostile to God's creative goodness was Jonah, the 'dove'! Far from threatening God's purposes, it was the great sea monster which was to be the means of the prophet's salvation.

Cast into the sea, Jonah was lost in a morass of chaos and evil. By accumulating the images of storm and sea, the story-teller is saying that things were as bad as they possibly could be for Jonah. He was lost. Moreover, he had brought all this evil upon himself. The prophet Micah speaks of God's delight in steadfast love and compassion, and his unwillingness to retain his anger for ever. He refers to forgiveness as God casting 'all our sins into the depths of the sea'.[16] Jonah sank into the depths of the sea weighted down by his sin. But even in the face of all this, the writer asserts that God is in control of all the evil forces mustered against the prophet, including his own disobedience. Indeed, God plays with these very forces, using them to effect his will. In the depths of the ocean the great fish will prove to be the very

[15] E.g. Job 38:8–11; Jer. 5:22, which refer to Yahweh's power over the sea. In the new heavens and the new earth there will be no sea, cf. Rev. 21:1.
[16] Mic. 7:19.

place where Jonah will meet his God. Can Jonah, perhaps symbolizing God's people and storming in all his chaotic hostility against God, now be tamed? Centuries later Paul would write,

> For I am sure that neither death, nor life, nor angels, nor principalities, nor things present, nor things to come, nor powers, nor height, nor depth, nor anything else in all creation, will be able to separate us from the love of God in Christ Jesus our Lord.[17]

Swallowed

The word 'swallow' or 'gulp' emphasizes the speed of the action: Jonah disappeared in an instant. At this point the reader is by no means intended to think in terms of his survival. Elsewhere, the same imagery is used of the glorious city of Samaria. She was gulped down as if by a person eating a ripe fig.[18] In the language of the Psalms the word is often rendered 'swallowed up' or 'devoured', and means annihilated.[19] The Hebrew word can also mean 'destroyed'.[20]

When describing the horror of the Babylonian invasion of Jerusalem in 587 BC and the subsequent exile, the prophet Jeremiah uses a striking metaphor:

> Nebuchadrezzar the king of Babylon has *devoured* me,
> he has crushed me;
> he has made me an empty vessel,
> he has swallowed me like a monster;
> he has filled his belly with my delicacies,
> he has rinsed me out.[21]

And

> . . . I will punish Bel in Babylon,
> and take out of his mouth what he has *swallowed*.
> The nations shall no longer flow to him . . .[22]

As in a fairy story where the monstrous dragon devours the heroine, Babylon had swallowed Israel. In the way a person might empty a container full of delicious delicacies, so Babylon had wiped Jerusalem

[17] Rom. 8:38–39.
[18] Is. 28:4.
[19] Pss. 21:9; 35:25; 69:15; 106:17; 124:3.
[20] Lam. 2:2, 5, 8, 16.
[21] Jer. 51:34 (my italics).
[22] Jer. 51:44 (my italics).

clean off the face of the earth. Using the language of Babylonian and Canaanite mythology, Jeremiah speaks of Babylon as *tannîn*, translated as 'dragon' (RV), 'serpent' (NIV) and 'monster' (RSV) on account of her cruel destruction of both people and land during the period of exile (597–582 BC). But, he claims, God would cause the dragon to spew out Israel. Then the little nations would no more flow to Babylon like plankton into the jaws of a huge sea creature.

This is the powerful language of imagery and metaphor. Babylon is not literally a great monster and she does not literally swallow Israel, but the imagery vividly focused the horror of exile. Something fundamentally disordered was destroying creation. The metaphor of Babylon as a dragon highlights the inhuman and terrifying cruelty of her triumph over little nations. Devastation and exile had been actual, literal, historical events. Graphic poetic imagery colours the language used here by Jeremiah to describe these events, offering a different kind of perspective from that provided by an historical account. The language gives a feeling of the sheer horror and fear experienced in those cruel days.

As we have already seen, no date is given in the book by which we may be certain of its provenance, but God's call and Jonah's response to God were real. That God calls men and women to love and serve him is abundantly plain from Scripture and personal experience. Equally plain is the reality that many of us resist or are simply deaf to God's call. The fact that we do not always hear God does not mean that we are not being called by him. It simply means that humankind is most often either deaf or resistant to God's word. When speaking of people's sheer stubbornness, north-country folk often say, 'There's none so deaf as them as winna hear!'

Jonah is a powerful image of our resistance to God. At first sight, being devoured by the great fish could appear to be a punishment. After all, what kind of God would tolerate such open opposition? But the narrator twinkles with humour, for this great fish was actually appointed by God as part of his rescue operation. Unlike Jonah, the gigantic fish meekly obeys the call of its Creator. We read that the prophet was swallowed by the fish, but we know that before being consumed by the fish, he was consumed by opposition to God on the matter of the pagans. His hostility towards the Lord on this matter called into question his capacity to be faithful to God in any other way, for it betrayed a fundamental misunderstanding of the nature of Yahweh. Most especially, being swallowed by opposition to God's call and consumed by the fish refer to his journey towards death reaching its climax. God's call had invited Jonah to expand his heart. His refusal signifies his sin and rebellion. Jonah's descent to *Sheol* in the belly of the fish speaks of his death.

Three days and three nights

Particular stress is laid on the phrase 'three days and three nights', as if to emphasize the length of Jonah's internment. The only other place where this exact expression is used in Scripture is Samuel 30:12. Here, an Egyptian is found by the wayside. He had not eaten bread or drunk water for 'three days and three nights'. He was approaching death and his survival was in doubt. In realistic terms, 'three days and three nights' in the belly of the fish denoted death. The longer Jonah remained inside the fish, the less was his likelihood of survival. When John tells us of Jesus going to Bethany and finding that his friend, Lazarus, had been in the tomb for four days, he is underscoring the fact that Lazarus was dead.[23] A similar point is made by Luke: since it was three days since Jesus had been crucified, any hopes of deliverance were dashed.[24]

The prophet Hosea depicts the shallowness of Israel's hope that their repentance would persuade God to revive them after two days, by raising them up on the third day.[25] The context shows that the prophet was referring to Israel's complete misapprehension of the depth of her need of radical repentance. The people were unaware of the extent of their alienation from God and, while Yahweh longed to restore them, he could not be manipulated by acts of repentance which had no depth.

In Jonah the expression 'three days and three nights' could simply mean 'a few days'. On the other hand, the link with '*Sheol*' in 2:2 might suggest that the phrase echoed a mythological idea concerning the length of time a journey took to get from the land of the living to *Sheol*. Taken together, this combination of images associated with death in 1:17 points to the prophet's death. Yet the actual words are missing; it does not say, 'And Jonah died.' Instead this omission, combined with the phrase 'three days and three nights', creates an expectation: death is not the end of Jonah.

From the belly of *Sheol* (2:1–9)

> Then Jonah prayed to the LORD his God from the belly of the fish, saying '. . . out of the belly of Sheol I cried . . .' (vv. 1, 2)

It was from 'the belly of Sheol', a unique phrase in the Bible, that Jonah prayed. The 'belly' of the great fish is paralleled with the

[23] John 11:17.
[24] Luke 24:21.
[25] Hos. 6:1–3.

'belly' of *Sheol* (2:2). The word translated 'belly' could equally well be rendered 'womb', as in Genesis 25:23, or 'entrails', as in 2 Samuel 20:10, or 'heart', as in Psalm 22:14, or 'insides'. Here in Jonah 2:1 it is popularly assumed to mean 'stomach', since, at Yahweh's command (2:10), the fish vomits out the prophet. But the word is best taken to mean 'insides' or the 'innermost part'. The writer is not specific. He is less interested in the fish's anatomy than in the nature of Jonah's flight and God's deliverance. Clear resonances with the innermost, secret part of the ship where Jonah had found a place to sleep (1:5) are intended. Being in the 'belly' or innermost part of *Sheol* is the nemesis of Jonah's longing to be in a secret hiding place. Here, at last, from the deepest, darkest place, the prophet prays.

Concerning this place, Erich Fromm has written,

> We find a sequence of symbols which follow one another; going into the ship, going into the ship's belly, falling asleep, being in the ocean, and being in the fish's belly. All these symbols stand for the same inner experience: for a condition of being protected and isolated, of safe withdrawal from communication with other human beings. They represent what could be represented in another symbol, the foetus in the mother's womb. Different as the ship's belly, deep sleep, the ocean, and the fish's belly are realistically, they are expressive of the same inner experience, of the blending between protection and isolation.[26]

Prayer

We would be justified in believing the belly of *Sheol* to be Jonah's tomb, but the prayer now on the prophet's lips transforms the belly of the fish into a place of potential new life, a womb.

Jonah's flight from God is equivalent to a refusal to be born anew. To refuse life is to choose death. His withdrawal from communication and human community, his running away and hiding, amount to his denial of the God-given human need of communion. God has created human beings for fellowship with himself and community with others. The God who is 'three-persons-in-one' creates humankind in his image. Therefore, everything which colludes with competitive hostility, angry withdrawal and isolationism leads away from the image of this three-personed God. Wherever it is found, in either church or world, the attempt to live in disregard of God and others leads to spiritual death.

[26] Assembly of Rabbis, p. 999.

Our search for safety or security in places that we can call our own is endless. God's glorious creation is not only a place of awesome wonder; it is also a place of horror and brutality. Such reality is often too painful for us to contemplate. Violence not only exists in the physical world, such as in natural disasters and earthquakes, but also in the secret, hidden world of the human heart and imagination. This is something we are often tempted to avoid. Only the Spirit of the living God can tease out and release us from the power of destructive violence within. We may hide in the comforts offered by such things as materialism, the status offered by a respectable profession, the self-respect offered by membership of the Christian community, the personal conviction that we hold to the 'true faith'. In these and other ways we defend ourselves, guarding our reputations by means of different social conventions. We may sometimes use the respectability they offer as a safe hiding place. Even the current fashion of filling our diaries with our everyday busyness can become a barrier against our being open to God.

By hiding or protecting ourselves from God's reality we become deluded. Like Jonah, we might dig our hiding places so deep that we become entombed. We may become blind to the unsavoury reality within us, and deaf to the cries of those around us. We can even build our defences so high that it takes some kind of disaster before we can be exposed to God's reality.

To pray is to admit that Another Reality, One which is distinct from our own, exists. It is a Reality which is different from ours and possibly therefore threatening. It is a Reality which constantly seeks to be in relationship with us. The Lord God is this Reality. Yahweh is the only safe hiding place, the only secure refuge. Only here may we acknowledge and expose our total defencelessness, powerlessness and vulnerability. To unmask ourselves in prayer is to begin to discover who we really are in the presence of this faithful One. In prayer the heart, eyes and ears of the human soul are opened to the possibility of being touched and healed by this Other Reality, the brooding Holy Spirit of God. Prayer is the breath of life. It is Jonah's last hope.

2:1–10

6. Jonah calls upon the Lord

The psalm (2:1–9)

In approaching the psalm we must begin by acknowledging the change in literary genre from narrative to poetry. Here the narrative storyline modulates into poetic language. The psalm is more than a simple continuation of the narrative. As in other passages of Scripture, the change from narrative to poetry replays the events in a different key. The songs of Moses and Miriam in Exodus 15 rise out of the events of Exodus 14, sounding fresh depths of praise and joy. Similarly, David's lament over the deaths of Saul and Jonathan in 2 Samuel 1 discloses to the reader the depths of his grief. In both these instances the psalm invites the readers to enter more fully into the meaning of the events.

The psalm in Jonah 2 draws on other psalms, using vivid language to depict Jonah's experience. It shows Jonah reflecting on what has happened. By using poetic language the writer is able to supply further colour to the character of Jonah. The reader learns that he is not simply 'a Hebrew'; he is a particular person with particular character traits which affect his response to God. We also become aware of a certain irony in the psalm, which reflects Jonah's ambivalence. We were told in 1:1 that the prophet had fled from Yahweh's presence. Quoting from Psalm 31:22, Jonah believes he was cast out from God's presence (2:4a). Wherever the balance of truth lies, the psalm now on Jonah's lips clearly suggests he is very relieved that God has not fled from him!

In the same way that the brief narrative framework found in 1:17, 2:1 and 2:10 formed a chiastic pattern, so also does the psalm itself. Verses 2:2–9 may be set out as follows (italics mine):

A I called to the LORD, out of my distress,
and he answered me;
B out of the belly of Sheol I cried,
and thou didst hear my voice.

C For thou didst cast me into the deep,
into the heart of the seas,
and the flood was round about me;
all thy waves and thy billows
passed over me.
D Then I said, 'I am cast out
from thy presence;
how shall I again look
upon thy *holy temple*?'
E The waters closed in over me,
the *deep* was round about me;
F weeds were wrapped about my head
at the roots of the mountains.
G I *went down* to the land
whose bars closed upon me for ever;
F1 yet thou didst *bring up* my life from the Pit,
O LORD my God.
E1 When my soul fainted within me,
I remembered the LORD;
D1 and my prayer came to thee,
into thy *holy temple*.
C1 Those who pay regard to vain idols
forsake their true loyalty.
B1 But I with the voice of thanksgiving
will sacrifice to thee;
what I have vowed I will pay.
A1 Deliverance belongs to the LORD!

Setting the psalm out in this way may, at first sight, appear contrived and irrelevant to the task of exposition, but it is a very common trait of Hebrew poetry to use literary forms such as the chiasmus to help carry meaning. In working to recognize these forms, fresh insight may emerge. A closer look at the chiastic pattern in Jonah 2 reveals clues concerning the focus of the psalm. We find that while most of the psalm shows Jonah quoting different parts of the Psalter, the wonderfully graphic words of 5b and 6a, which culminate in the climax in verse 6b (G), are unique to Jonah:

> The deep was round about me;
> weeds were wrapped about my head
> at the roots of the mountains. I went down
> to the land whose bars closed upon me forever.[1]

[1] Magonet (1983), p. 49.

This climax portrays Jonah at 'death's door', imprisoned for ever in the land of *Sheol*. But this is the turning point. He can descend no further. Magonet suggests that Jonah needed new words to express his experience. In the chiastic arrangement suggested above, these new words, reaching to the heart of Jonah's position, are at the centre of the psalm helping to focus that possibility of meaning. His self-centredness is dispelled as the awful truth of his descent to the Pit becomes clear to him. 'At the moment of greatest darkness and despair, when no human action (certainly not his own) can release him, God breaks through all these suffocating layers, and draws his life out to safety.'[2]

The central focus of the psalm is Jonah's lowest point. Working outwards from this central point (G), the other aspects of the psalm which emerge in the chiasm include:

F Jonah goes down: this is an allusion to his descent in chapter 1. It contrasts with God bringing him up from the Pit or *Sheol* in **F1**.

E Jonah speaks of the 'deep', that is, *tᵉhôm*, the fearful reality spoken of in Genesis 7:11, Exodus 15:5 and Isaiah 51:10 which threatened Jonah's very life. It was at this point, when his life was ebbing away, that he remembered the Lord in **E1**.

D Jonah claims he is cast out from God's presence. Here the presence of God is paralleled in **D1** with God's holy temple. His claim is matched by the statement that God heard him in his holy temple in **D1**.

C Jonah claims that God hurled him into the sea. That this is intended as a reminder of events in chapter 1 is corroborated in **C1**, where he alludes to the mariners who actually hurled him into the sea as idol worshippers.

B Jonah cried to God from the innermost parts of *Sheol*, and God heard him. Surely there is an ironic echo here to Jonah's singular failure to answer God when he first called the prophet (1:2). Mercifully God has heard him in his distress and he offers thanksgiving, sacrifice and vows in **B1**.

A Jonah calls and God answers. God comes to the rescue of his reluctant prophet and Jonah offers praise in the words 'Deliverance belongs to the LORD' in **A1**.

Jonah in distress

Despite the book's interest in the theme of repentance, a theme which comes to the fore in chapters 3 and 4, repentance is not

[2] Ibid., p. 51.

referred to in Jonah's psalm. Here we see him finally calling on God in prayer because of his distress. The setting of his psalm in the 'belly of Sheol' naturally inclines us to sympathize with the prophet. His circumstances must surely justify the self-centredness evident throughout these verses. To this extent there is a realism about the prayer. Many of us, when caught in very difficult circumstances, may find we have little thought to give to God; instead, our overriding concern is to find help and a way out of all that causes us distress. Ultimately, we may be driven to prayer as a last resort, and, like Jonah, we may promise to praise God when he rescues us.

Whether for Jonah or ourselves, the great wonder of this kind of prayer is that our Lord, in his great love towards us, condescends to deliver us out of our frequently self-inflicted mess. Here is a God more willing to hear than we are to pray, a God who knows the words on our lips before we speak them, but who longs for us to speak them so that we may know he has heard our prayer.

Jonah's reference to 'those who pay regard to vain idols forsak[ing] their true loyalty' (v. 8) may be an indirect acknowledgment of his guilt in forsaking Yahweh. More likely, however, these words refer to the pagans whom God had called Jonah to address. Here he dismisses them as paying regard to 'vain idols'! In fact, the pagans, unlike the believers, do not know whom to call upon in their distress. Jonah was called to make God's ways known to these very people whom he here dismisses. Jonah remains locked into a way of thinking. Perhaps such total self-absorption is a picture of hell? In calling the fish to spew him out, God is indicating that the key to Jonah's new life lies with the very pagans, the Ninevites, whom the prophet so desperately struggled to avoid.

The chiastic arrangement of the psalm highlights another aspect of Jonah's self-understanding. In C he speaks of God casting him into the deep, but the parallel in C1 recalls the pagans who, as we know from 1:15, had thrown him overboard. Jonah knew that God would still the storm when they threw him overboard. He knew that God would respond to the sailors' action in this way and so, in effect, it was true that God had thrown him into the sea through the action of the sailors. But here in 2:8 he overlooks the costliness of their obedience. Their response contrasted sharply with Jonah's own disobedience, to which he does not allude in the psalm. Yet here he refers to them as idolaters. It is as though he saw himself as an innocent victim offering his life for the sailors, rather than as a renegade prophet whose disobedience had caused the storm in the first place. Contrasting himself with them, he promises thanksgiving, sacrifice and the payment of vows to the Lord. Those listening to the story know that the sailors were there first. Like God-fearing Noah, they have already offered their sacrifices to the Lord in thanksgiving for their deliverance.

An alternative possibility in relation to C and C1 is that Jonah was now admitting that *he* had forsaken his 'true loyalty' by fleeing God's presence. The 'son of faithfulness' had been unfaithful to God, so C could then be an admission that he had been justly punished by God throwing him into the heart of the sea. In view of the contrast Jonah makes between those who forsake their true loyalty and himself in verse 9, it is unlikely that this is his admission of sin.

Whichever interpretation is preferred at this point, it is offset by the immeasurably generous grace of the Lord. Jonah calls on God and, like an obedient servant, the Lord hears and answers his prayer. The Lord does not argue with Jonah, reprove him or make him suffer more than he already has suffered; he does not humiliate or chastise him, correct or punish him further. Instead, in the prophet's words,

> I went down to the land
> whose bars closed upon me for ever;
> yet thou didst bring up my life from the Pit. (v. 6)

Were the whole chiastic pattern to be laid on its side, with A at the left-hand and A1 at the right-hand side of the page, we would see Jonah's steady descent to death's door (G) followed by a gradual ascent. In the process of deliverance, however, it is not clear that we would see a change in Jonah's attitude towards those to whom God was calling him. In this context verse 8, with its specific reference to 'true loyalty' (*ḥeseḏ*), may offer us a clue to the intended audience of the book. In other words, here the writer offers a maxim to an imaginary congregation:

> Those who pay regard to vain idols
> forsake their true loyalty. (v. 8)

The word 'forsake' is used in relation to a doe forsaking her fawn, parents forsaking a child, and a wife leaving her husband.[3] It is frequently used in connection with forsaking the true God.

> Then men would say, 'It is because they forsook the covenant of the LORD, the God of their fathers, which he made with them when he brought them out of the land of Egypt.[4]

[3] Jer. 14:5; Ps. 27:10; Prov. 2:17.
[4] Deut. 29:25.

The theme of the people of God forsaking the Lord is central to the book of Jeremiah.

> Be appalled, O heavens, at this,
>   be shocked, be utterly desolate, says the LORD,
> for my people have committed two evils:
>   they have forsaken me,
> the fountain of living waters,
>   and hewed out cisterns for themselves,
> broken cisterns,
>   that can hold no water.[5]

In Jonah 2:8 those who forsake their 'true loyalty' (RSV), or their 'own mercy' (RV), or the 'grace that could be theirs' (NIV), are those who forsake the true God, Yahweh, and worship gods of their own making. They are breaking the covenant bond characterized on God's part by *ḥeseḏ*, that is, God's pledged and faithful love towards his people. The author portrays Jonah as one who has tried to escape his 'true loyalty'. Jonah imagines that it was the sailors who worshipped vain idols when, in fact, it is he who has been unfaithful to Yahweh. It could be that the book of Jonah was being addressed to those who had forsaken their love of the Lord, preferring instead empty things. Such people would be Israelites, like Jonah. On the lips of Jonah there is much irony in the words of verse 8. As we shall see, he longed for a god who was made in his own likeness rather than the Creator in whose image Jonah was made. Jonah's dream-god was, in effect, theologically and morally bankrupt, no better than the empty idols of the pagans.[6] All who long for such a god forsake their 'true loyalty'.

Drowning

The vivid description of drowning (vv. 3–5) depicts Jonah's descent into *Sheol*, the place of the dead. He was plunged into the wild sea (v. 3), becoming entangled with reeds (v. 5) until he reached the very bottom, 'the roots of the mountains' (v. 5). There he was imprisoned, serving a life sentence (v. 6). Picking up the theme of Jonah's descent from chapter 1 (1:3, 5), verse 6a speaks of him going 'down' to the land of the dead. Here his descent is halted, his flight from the presence of God ended. Yet it is here, in the innermost depths of *Sheol*, that Jonah meets God (v. 6b).

[5] Jer. 2:12–13.
[6] Ps. 31:6 is the only other instance where this same expression, 'vain idols', is found.

Sheol

Referring to the creation of the cosmos, Genesis 1:7 speaks of the 'waters which were under the firmament'. Ancient Semitic cosmology imagined there were waters surrounding the earth. The waters were separated by the 'firmament', a Latin term[7] used to translate the Hebrew word *rāqîa'*, a pounded brass dome over the earth.[8] This subterranean ocean under the firmament was regarded by some to be the place of *Sheol*, a Hebrew term meaning both the grave and the netherworld, the lowest possible place in creation.[9]

Jonah 2:6 speaks of *Sheol* as if it were a city with gates. A similar image is found in Job.[10] The 'roots', the deepest extremities of the mountains, and the 'bars' of the underworld are expressions of Ancient Near Eastern and Old Testament imagery which point to the power of death to imprison its captives.[11] Isaiah speaks of death's insatiable appetite,[12] an image which corresponds to *Sheol* 'swallowing' its prey.[13] The journey to *Sheol*, also known as 'the Pit', its location and its 'bars', point irrevocably to the finality of death. There was no escaping its power. In Hosea we see death and *Sheol* personified as a tyrannical ruler.[14]

One of the many theological themes in the book of Jonah concerns the supreme Lordship of God. All creatures were at his command. Nothing was outside his concern or the sphere of his power, not even death itself. God's might, of its very nature, must therefore include the possibility that he would deliver someone from death.[15] He, who alone was Creator and Saviour, would not be limited by the bars of hell. Nor would he be limited by a frightened and obstinate prophet whose narrow-mindedness had led him to the place of the dead. In this kind of situation the poetic hyperbole of Amos 9:2–4 had to bear a close resemblance to truth. It is here that Jonah's disobedience towards God becomes the occasion of a daring foray into theology. Speaking of God's unrepentant people, Amos says:

[7] The Latin is *firmamentum.*

[8] The verbal root of *rāqîa'* is *rq'*, meaning 'to hammer'. It is used to speak of God's creative action of spreading out the earth, cf. Job 37:18; Ps. 136:6; Is. 42:5. See also 'Cosmology', in Ryken, Wilhoit, Longman III (eds.), p. 170.

[9] E.g. Job 11:8; Prov. 9:18; Is. 7:11; Matt. 11:23.

[10] Job 17:16.

[11] Ps. 18:5.

[12] Is. 5:14.

[13] Ps. 141:7; Prov. 1:12.

[14] Hos. 13:14.

[15] Ps. 49:13–15.

> Though they dig into Sheol,
> from there shall my hand take them . . .
> and though they hide from my sight at the bottom of the sea,
> there I will command the serpent, and it shall bite them.
> (vv. 2, 3)

Jonah's determination to run from the presence of the Lord was a flight to death. By God's mercy, the great fish swallows Jonah, rescuing him from death by drowning – but in its belly, the belly of *Sheol*, the place of the dead, he discovers the God from whom he has fled waiting to meet him.

As we have seen, death and *Sheol* were personified as having insatiable appetites.[16] In a courageous play on this metaphor, however, the Lord of life reverses the curse of the grave by 'swallowing up death for ever'.[17] In Jonah we find that the great fish was sent to swallow, that is, to destroy. It was the heart of Jonah's condemnation, a seal on his act of death. The journey of Jonah the runaway ended in *Sheol*. It is most wonderfully while he is at the nadir of his misery that he rediscovers the permanence of grace. In the place of death he is met by God's grace and realizes that he can never escape it. Jonah discovers God in *Sheol*. The God whom Jonah thought he knew proved to be altogether different from what he had expected. He was already present in the place where Jonah had sought his absence. The writer envisions God rescuing Jonah from death, not near-death but actual death. Boldly he envisages the implications of the belief expressed in Psalm 139:7–8:

> Whither shall I go from thy Spirit?
> Or whither shall I flee from thy presence?
> If I ascend to heaven, thou art there!
> If I make my bed in Sheol, thou art there!

In telling of Jonah being swallowed by a great fish, the writer is interested in much more than a humorous story. He is playing with the daring possibility of a person, or nation, descending into *Sheol*, into the very place of the dead, there to be met by God *and restored to life*.

This profound and vivid imagery of death as a prison house with bars is the background to the words of Jesus to the disciples in Matthew 16:18: '. . . and the powers of death shall not prevail against it', that is, the church (*ekklēsia*). This most powerful Lord would

[16] Is. 5:14.
[17] Is. 25:8.

defeat death. Its power would be broken and its sting neutralized by his presence. Jesus goes on to say that the keys of the kingdom of heaven would be given to the people of God (*ekklēsia*). They were called to share in the nature and work of their Redeemer God who, in Jesus Christ, was recreating humankind in his image by unlocking the gates of death's deepest prison house.

Fall of the Northern kingdom in 721 BC

In considering this possibility of Israel's restoration we must look at Amos and Hosea, prophets in the Northern kingdom of Israel, possibly contemporary with Jonah son of Amittai (see time chart and map, pp. 216–218). These prophets struggled with the wickedness of Israel who, at that time, was bent on a course of national self-destruction in the face of Assyrian ascendancy. In the event, the prophets were unsuccessful in urging repentance on God's wayward people, and after a three-year siege of her chief city, Samaria, the nation was dragged cruelly into exile by Sargon II, king of Assyria, in 721 BC. Israel was dispersed among the nations. The fall of the Northern kingdom is predicated on the wickedness of Israel and especially her failure to respond to the message of the prophets.[18]

Before this, however, 2 Kings 14:25 tells us how the word of the Lord through Jonah, son of Amittai, strengthened the hand of Jeroboam II as he restored Israel's ancient borders. The writer puts it like this:

> [Jeroboam] restored the border of Israel from the entrance of Hamath as far as the Sea of the Arabah, according to the word of the LORD, the God of Israel, which he spoke by his servant Jonah the son of Amittai, the prophet, who was from Gath-hepher.

The achievements and successes of Jeroboam II during his long reign in Israel are ignored by the prophetic historian of 2 Kings. His main interest was how the word of the Lord brought deliverance to his people Israel. It is through the Lord's word to the prophet, acknowledged here, that God in his mercy saved his beleaguered people in their distress. Jonah became God's instrument in saving Israel. The king's actions accorded with the word of the Lord through Jonah, and Israel prospered.

The word of God through Amos and Hosea, who may have been Jonah's later contemporaries, met with no equivalent success. The

[18] 2 Kgs. 17:13–14.

people continued to enjoy their prosperity, taking it to be a sign of God's mercy and blessing, and dismissed their prophetic assaults. Referring to Hamath and the Brook of Egypt, Amos points to the extension of Israel's borders as having created a greater opportunity for the enemy to destroy Israel.[19] Hosea later taunts Israel for seeking to make alliances with Assyria.[20] He says that she prefers Assyria to Yahweh. Israel's political advances during the reign of Jeroboam II had made her arrogant. Her religious zeal, shown vividly in Amos 4 where the Israelites exceeded the requirements of the law in their offerings, served only to reflect her arrogance; it was a cloak for her greed.

As the threat of Israel's final defeat looms ever nearer on her northern horizon, we can hear Amos's terrible words of judgment on arrogance, greed and pretence echoing through the desolate hill-sides of the recently enlarged borders of the Northern kingdom as its inhabitants were forcibly exiled:

> Though they dig into Sheol,
> from there shall my hand take them;
> though they climb up to heaven,
> from there I will bring them down.
> Though they hide themselves on the top of Carmel,
> from there I will search out and take them;
> and though they hide from my sight at the bottom of the sea,
> there I will command the serpent, and it shall bite them.
> And though they go into captivity before their enemies,
> there I will command the sword, and it shall slay them;
> and I will set my eyes upon them
> for evil and not for good.[21]

Assyria was the nadir of Israel's flight from God. It was the place of death for Israel. But could it possibly be that even there they were not out of God's reach? Would God come in mercy towards his people and restore them again, as he had done according to the word of Jonah in 2 Kings 14:25? Or would he come to them in judgment for their disobedience?

Sheol's destruction

Using the same word 'swallow' as in Jonah 1:17, Hosea refers to Israel's earlier alliance with Assyria:

[19] Amos 6:2–11.
[20] Hos. 9:9f.
[21] Amos 9:2–4.

> Israel is swallowed up;
>   already they are among the nations
>   as a useless vessel.[22]

Politically, international alliances could be of great value to a small nation seeking to ensure its own security and prosperity, but such alliances suggested to Hosea that Israel was turning her back on Yahweh, the true source of her well-being. She was walking away from life and going towards death. This image echoes Jonah's flight from God and his being swallowed by the fish. Just as there was an ambivalence about the fish which swallowed Jonah, so the picture of Israel being swallowed by the nations carries the same ambivalence. On one level the fish appears to rescue Jonah from death, while on another level it is a symbol of his death. On the one hand, entering into an alliance with Assyria appeared to rescue Israel from danger and offer her security, but on the other hand it signalled her death. Jonah and Israel had chosen death in place of life.

Reflecting on this, Hosea looks towards the destruction of death and *Sheol*. With stunning confidence in God's power to redeem his own even from death and *Sheol*, Hosea says of God:

> Shall I ransom them from the power of *Sheol*?
>   Shall I redeem them from Death?
> O Death, where are your plagues?
> O *Sheol*, where is your destruction?
>   Compassion is hid from my eyes.[23]

He asserts that God had no intention of changing his mind ('Compassion is hid from my eyes') about this decision to vanquish death; he intends to show no compassion or softening in his attitude towards death and *Sheol*. They and all their associates were doomed. Again using the same word and building on the imagery of Hosea, Isaiah 25:8 says of God: 'He will swallow up death for ever.'

Does the appearance of this theme concerning the destruction of death in the eighth-century prophets point to something they shared in common? Might it have arisen from within the context of the awful possibility with which they were faced, namely the total annihilation of Israel, the Northern kingdom? Could there possibly be any hope for Israel? Maybe it is in the context of this pressing question that the book of Jonah has its particular impact and message. Israel had forsaken her true loyalty. Was the writer suggesting that

[22] Hos. 8:8.
[23] Hos. 13:14.

Yahweh was able to deliver even the unfaithful and disobedient from the power of *Sheol*?

Before moving on, it is worth noting here that in his letter to the Corinthians, Paul, combining the words of Isaiah and Hosea, writes,

> Death is swallowed up in victory.
> O death, where is thy victory?
> O death, where is thy sting?[24]

For Paul salvation is of God's free grace. It can be neither earned nor deserved. It is pure gift to be received. His formulation arises directly out of the same nexus of concerns which the eighth-century prophets faced: namely, what was God's relationship to the disobedient whose flight from God's presence was leading them to death?

Death swallowed by grace

Maybe this key question lies close to the heart of the book of Jonah. The language in the book is metaphorical. The writer is not simply writing a newspaper report of what happened to an Israelite prophet. He is grappling theologically with human experience. The experience is that of a person who seeks to avoid the call of God. In particular the person in question is a religious person, familiar with Scripture, worship and the core beliefs of his faith tradition. What happens when such a person, or such a nation as Israel, runs away from God? To run away from the source of life and love is to run towards death. We see that God gives Jonah the freedom to run away, but even as he reaches his destination God is waiting to meet and deliver him.

It is as though the writer is pondering the depths of God's word in Hosea 11:8–11. How would a faithful God who is both just and merciful deal with the disobedient? This is not expressed in terms of their breaking the commandments, but in terms of his people falling out of love with their Saviour God. Being a believer in this God is about the gift of his presence. It is less about doing the right things and more about being in his presence. 'Righteousness' is not sinless perfection, but guiltlessness. It is as we live in his presence that our lives are transformed.[25] Such transformation energizes and informs the human spirit to a life of moral courage and right living within the human community. To flee God's presence is to be cut off from

[24] 1 Cor. 15:54.
[25] John 15:4f.

the very source of life. It is our failure as God's people to live out our knowledge of him in our lives that raises the question, 'What will God do with us?' In the book of Jonah we are shown a sweet reasonableness in God's dealings with the disobedient which contrasts markedly with Jonah's self-righteous and sullen response. In the face of God's gracious generosity Jonah is angry (4:2), a clue to his religiosity being driven, not by the love of God, but by self-interest and self-pleasing, the religious characteristics hinted at in Amos 4 and 5.

In the way that the merciful God provided protection for Adam and Eve,[26] so, in his flight from God, Jonah finds himself surrounded by the selfsame God. Remarkably but realistically, his restored life shows that his deliverance from the fish, although a dramatic story, has little effect on him either morally or in terms of his belief in God's goodness. Here we begin to see that God's power is not challenged by sea monsters, dragons and the leviathan, or by the chaotic forces of wind, storm and tempest, or even by death itself, but by his own people.

The undying mercy of God

In Scripture God's justice is about his right dealings with his people. In the book of Jonah the writer claims that the true nature of Israel's God is most fully expressed by the quality of his mercy. It is in mercy that he deals with Jonah. This is shown in his compassion towards the prophet, the sailors, the people of Nineveh and even its animals. The absolute prerogative of any ruler is mercy. This was not, however, a characteristic much in evidence among the powerful Assyrian rulers in their dealings with defeated nations. It is in contrast to these fearsome rulers that we see Yahweh's power not depending on cruel brutality and oppression but being shown in his undying capacity for mercy. God's persistence with Jonah is a sign of this mercy and reflects the true nature of his justice.

Prayer elicits mercy

The conclusion of the psalm in 2:9 echoes 1:16. As the sailors celebrated their deliverance with sacrifices and vows, so Jonah promises to do the same. His final statement is one of the most profoundly significant sayings in Scripture:

[26] Gen. 3:21.

'Deliverance belongs to the LORD!'

The word for 'deliverance' or 'salvation' is from the Hebrew *yᵉšûʿâ*. The names Joshua, Hosea, Isaiah and Jesus all derive from this same Hebrew word.[27]

Salvation is of the Lord. It belongs to him. It is not of the Jews, the Christians, the Muslims, the righteous or the holy; it is of the Lord. It is true that, when speaking to the Samaritan woman, Jesus said to her, 'Salvation is from the Jews.'[28] In saying this, he referred to God's choice of a particular people through whom he would make himself known to all people. His word and will are revealed through the ongoing work and dialogue which characterizes such a relationship. The Lord is known through his dealings with his people and through his people's response. In speaking to the Samaritan woman, Jesus was not making a triumphal claim concerning Jewish superiority. The Jewish people did not *possess* the living truth any more than Jonah did. Rather, the One who was 'the way, the truth and the life' walked their streets in the person of Jesus. The Jews were living witnesses called to testify to the dynamic reality of God's salvation. Nevertheless, we are told in the same Gospel that 'his own people received him not'.[29] Scripture testifies to the experience that God's chosen people frequently fail in their calling. In this Jonah is no exception. Those who claim to be God's people must tell the story of his salvation, bear witness to it, be transformed by it and know its joy – but ultimately their salvation is of the Lord. Deliverance does not belong to them, be they Jews or Christians. It is from the living Lord, who unfailingly persists in wooing the hearts of his people. The living God is not in the pocket of any people. His deliverance is divinely dynamic.

The psalm shows how Jonah's experience of deliverance was an expression of the Lord's unfailing mercy. He called to the Lord in his distress and the Lord answered him. The Lord's response to the prophet's call restored a broken relationship. The prophet's action, spurred by his realization that ultimately God was all that he had, opened the door to new life and fresh possibilities. Jonah's declaration of God's power to save, 'Deliverance belongs to the LORD', is the consequence of his statement in 1:9, 'I fear the LORD, the God of heaven, who made the sea and the dry land.' Significantly, Jonah is proclaiming that salvation comes from Yahweh, not from his own world view. The prophet appears to be shifting his ground.

[27] Matt. 1:21, 'You shall call his name Jesus, for he will save his people from their sins.'
[28] John 4:22.
[29] John 1:11.

'Vomited out' (2:10)

> And the Lord spoke to the fish, and it vomited out Jonah upon the dry land. (v. 10)

The psalm began with the prophet calling on Yahweh. It concludes, after an uncertain struggle, with Jonah's dramatic affirmation that 'Deliverance belongs to the Lord!' Upon this great climax, the fish, at the command of Yahweh, vomits out Jonah upon the dry land. The writer's use of the word 'vomit' here is curious. We might imagine the prophet being thrown out of the fish's mouth, or even walking out. The writer does not say that the fish spat Jonah out, or even coughed him up! No, the text says Jonah was 'vomited out'. Holbert suggests that the fish is so sickened by Jonah's hypocritical piety at this point that 'It is no wonder that immediately after Jonah shouts, "Deliverance belongs to Yahweh!" the big fish throws up!'[30]

Undoubtedly, the fish spews him out in obedience to the word of Yahweh, but the word used suggests the fish's repugnance towards Jonah. That Jonah's prayer is met by Yahweh addressing the fish rather than Jonah is a corroboration of the same view. Like the psalmist, however, Jonah had divine company in the fish's belly: 'If I make my bed in Sheol, thou art there!'[31] Yahweh and the fish collaborated to deliver Jonah and send him on his way. Now he faces not oblivion but God, not security but challenge, not death but life. Surely this is a new beginning for a born-again prophet? The Lord had shown his readiness to deliver his disobedient people, but were they capable of being transformed?

Liturgical prayer

We may assume, contrary to some, that the silent Jonah of chapter 1 and the voluble Jonah of chapter 2 are one and the same person. In the psalm the writer has put into the mouth of the pious but disobedient Jonah a prayer which draws on material with which he was familiar from regular worship. In his need he recalled these words from the Psalter, and in so doing he opened a door, allowing God to meet him.

The value of liturgical prayer is that frequent repetition can fill the memory of the human heart with words, phrases and images that become a rich treasury from which to draw in times of distress. It sometimes happens when a person is in great need that familiar and

[30] Holbert, p. 353.
[31] Ps. 139:8.

treasured passages of Scripture become freshly meaningful. Familiar words can recreate images and emotions which come to the surface of our minds with power to reawaken a heart which is closed, or to mend a heart which has been broken. So gracious and compassionate is this God that he responds to the saying of words which may, for a while, have lost their meaning for us.

Jonah's grave was emptied when he decided to work with the Creator-Redeemer God. This meant empty formulas being transformed into words with meaning and life. Such formulas cannot contain or express the extent to which God's passionate love and mercy will go in order to bring salvation to the world,[32] but they can point to the way. Jonah was learning that 'truth' is a way of living with God and not only a propositional statement. It is in going with God that we open ourselves to new life, to transcending ourselves. Thus life with God is a perpetual new beginning from the ashes of our past as we strive to walk with our Saviour. As Jacques Ellul comments, 'This man [Jonah] is really dead and really brought to life again.'[33] But, as the morning dew is short-lived,[34] so too is this sense of triumph, as we shall see.

[32] John 3:16.
[33] Ellul, p. 2.
[34] Hos. 13:3.

The Hound of Heaven

I fled Him, down the nights and down the days;
I fled Him, down the arches of the years;
I fled Him, down the labyrinthine ways
Of my own mind; and in the midst of tears
I hid from Him, and under running laughter.

Now of that long pursuit
Comes on at hand the bruit;
That Voice is round me like a bursting sea:
'And is thy earth so marred,
Shattered in shard on shard?
Lo, all things fly thee, for thou fliest Me!
Strange, piteous, futile thing,
Wherefore should any set thee love apart?
Seeing none but I makes much of naught' (He said),
'And human love needs human meriting:
How hast thou merited –
Of all man's clotted clay the dingiest clot?
Alack, thou knowest not
How little worthy of any love thou art!
Whom wilt thou find to love ignoble thee
Save Me, save only Me?
All which I took from thee I did but take,
Not for thy harms,
But just that thou mightest seek it in My arms.
All which thy child's mistake
Fancies as lost, I have stored for thee at home:
Rise, clasp My hand and come!'

Halts by me that footfall:
Is my gloom, after all,
Shade of His hand, outstretched caressingly?
'Ah, fondest, blindest, weakest,
I am He whom thou seekest!
Thou dravest love from thee, who dravest Me.'

(Francis Thompson, 1859–1907)

3:1–10

7. A persistent God

Literary features

Once again the events in these verses are framed by the actions of God.

A Then the word of the LORD came to Jonah the second time, saying, 'Arise, go to Nineveh, that great city, and proclaim to it the message that I tell you.'

B So Jonah arose and went to Nineveh, according to the word of the LORD.

C Now Nineveh was an exceedingly great city, three days' journey in breadth. Jonah began to go into the city, going a day's journey. And he cried, 'Yet forty days, and Nineveh shall be overthrown!'

D And the people of Nineveh believed God; they proclaimed a fast, and put on sackcloth, from the greatest of them to the least of them.

D1 Then tidings reached the king of Nineveh, and he arose from his throne, removed his robe, and covered himself with sackcloth, and sat in ashes.

C1 And he made proclamation and published through Nineveh, 'By the decree of the king and his nobles: Let neither man nor beast, herd nor flock, taste anything; let them not feed, or drink water, but let man and beast be covered with sackcloth, and let them cry mightily to God; yea, let every one turn from his evil way and from the violence which is in his hands. Who knows, God may yet repent and turn from his fierce anger, so that we perish not?'

B1 When God saw what they did, how they turned from their evil way,

A1 God repented of the evil which he had said he would do to them; and he did not do it.

At the opening the Lord calls Jonah a second time to go to Nineveh (A). At the end (A1) he changes his mind about punishing Nineveh. Jonah's decision to obey (B) corresponds to God's change of mind (B1). The sheer brevity of Jonah's message to Nineveh (C) is contrasted with the detailed proclamation (C1) of the king concerning repentance. The response of the people (D) finds its focus in the response of the king (D1). Finally, the actions of the great king of Nineveh (D1) are matched by the repentance of the Great King (A1).

A taste of freedom (3:1–3)

> The word of the LORD came to Jonah the second time, saying, 'Arise, go to Nineveh, that great city . . .'

Notice how, in calling Jonah a second time, Yahweh graciously makes no reference to the prophet's previous failure. Neither does he remind Jonah of his deliverance from *Sheol*, nor of his promise, 'What I have vowed I will pay' (1:9). In fact, there is a certain humility on God's part as he calls on Jonah a second time. God's words carry no rebuke for Jonah and no warning of what will happen if he fails to respond once again. The call respects his humanity and assumes he has the capacity to respond. It assumes he will accept his vocation to go to Nineveh. The possibility still exists that he will resort to flight. He is still free to say either 'Yes' or 'No'. We might imagine the story-teller at this point altering the pace of his words by drawing them out a little, bringing his listeners to the edge of the precipice before releasing the tension.

> So Jonah arose . . . and . . . went . . . to . . . Nineveh. (v. 3)

One might imagine the physical release of tension which would follow those words. 'At last!' The word of God came to Jonah a 'second time', and this time the prophet did as he should. Jonah is the only biblical prophet who had to have his assignment given twice.

At this point we need to remember where Jonah has been since his first call. He has been to hell and back, reached out to God for help as the sailors had done, and experienced God's deliverance. At the very least he would not want to go through all that again! Jonah cannot possibly be the same person. He has a new start and the fruits of his experience must be brought to bear in a real situation, no matter how fearfully difficult the situation may seem. God's work of salvation has no credibility or cash value unless it impinges on the real world. It cannot be privatized, becoming the personal possession of individuals. It cannot be customized, being tailored to suit the particular predilections and fancies of those concerned with theological nicety or human fulfilment. The pursuit of theological precision, as of personal well-being, identity, sense of meaning, destiny, ambition or security, will always prove elusive and empty when sought for its own sake. Scripture urges the pursuit of God alone. 'Seek me and you shall live'[1] and 'Seek first his kingdom'[2] are two among many possible passages which urge this orientation in our living. Augustine also reminds us that our hearts are restless until they rest in him. That restlessless can divert our energies into all kinds of good causes, but each may become a diversion from the real thing. An example for many of us may be the subtle temptation to give our life's energies to maintaining 'Church-ianity' rather than to living 'Christ-ianity'.

An unreasonable call

So often, however, God's call is just unreasonable. In the New Testament Jesus calls fishermen and tax collectors to follow him. As we read the stories we are amazed by the instant obedience of these people. Attempts to rationalize their immediate response are scrutinized by Bonhoeffer.[3] He counters that it misses the point to say that those whom Jesus called must have known him and been familiar with his teaching and considered carefully the cost of following him before he called them. The point of the call narratives is that when God calls, the only response is to obey whatever the cost. Those who follow are called to take up their cross, a symbol of torture and death. Such a call is surely unreasonable, as Jonah's initial response to God's call so shockingly demonstrated.

God does not, however, negotiate with the prophet to arrive at a mutually agreeable calling. Certainly the call remained as unreasonable in chapter 3 as it had been in chapter 1. In terms of our limited human understanding, God's ways sometimes appear not only unreasonable, but eccentric and anarchic. Those he calls to inherit the kingdom of God, for example, are as likely to be tax collectors and prostitutes as scribes and Pharisees. God does not easily give up on anyone and Jonah, the disobedient prophet, has had a life-changing experience which took him beyond the bounds of reason and popular theology. It took him to a place where he was utterly helpless. It was in *Sheol*, of all places, that he received a taste of freedom.

[1] Amos 5:4.
[2] Matt. 6:33.
[3] Bonhoeffer, p. 48.

He had experienced the worst that could happen; he had been to the land of *Sheol*, whose bars closed upon him for ever, and yet he was delivered by God.

The One who calls is the One who liberates; he frees his people from slavery in Egypt, calling them out into the wilderness to worship and serve him. God's people in Egypt were no more deserving of God's deliverance than Jonah. This work he does for his own name's sake, that all should know what kind of God he is. He leads them out and he meets their needs, sustains, teaches and continues with them so that they may finally inherit the Place of Promise. Being called out into the wilderness was no strange innovation, and neither was the concept of Yahweh having concern for pagans. Perhaps it was the awful realization that God wanted Jonah to participate directly in these things that was so unreasonable. It was much more comfortable simply to reflect on them in prayer and meditation. Was believing insufficient? Did he really have to *do* something? As it happens, no direct reference is made in the book of Jonah to the liberating, life-giving event of the exodus, but it would have been as familiar to Jonah as the story of the cross and resurrection is to the Christian believer.

It is easy as Christians to affirm the historicity of our faith, and to claim its truth and sufficiency for salvation. It is much less easy to face the call to experience it in ways which will change our lives. Even in small things, such as our everyday relationships, the way we spend our money, the way we vote, use the world's resources and bring up our children, we face the challenge of God's call. Almost inevitably it will involve going against the status quo, challenging the accepted norms, be they of church or community, and going out in faith as Abram and Israel – and Jonah – did, not knowing what lay in store for them. It is the going forward in faith, with no other security than obedient response to the call of the liberating Lord, that is true freedom. The call takes us into the frighteningly unfamiliar, which tests our faith. We learn of its strength and authenticity when we are weak and vulnerable, walking along unknown roads and among strange people. God's people were called to go to strange places. Abraham was called to leave his family home in Ur of the Chaldees with its familiar culture and religion. Even worse, he was later called to slay his only son, his beloved Isaac in whom resided all his hopes and the covenant promises of God himself. Jacob struggled with the Stranger, emerging as a cripple. Jonah was called to go to the great city of Nineveh. We long to emerge intact, to retain our equilibrium, to remain strong. God calls us to places where we will be weak, vulnerable and exposed to the cross, to death, for only then can we know the power of his resurrection.

Why was Jonah sent to Nineveh?

God speaks of it as 'that great city' (1:2; 3:2), a city important to God (3:3 NIV), a city about which he is concerned. The name of the city is on God's lips at the beginning and end of the book. Maybe God intended to demonstrate the effectiveness of his own word to that exceedingly great city, whose very name conjured up images of power and glory. It represented the zenith of cultural civilization in its day, and as such was attractive to many of God's people long before they were exiled to Assyria in 721 BC.[4] Maybe God's concern for this great city is an image of his concern for all great cities even today. Large cities, often characterized by their extensive power and wealth, often have a downside seen in gross poverty, neglect, drugs trafficking and human exploitation. While their resources frequently lead to considerable influence beyond their own boundaries, life in the city can also harbour corruption on a large scale. In the vision of the city of God, the holy city, all evil and suffering is overcome.[5]

By addressing Nineveh, it could also be that God intended to show the effectiveness of his word to his own people in the great city of Jerusalem. It could be that the prophetic writer of Jonah is addressing God's people by telling them a story concerning Nineveh. Maybe Nineveh's response to the word of Yahweh would be the eye-opener God wanted for his own people. They might then begin to see that even that great city repented, while they themselves remained deaf to God's word and stubbornly unrepentant. While she need no longer fear Nineveh, for even that great city was subject to Yahweh, Israel did indeed need to fear the great King, Yahweh, before whom even the great king of Nineveh prostrated himself in sackcloth and ashes.

Although the city was finally destroyed by a coalition of the Medes, Babylonians and Scythians in 612 BC,[6] Nineveh's repentance is held up by Jesus as standing in stark contrast to the continuing obduracy of his own contemporaries: 'The men of Nineveh will arise at the judgment with this generation and condemn it; for they repented at the preaching of Jonah, and behold, something greater than Jonah is here.'[7]

Mercifully, Jonah was called to one particular city, not to the whole world. It is frequently the case that the specificity of God's call

[4] 2 Kgs. 16 – 17.

[5] Rev. 21.

[6] The fall of Nineveh is recorded in the Babylonian Chronicle for 616–609 (British Musuem).

[7] Matt. 12:41.

to us is associated with our existing awareness of need in that place. The Christian's awareness of the world's needs represented in our great cities may well be the first step to hearing God's call to go to those cities and meet with the Christ already suffering there.

Mission

The word 'mission' is not found in the pages of Scripture, but there is a good deal in the Bible about God 'sending' men and women into the world. For the New Testament writers, Jesus Christ is the *apostolos,* the One who is 'sent' by God.[8] Jesus is the One whom God sends into the world, and to the lost sheep of the house of Israel, to do his Father's will. The Old Testament prophets and the New Testament disciples are drawn into God's sending of Jesus. They are to deliver a message and to live a life, God's life, in the world.[9]

The particular insight concerning mission which we discover in the book of Jonah is that the prophet is not simply sent to the house of Israel. Surprisingly, he is sent to the pagan city of Nineveh. Is there a foreshadowing here of the One to come who would send his disciples into all the world? Moreover, does Jonah's response to God's call in any way prefigure our own?

Mission is about extending the boundaries of our life, whether it be the life of a church or an individual believer. Jesus speaks to the disciples of having sheep that are not of this fold.[10] The boundaries of the sheepfold must therefore be extended and enlarged so that these, too, may be brought in. This inevitably leads to a loss of control on the part of those called to engage in God's mission, but their task is to be obedient to God's call, not to control it. It is, after all, God's mission and not ours. The missionary history of the British churches over the last two hundred years saw much courageous self-sacrifice and bore much fruit. Less happily, a reluctance to give up control of new, young churches resulted in the foisting of Western church structures onto African and Asian communities. The task to which we are called, and the work to which we are sent, is greater than we can possibly ever know. The extent of God's mission is boundless. Our success will only ever be limited.

In Jonah we see, for whatever reason, that the prophet found it impossible to conform his life to God's call. His initial attempt at

[8]Heb. 3:1.
[9]For the Hebrews this life is characterized in the teachings of the Torah.
[10]John 10:16.

running away from the God who called him is evidence enough. He is not alone in this. Jeremiah complained openly about God's treatment of him.[11] He described how God's word had shaped his life, yet complained that God had proved to be a disappointment to him: 'Wilt thou be to me like a deceitful brook, like waters that fail?' Responding to this accusation, God urged Jeremiah to abandon his self-concern and repent of his complaining so that he may be restored to serve him: 'so you may stand before me.' The prophet of the Lord is called to be the Lord's mouthpiece.[12] Such a one who is called to this service will, as Jeremiah 15:19 puts it, 'utter what is precious and not what is worthless'.

Since, in common with Jeremiah and Jonah, many of us find that our lives cannot fully reflect the life of God, we become wholly dependent on living before him humbly in a state of repentance and forgiveness. In standing before God a second time, we see that Jonah had been granted the grace of repentance. Here lay the hope of a new beginning.

The 'go' of the gospel

At last, Jonah goes – literally, he *walks* to Nineveh. Geographically this was a demanding journey of about 900 miles across desert routes. The Hebrew word *hālaḵ*, with its basic meaning of 'walk', is used here for the first time in Jonah. In chapter 1 he 'went down'.

The concept of 'walking' is at the very heart of the gospel. When Jesus walked along the pathways and tracks of Galilee and Judea he showed us the life of God in the world. He showed us the way God walks in the world. In Hebrew thought, walking – *hālakah* – is walking through life following the way of God's teaching. The Lord God called Abraham, saying, 'Walk [*hālaḵ*] before me, and be blameless.'[13] This was not simply an instruction concerning Abraham's mode of transport! Nor was it to do with the number of miles he covered. It was to do with his way of living. He was called to walk in God's ways.

Jonah's response to God's second call was to walk in God's ways. In going or walking to Nineveh, Jonah needed to cross more boundaries. There were the obvious territorial ones, but there were others, too. He crossed the cultural and religious boundaries between Israelite and Gentile, between the holy and the unclean, the sacred and the profane. He would also pass from being one of the righteous

[11] See Jer. 15:16–19.
[12] Exod. 4:11–16.
[13] Gen. 17:1.

who stood in the presence of God to being an alien in a strange and wicked city.

In crossing boundaries Jonah discovered that God had already been that way. God was even waiting to meet him in *Sheol*. As God's people 'go', they find him already waiting to meet them in the strange and frightening place. If God were content to remain comfortably within the boundaries his people create for him, there would be no gospel. He would be in their control. Such a state of affairs is a denial of the existence of a Creator God. Jesus Christ crossed between heaven and earth to walk in our streets and cities. He crossed the threshold between death and life to assure his people of his unfailing presence. He crossed the social, religious and political divides of his day so that all might be drawn to him. In Christ the world sees a God who gets up and goes to meet his people. That is the sort of God he is. God is not territorial. Mission involves taking risks, traversing boundaries, crossing over into dangerous places only to discover that God is already there.

In Acts 10, Luke tells us of a struggle which Peter had to face. Following a perplexing dream, he was sent for by Cornelius, a devout, God-fearing centurion, to meet him in Caesarea. The Gentile and his household wanted to hear the words of the Lord and, when Peter spoke to them, God's Spirit was 'poured out . . . on the Gentiles'.[14] As if doubly to underline its importance, Luke records Peter's account of this event again in chapter 11, concluding it with the words of the stunned disciples, 'Then to the Gentiles also God has granted repentance unto life.'[15] However, not even Peter found walking across this boundary an easy matter. He felt threatened by his colleagues. Paul tells us of his conflict with Peter, who was afraid of the Jewish faction which was seeking to block the full admission of Gentiles to faith.[16] Initially obedient to God's call, Peter's subsequent compromise concerning the Gentiles must have been a cause of grief and perplexity to many.

God may take us through the entrails of *Sheol* so that we can know in our hearts the meaning of faith in him. This strange and barren wilderness can lead us to the Place of Promise where we are free from the inhibitions that bind us and bog us down in the mire of complacency and false security. But it is no easy journey.

For Jonah, a journey to Nineveh could not possibly be as arduous and life-threatening as his abortive voyage to Tarshish had proved. That journey had led him to the gates of *Sheol*; the gates of Nineveh

[14] See Acts 10:10–48.
[15] Acts 11:18.
[16] Gal. 2:11–13.

would be as nothing compared with those gates! So he got up and went. He did something highly unusual, showing an extravagant gesture of openness to worlds unknown.

Kerygma

> '. . . and proclaim to it the message that I tell you.' (v. 2)

There is a difference here in the words put into the mouth of God from those found in his first call of Jonah. In 1:2 he is told to 'cry against it; for their wickedness has come up before me'. Now, in 3:2, God says, 'proclaim to it the message that I tell you.'

The Hebrew word rendered 'message' is translated in the Septuagint (LXX) by the Greek word *kerygma*. Jonah was to be a herald proclaiming a message, that is, *kerygma*. The substance of the message is not given, but may we not suppose that it was in some way connected to the deliverance Jonah had experienced from the belly of *Sheol*? Was he not now being given an opportunity to 'pay his vows'? Might we not hope that his message found its focus in his climactic cry, 'Deliverance [*yᵉšû'â*] belongs to the LORD' (2:9)?

The word *kerygma* came to have particular significance in the life of the early church. In the New Testament it is used to describe the substance of the apostolic 'preaching' or 'proclamation'.[17] As Paul himself claims, it was the manner as well as the substance of the proclamation which was to be effective in changing lives.[18] The only other occurrence of the word in the Greek Old Testament is in 2 Chronicles 30:5, but its use in Jonah 3:2 is significant for our understanding of its use in the New Testament. As we shall see,

> The preaching of Jonah was followed by the repentance of the Ninevites . . . Christian preaching does not persuade the hearers by beautiful or clever words – otherwise it would only be a matter of words. It takes place in the spirit and in power. It is thus efficacious.[19]

In his correspondence with the church at Corinth, Paul writes,

> When I came to you, brethren, I did not come proclaiming to you the testimony of God in lofty words or wisdom. For I decided to know nothing among you except Jesus Christ and him crucified. And I was with you in weakness and in much fear and trembling;

[17] Rom. 16:25; 1 Cor. 1:21; 15:14; Titus 1:3.
[18] 1 Cor. 2:1–5.
[19] Limburg, p. 75.

> and my speech and my message [*kerygma*] were not in plausible words of wisdom, but in demonstration of the Spirit and power, that your faith might not rest in the wisdom of men but in the power of God.[20]

Paul stresses that his bearing reflected not a triumphalism (such as has since characterized much of Christianity) but a humble dependence on the crucified Christ. It was not his skill with fine words and attractive preaching which had power, but the outworking of God's presence in his life.

In similar vein, the Japanese Christian and theologian Kosuke Koyama writes a moving dedication in his book *Mount Fuji and Mount Sinai*, 'To the memory of Herbert G. Brand (1865–1942), through whose preaching, *in broken Japanese*, my grandfather was converted to Jesus Christ' (italics mine). What a testimony to the way of walking, the crossing of boundaries and the living proclamation of the message.

Nineveh

> Now Nineveh was an exceedingly great city, three days' journey in breadth. (v. 3)

It is not immediately obvious how we should read the phrase 'three days' journey in breadth'. It may be that, as Jonah set out, the narrator himself was amazed. It is as though he muses on the folly of God's call to Jonah as he describes the great city. Nineveh was 'exceedingly great'. Another equally proper way of translating the Hebrew would be to say that it was 'a great city even in God's sight'. It was so large that it was literally a 'three-day walk' across.

If the great city were a three-day walk across, that would make it in the region of forty miles in diameter. Even after the city boundary was enlarged by Sennacherib (704–681 BC), however, the diameter was no more than a mile at its widest point. In 4:11 the population of the city is given as 'more than a hundred and twenty thousand', a figure which archaeological sources would support.

Biblical writers were perfectly capable of providing precise measurements and other similar details when they were needed, yet here such precision is missing. Maybe we have lost our understanding of an ancient Hebrew idiom. Or maybe, as Stuart suggests, a 'three-day city' was a *terminus technicus* in diplomacy.[21] A further possibility is

[20] 1 Cor. 2:1–5.
[21] Stuart, p. 488.

that the story-teller intends it as a reminder of Jonah's journey to Sheol (1:17). Or perhaps the narrator was reminding his listeners (in the unlikely case that they had forgotten!) that Nineveh was 'a very great city'. The effect is to heighten the tension. Jonah . . . *goes*; he goes to . . . *Nineveh*; it was an . . . *exceedingly* great city! Whatever is meant by the phrase, Wolff comments aptly that the listener 'is not supposed to do arithmetic. He is supposed to be lost in astonishment, so that he can take in the events that follow in an appropriate way.'[22]

Jonah's proclamation

> And he cried, 'Yet forty days, and Nineveh shall be overthrown.' (v. 4)

Jonah enters the city. At last he does what the Lord has commanded. He cries out. He proclaims the message in a terse and taciturn fashion, a message which, on first hearing, is hardly hopeful! Nevertheless, the Ninevites received the warning of their overthrow. They were given 'forty days' in which to consider their position, the number 'forty' indicating a period of time frequently associated in Scripture with an encounter with God.[23]

There are two things to note about the word 'overthrown' (*hāp̄aḵ*). First, it is indissolubly linked in the biblical tradition with the overthrow of the cities of Sodom and Gomorrah described in Genesis 19:21, 25, 29. By using this particular word, the story-teller reminds the hearers of an earlier cataclysmic event. It may awaken in them a sense of justice having been done: as the cities of the plain got what was coming to them, so Nineveh deserved to be overthrown for her wickedness. However, the word equally means a turning upside-down, a reversal, a change, a deposing of royalty, or a change of heart. Deuteronomy 23:5 reads, 'The LORD your God turned [*hāp̄aḵ*] the curse into a blessing for you, because the LORD your God loved you.' There are other examples of the word being used in this way.[24] The message of Jonah could therefore be understood as meaning, 'In forty days Nineveh will have a change of heart.' As the Jewish expositor Rashi comments, 'The word "overthrown" has two senses, good and bad. If they do not repent they will be "destroyed". But if they repent they shall indeed be "overthrown", for they will have changed from evil to good.'[25]

[22] Wolff, p. 148.

[23] See Gen. 7:4; Exod. 16:35; 24:18; 34:28; Deut. 8:2; 1 Kgs. 19:8; Matt. 4:2; Acts 1:3.

[24] 1 Sam. 10:6; Ps. 105:25.

[25] Assembly of Rabbis, p. 1005.

The turning point

And the people of Nineveh believed God . . . (v. 5)

This phrase is the turning point of the book. The narrative has led to this point and the rest of the story is a working out of the consequences for Jonah of God's response to Nineveh's repentance. Without this response on the part of the people of Nineveh there would be no tale to tell, therefore much is made of it.

We have seen that Nineveh was by all accounts an outstanding city. True to form, her act of repentance was no exception. As if to underline the thoroughness of Nineveh's repentance, the writer devotes five verses to a full description of the event.

Indeed, Jonah had barely finished speaking before 'the people believed God'. Instantaneously their actions reflect their belief: they proclaim a fast and cover themselves with sackcloth. The city's repentance was great: 'from the greatest of them to the least of them' (v. 5), both 'man' and 'beast' (v. 7). The reference to both ends of the spectrum, 'great' and 'least', 'man' and 'beast',[26] shows that Nineveh's change of heart involved everything. It was not half-hearted or shallow. It was total.

Of their own accord the people of Nineveh undertook to be reconciled with God. They did not wait for orders from their king. It was they who inspired the king to join them in the act of contrition. A ruler both influences and reflects the public opinion of his subjects, for good or ill. Their response could not have been more different from Jonah's initial reaction to God's call. The contrast is stark.

Animals fast and pray

As if to underline the totality of Nineveh's response, even the animals are included. They are portrayed as sharing fully in the repentance of the city, fasting from food and drink, being clothed in sackcloth, and even being called on to 'cry mightily to God' (v. 8).

As we have already seen, animals are believed to play significant roles in the drama of salvation. The prophet Joel describes their conditions in a time of drought:

> How the beasts groan!
> The herds of cattle are perplexed
> because there is no pasture for them;
> even the flocks of sheep are dismayed.

[26]This is a literary device known as merismus.

> Unto thee, O LORD, I cry.
> For fire has devoured
> the pastures of the wilderness,
> and flame has burned
> all the trees of the field.
> Even the wild beasts cry to thee
> because the water brooks are dried up,
> and fire has devoured
> the pastures of the wilderness.[27]

In better times, the psalmist provides a vision of the goodness of creation in which all are mutually dependent on one another and on God.

> The young lions roar for their prey,
> seeking their food from God.[28]

The solidarity of human beings and animals is referred to by the writer of Ecclesiastes:

> For the fate of the sons of men and the fate of beasts is the same; as one dies so dies the other. They all have the same breath, and man has no advantage over the beasts; for all is vanity. All go to one place; all are from the dust, and all turn to dust again. Who knows whether the spirit of man goes upward and the spirit of the beast goes down to the earth?[29]

In an agrarian society where human beings and animals are interdependent, it is natural that the beasts should be included in the repentance of the city. Judith 4:10 makes mention of animals being clothed in sackcloth, and Herodotus, the Greek historian, describes a Persian cavalry unit shaving their horses and oxen out of grief over the death of their leader. Even so, we may be rendered speechless as we imagine the practical implications involved in taking these statements literally!

In the story of Noah's ark, all species of animals shared with humanity in both the calamity of the flood and the eventual deliverance. The story tells how, in the ark, they were miraculously preserved together and together shared a new beginning.[30] While significant differences are indicated in Genesis 1:24–31, these verses

[27] Joel 1:18–20.
[28] Ps. 104:21.
[29] Eccles. 3:19–21.
[30] Gen. 6 – 9.

speak of the animals sharing the same day of creation with humankind. We may suppose from this an intended and close relationship between these two orders of creation. It is this mutual interdependence between human beings and animals that underlies the inclusion of animals at Nineveh.

Moving from the 'least' to the 'greatest', we now come to the climax of the city's great repentance, shown by the response of the king of Nineveh. Such a 'great city' would have had a great ruler. Indeed, he was known as 'the great king'.

The king of Nineveh (3:6–9)

The king gives expression to his belief, and that of the people of Nineveh, by acting appropriately. The writer depicts the king of Nineveh as following in a particularly noble tradition:

> . . . he arose from his throne,
> removed his robe,
> and covered himself with sackcloth,
> and sat in ashes. (v. 6)

There is something deliberately dramatic about these words. They are vividly pictorial. There is a beautiful symmetry in the way the actions of the king are set out. The action begins with him rising from his throne and ends with him sitting in ashes. Between these two resting places he has taken off his royal robe and covered, or 'hidden', himself in sackcloth. Not even David's repentance, after he had heard the words of Nathan the prophet, is so lucidly portrayed. In that story it is only after King David has been told that his child is dead that we are told, 'Then David arose from the earth, and washed, and anointed himself, and changed his clothes.'[31] The story of Ahab shows the king adopting a similar response on hearing the words of the prophet Elijah: 'he rent his clothes, and put sackcloth upon his flesh, and fasted and lay in sackcloth, and went about dejectedly.'[32] God's response to Ahab was to delay the judgment.

The response of these kings to the words of the prophets was unusual. Perhaps more common was the response of Jehoiakim, king in Jerusalem. On hearing the words of the prophet Jeremiah read to him by the scribe, 'the king would cut them off with a penknife and throw them into the fire in the brazier. Yet neither the king, nor any of

[31] 2 Sam. 12:20.
[32] 1 Kgs. 21:27–29.

his servants who heard all these words, was afraid, nor did they rend their garments.'[33] Such brazen hostility towards God was all the more shocking coming from a descendant of David and a king of Jerusalem.

The pagan king of Nineveh, however, knew that fasting and the usual outward signs of repentance alone were insufficient. He added a totally new dimension to them by urging on the people the idea that the pattern of evil and violence had to be broken: 'let every one turn from his evil way and from . . . violence' (v. 8). 'It is not said of the men of Nineveh, "And God saw their sackcloth and their fasting," but "God saw their works, that they turned from their evil way."'[34]

This theme is also found in the prophet Isaiah:

> Is not this the fast that I choose:
>   to loose the bonds of wickedness,
>   to undo the thongs of the yoke,
> to let the oppressed go free,
>   and to break every yoke?
> Is it not to share your bread with the hungry,
>   and bring the homeless poor into your house;
> when you see the naked, to cover him,
>   and not to hide yourself from your own flesh?'[35]

The wholehearted, trusting response of the king is all the more remarkable since it would appear from verse 9 that there was no guarantee of God's intention to relent even if the Ninevites turned to him. As the great king of Nineveh urged the people and the animals to cry mightily to God, all that underlay his words was a hopeful but poignant 'who knows?' or 'perhaps':

> Who knows, God may yet repent and turn from his fierce anger, so that we perish not? (v. 9)

The king's call that all Nineveh should cry to God for deliverance echoes the same hope in the 'who knows?' or 'perhaps' of the mariners in 1:6 and 1:14, and uses the same Hebrew word. Once again we see the effectiveness of such cries in the heart of the Creator God. The same desperate hope, 'perhaps', quivered on the lips of David as he fasted in the hope that God would save his child. He cried, 'Who knows whether the LORD will be gracious to me?'[36] At

[33] Jer. 36:23–24.
[34] Assembly of Rabbis, p. 1007.
[35] Is. 58:6–7.
[36] 2 Sam. 12:22.

another time, when the nation of Israel was being devastated by locusts, the prophet Joel urged the people:

> ... rend your hearts and not your garments.
> Return to the LORD, your God ...
> Who knows whether he will not turn and repent,
> and leave a blessing behind him?'[37]

There was no guarantee that Nineveh's fasting would bring about the desired response. God was their only hope. They believed that the God, *'ᵉlōhîm*, proclaimed by Jonah had the power to deliver them from impending disaster. They also believed that their evil and God's 'fierce anger' were connected, and that their change of heart might create a change of heart in God. This was bold belief indeed – and, we are told, it paid off.

Whoever this great king of Nineveh was, he possessed a great capacity for humility in the presence of God's word. This of itself is striking and contrasts with Jonah's initial response to God. The king's response highlights a tendency sometimes seen in those who, like Jonah, claim to know God. They may show less capacity for humility in God's presence and more resistance to God's word than those who make no such claims. Christian leaders may be tempted to presume they know the mind of God on various matters. Jonah claims as much in 4:2, and yet he discovers that it is only in making the journey, in walking with God, that his ways are revealed. Leadership can never be a matter of knowing God's way in advance; only in the walking can it be known.

The great king saw a possible answer to his difficulties in the words of a foreign prophet. His response may have been driven by opportunism, but it reveals an amazing degree of humility. 'Who knows?' Here, the story of the small-hearted Jonah touches on learning the lesson of humility in the presence of the Lord God. How surprising it must have been to discover that the lesson had already been learnt by the great king of Nineveh.

Believing

It is interesting to see that when the writer says 'they believed God' in verse 5, he uses the same Hebrew word for 'believed', *'āman,* as that found elsewhere in Scripture. In describing Abraham's response to the Lord binding himself to the immutable covenant promise, Genesis 15:6 reads, 'And he [Abraham] believed the LORD; and he

[37] Joel 2:13–14.

reckoned it to him as righteousness.' And in describing the response of Israel to their deliverance at the Red Sea, Exodus 14:31 reads, 'And they believed in the LORD and in his servant Moses.'

In biblical narratives the act of 'believing' is much more than accepting certain credal statements about God. As in the two illustrations above, belief is an action of trust resulting from an experience of God's deliverance. It is not the clarification of a concept or the recital of a theological formula. Belief is a fundamental life commitment arising out of an experience which is unshakeably true. A credo is an articulation of such a truth, out of which a person lives his or her life. Attitudes are formed and values established on the basis of this truth. Such attitudes and values, in turn, set the moral compass which undergirds and guides action.

The creeds recited in the liturgies of the Christian church do not articulate philosophical propositions about God and the world. Rather, they should be understood as having a similar literary energy as that characteristic of a hymn. They express a formulation of a truth which lies at the heart of the Christian's life commitment. That commitment is made and proclaimed in words of faith. It is based on the experience of the people of God, who have subsequently interpreted events of Scripture as witnessing to the truth.

The truth which the Ninevites recognize is God's readiness to be merciful. They cast themselves on his mercy and discover that he is merciful. 'Deliverance belongs to the Lord.' Perhaps one of the most wonderful truths lying at the heart of the book of Jonah is that God turns to those who turn to him. Even more wonderful is the truth that he does not turn away from those who, like Jonah, turn away from him.

Nineveh's 'belief in God' was not simply an assumption that God existed. As James says, 'Even the demons believe [that he exists].'[38] The Assyrians were a most religious people: they shaped their national life according to their belief in the goddess of war, Ishtar. Their 'belief' was a commitment to the character of their god. But people are known to welcome other gods if they can provide what is needed. Nineveh is depicted as needing deliverance from 'evil'. As the cries of the Israelites had come up before God when they suffered in Egypt,[39] so the *rā'â* of the Ninevites had come up before him. They may have suffered natural disaster such as earthquake or famine; they may have suffered political disaster such as defeat at the hands of their enemies and internal rioting. Any such disaster accompanied by, indeed compounded by, a weak ruler or a total

[38] Jas. 2:19.
[39] Exod. 2:23.

eclipse of the sun could have conspired to make the people and king of Nineveh receptive to the words of a foreign prophet.[40] Or, as in the case of Sodom, their need may have been for deliverance from their moral perversity. Whatever it was, they needed to recover their strength; the God of Israel offered them relief from their struggles if they repented.

Rather like the disciples by the Sea of Galilee who, on hearing the call of Jesus to 'Follow me', immediately left their nets to follow him, so the people of Nineveh respond unquestioningly. Similarly, Abraham, whose home town of Ur was part of the agglomeration of cities in the region of Babylon, when he heard the call of Yahweh to 'Go from your country and your kindred . . .', immediately 'went, as the LORD had told him'.[41]

The king of Nineveh is portrayed as welcoming the words of God and responding with a wholeheartedness which acknowledges Yahweh alone as the King of kings. The portrayal of the king in these verses is of an ordinary human being joining with his people in the hope of receiving help. There is a suggestion here that repentance has the effect of rehumanizing people, that repentance is the retrieval of humanity and the dropping of all pretentious roles. The great king becomes a supplicant, one with the least in his kingdom. The act of repentance renews and revitalizes the human–divine bond once broken in the garden. Repentance opens the eyes of our soul to reveal the Lord, the One about whom Jonah claimed to know so much (4:2).

God's response and moral symmetry (3:10)

> When God saw what they did, how they turned from their evil way, God repented of the evil which he had said he would do to them; and he did not do it. (v. 10)

God's action here corresponds to Nineveh's 'turning from evil' (3:8). This is shown by an exact parallel in the words used:

A Let every one *turn* from his *evil* way and from the violence which is in his hands. (v. 8b)

B Who knows, God may yet *repent* and turn from his fierce anger, so that we perish not? (v. 9)

[40] These possible causes of Nineveh's plight are outlined by Stuart (drawing on Wiseman), p. 493–495.

[41] Gen. 12:1, 4.

A1 When God saw what they did, how they *turned* from their *evil* way, (v. 10a)
  B1 God *repented* of the *evil* which he had said he would do to them; and he did not do it. (v. 10b)

Yet again the narrator's literary skill underlines for us a dynamic sense of relationship between God and humankind. God is responsive to humankind. He responds to and reciprocates their actions.

God's readiness to relent is shown in the Hebrew word used here to speak of the divine 'repentance' (*nāḥam*). It is translated 'compassion' by the NIV and is a different word from that used of the 'turning' (*šûḇ*) of the Ninevites. When God saw that they 'turned away' (*šûḇ*) from their evil (*ra'*), he, in freedom, responded and 'turned away' (*nāḥam*) from the evil (*ra'*) that he had threatened to do to them. Putting it another way, 'he turned towards them in compassion' in response to their turning towards him in hope and penitence. But, in particular, the turning of the Ninevites was a matter of action, not merely good intention. As they changed their ways, God was relieved of the moral necessity of punishment, allowing him to do that which he always desires, that is, to bless humankind. God's desire to bless is shown in the sending of Jonah to call them to repentance. They respond wholeheartedly to the divine initiative of God's undeserved kindness.

The prophet Jeremiah, speaking of God's response to his people's evil, uses the same expression in 18:10. He speaks of the Lord 'repenting' (*nāḥam*) of the good he had intended to do when the people whom he had blessed turned to do evil (*rā'a'*).

This Hebrew word, *nāḥam*, which the prophets used to speak of a change of heart in God, is rich and complex. As the Jewish commentator Ibn Ezra has said, 'Words of Scripture are expressed in a language understandable to human beings.'[42] But the English word 'repent', which is frequently used to translate *nāḥam*, has become indissolubly linked with a 'repentance from sin' rather than a 'change of heart'. Inevitably, words collect associations and meanings which cause their true meanings to be overlaid. Rather like barnacles clinging to beautiful shells, so layers of usage cling to words, sometimes robbing them of their wealth. In the same way that an old oil painting needs to be cleaned, so such words need to be restored to allow their beauty and subtlety to shine through once more.

Is the beautiful literary symmetry in 3:9–10 intended to reflect a moral symmetry in God's relationship to humankind? Does God automatically reciprocate people's response towards him? If they

[42] Assembly of Rabbis, p. 1009.

bless him, will he bless them? If they respond to divine threats of devastation with a changed lifestyle, will they automatically be reprieved? And if people live as God requires them to live,[43] can they expect blessing and prosperity?

The story of Job, the cries of the psalmists and the experience of the prophets point to obedience being no guarantee of well-being.[44] Other psalms, as well as accounts of the wicked triumphing over the innocent and the gratuitous violence of the imperialists towards Jerusalem, only add to our perplexity about what may have been suggested by this literary symmetry.[45]

Jonah's approach to Nineveh was simple: the city was wicked and should be punished. God's approach to Nineveh was simple: the city had changed and should be delivered. Maybe the symmetry is intended to contrast the idea of God's justice with that of Jonah's. This would mean that a principle of God's attitude towards humankind is being shown, not an illustration of what might normally be expected to happen. While God's sympathy with sinful humanity is stressed in this story, Jonah shows himself to be hard-hearted and lacking in compassion or mercy.

God's dealings with humankind are best illustrated in the first instance by his dealings with his own people. Here we might turn again to the eighth-century prophet in Israel, Hosea. Pulled in one direction by his love for his wife and in another by her shocking adultery, the prophet recognizes that the same tension exists in the heart of the Divine. The following words highlight the tension between the nature of God's love and the claims of his truth. God agonizes over his people:

> How can I give you up, O Ephraim!
>   How can I hand you over, O Israel!
> How can I make you like Admah!
>   How can I treat you like Zeboiim!
> My heart recoils within me,
>   my compassion grows warm and tender.
> I will not execute my fierce anger,
>   I will not again destroy Ephraim;
> for I am God and not man,
>   the Holy One in your midst,
>   and I will not come to destroy.[46]

[43] Mic. 6:8.
[44] See Pss. 22; 44; 88; Jer. 15:15ff.
[45] See Ps. 73; Is. 53; 2 Sam. 13; Is. 5.
[46] Hos. 11:8–9.

In this climactic statement Hosea shows that God's overriding will is governed by his compassion (*nāḥam*). He will not come to destroy. Rather, as we read in 14:4, he will come with healing for their faithlessness and will love them freely. It is as his people realize this that, God says in 14:7, 'They shall return and dwell beneath my shadow.' God does not come to them in response to their repentance. Rather, recognizing their need, they come to God in response to his word of grace. His heart is already turning within him, his compassion growing warm and tender. Despite this, however, God did not prevent the Assyrians from destroying Israel in 721 BC. Both Israel and Jonah endured the storm and were taken to the place of death: it was the consequence of their disobedience. In the book of Jonah we see a God who did not desert his people in the exile.

We cannot tell whether there was some gracious fragrance about Jonah and his message which enabled the king of Nineveh to utter in hope the words 'Who knows . . . ?', while not presuming on God's mercy. God's concern for Nineveh was the concern of the Creator for his creation. He comes not to call the righteous, but sinners to repentance.

> And as he sat at table in his house, many tax collectors and sinners were sitting with Jesus and his disciples; for there were many who followed him. And the scribes of the Pharisees, when they saw that he was eating with sinners and tax collectors, said to his disciples, 'Why does he eat with tax collectors and sinners?' And when Jesus heard it, he said to them, 'Those who are well have no need of a physician, but those who are sick; I came not to call the righteous, but sinners.'[47]

Such an understanding highlights the agonizing tension existing in the heart of the Creator and Saviour of the world. That sublime tension is revealed in the cross of Christ. The fullness of God's compassion in the face of human frailty and sin meets with the fullness of his holiness in the man Jesus Christ. The outworking of this tension is seen in the passion of Christ, particularly as it is focused in the events of Holy Week. The resurrection of Christ shows that human sin is dealt with. God does not have to be persuaded to forgive: he has already made that decision. It is for humankind to claim the gift and allow it to transform the life of the world. In compassion and holiness God offers forgiveness to those who would destroy him, be they the self-righteous religious among his own people or the religious of other faiths.

[47]Mark 2:15–17.

The book of Jonah and other faiths

Does the story of Jonah have anything to say about our contemporary relationships with neighbours who espouse other faiths?

In considering this important question we first need to see that Jonah comes to us from the great stream of Hebrew tradition. This is renowned for the subtlety and depth of theological insight which it contains and which, even now, challenges Jews and Christians alike centuries later. Jesus of Nazareth, a Jew in the same stream of theological tradition as Jonah, reflects much of the prophet's approach in his parables and debates with religious leaders of his day. Paul, a Hebrew of the Hebrews, was also influenced by issues at the heart of this tiny text. In the Islamic tradition the story of Jonah is retold, focusing particularly on the prophet's repentance of his hatred towards the people of Nineveh. According to this version, Jonah's deliverance from this evil leads to Nineveh's deliverance from judgment and disaster.

We need to ask what it means that these three Abrahamic faith traditions hold this story in their sacred texts, a story which still has powerful resonances in relation to the repentance of faith communities. Such communities often prefer to contain God within the boundaries of their own traditions than to find him in the stranger and outcast. The book of Jonah challenges this exclusivist tendency by which boundaries are set which effectually make people outsiders. It is significant that in each of these three faiths, God is known for his mercy towards the penitents who show themselves willing to change.

A second approach points to Jonah, the Israelite prophet of Yahweh, being sent to the Ninevites. They were not Yahwists but worshippers of Ishtar. Jonah went at the command of the Lord God, Creator of heaven and earth, and Nineveh recognized his word. Their capacity for such recognition was a sign that they were made in the image of this God and were therefore capable of entering into their inheritance as God's people. Whether their worship of Yahweh was subsequently done in ways which Jonah would have recognized is not of interest to the writer. He does, however, assume that believers in other gods were capable of understanding and responding to God's word. The main focus of the text may be Israel's relationship to and responsibility towards other nations, a responsibility which presupposes that the truth of her faith would be measured in her embrace of others. Such inclusiveness is a reflection of the generosity and compassion of her Creator-Redeemer God.

In this respect it is instructive to notice that the Christian faith, as it has been understood and practised, is not a single, simple strand of belief. In different generations and in different climes it has been understood in different ways. To go with the Crusades to kill Jews and Muslims, for example, was at one time considered a true sign of Christian commitment. At other times, to maintain slavery was believed by Christians to be upholding God's created order. Yet again, to preach the importance of the Ten Commandments on the one hand, and to hang the poor who stole bread to feed their children on the other,[48] or to insist on the use of the 1662 Book of Common Prayer whether the culture was Inuit, Bantu or even twentieth-century England, and in some churches to insist on certain forms of episcopacy, have all been reckoned as true expressions of Christianity. Believers are always shaped and limited by the cultural context they inhabit.

The competition which has gradually grown up between the three Abrahamic faiths has resulted in untold damage, culminating in the twentieth-century Holocaust in which earlier Christian attitudes to Jewish people found a new and terrible expression.[49] Moreover, in common with peoples of other faiths, Christians often have difficulties in acknowledging fellow Christians from other cultures, denominations, theological traditions, persuasions and practices which are different from their own.

Nonetheless, transcending all plurality of faith and culture is the universal experience of suffering. Like no other it is a language common to all humanity. Suffering is an incomparable, uncomfortable and unwelcome language through which God speaks to the hearts of men and women. Eugene Heimler wrote:

> It was in Buchenwald that I learnt from Jews, Christians, Moslems and pagans, from Englishmen, Serbs, Rumanians, Albanians, Poles and Italians that I was only one more suffering insignificant man; that the tongue my mother taught me, and my Hungarian memories and the tradition of my nation, were nothing but artificial barriers between myself and others. For essentially, as Mankind we are one. A slap in the face hurts an Englishman as much as it does a German, a Hungarian or a Negro. The pain is the same . . . Our dreams, each dreamt in a different language, spell out the same dream in the language of mankind; all of us want peace, security, a life free from fear . . .

[48]Despite English practice, ancient Hebrew law did not prescribe the death penalty for theft of this kind.

[49]Considerable historical evidence of Christian (both Roman and Protestant, e.g. Luther) anti-Jewish behaviour is openly available.

> I learnt that within me, as in others, the murderer and the humanitarian exist side by side; the weak child with the voracious male. That I am not in any way superior, that I am not different from others, that I am but a link in the great chain, was among the greatest discoveries of my life.[50]

Jonah represents a comfortable believer. In the face of God's call to proclaim his word to people of a different faith and culture, he was unable to let his understanding of God and of his own faith community be challenged or changed. Such faithfulness to a limited vision leads to disaster. Such 'faithfulness' is ultimately unfaithfulness to the Living God.

[50] Assembly of Rabbis, p. 574.

Egocentric

What care I if God be
If he be not good to me,
If he will not hear my cry
or heed my melancholy midnight sigh?
What care I if he created Lamb,
And golden Lion, and mud-delighting Clam,
And Tiger stepping out on padded toe,
and the fecund Earth the Blindworms know?

He made the Sun, the Moon and every Star,
He made the infant Owl and the Baboon,
He made the ruby-orbed Pelican,
He made all silent inhumanity,
Nescient and quiescent to his will
Unquickened by the questing conscious flame
That is my glory and my bitter bane.
What care I if Skies are blue,
If God created Gnat and Gnu,
What care I if good God be
If he be not good to me?

(Stevie Smith, 1903–1971)

4:1–11

8. A prophet's anger and the Lord's pity

Jonah's anger (4:1–3)

But it displeased Jonah exceedingly, and he was angry. (v. 1)

On one level, Jonah's response to God's compassion was extraordinary. He had settled himself down to wait to see whether, in the space of forty days, Nineveh would be overthrown (3:4). There are many instances in the Bible showing that the 'forty day' time span was used to denote a period of trial or penance. In the event, nothing happened – no enemy invasion, earthquakes or plagues. Jonah's doubts about God were right: this was a God soft on sin and weak on justice. Jonah felt let down. In going to Nineveh at God's second call, the prophet had given God an opportunity to demonstrate the power of his judgment against the great city. He had faithfully held on to judgment, but had forgotten love. God held out both judgment and love, and love had prevailed.

In the New Testament Jesus speaks of there being much joy among the angels in heaven over one sinner who repents. But after all the effort involved, the repentance of the entire population of the great city of Nineveh brought no joy to Jonah, only intense anger. The words used clearly show that his anger was not just a matter of theological disagreement. Jonah was possessed by total opposition to God in this matter. Literally we read, 'But it was *ra'* to Jonah great *rā'â*, and he was angry.' We have noticed elsewhere the different nuances of this little word *ra'*. Here in 4:1 *ra'* is very specifically linked with anger. Jonah was not merely 'displeased', he was 'absolutely furious'. While God had turned away from the heat of his anger (3:10), Jonah was being consumed by the fire of the anger burning within him.

The contrast between Jonah's response to God's deliverance and that of the mariners' response to God's deliverance (1:16) is startling. When the storm was stilled 'the men feared the LORD exceedingly', but when the storm of God's anger towards Nineveh was stilled and he relented and showed compassion, Jonah 'boiled over with anger'. In what sense can it be said that Jonah 'feared' the Lord?

At another level, most of us will have some sympathy with Jonah. After all, many of us have been affected by leaders and nations who have acted wickedly. The current redistribution of land in Zimbabwe contributing to widespread famine in southern Africa; the theological justification of apartheid in South Africa; the intransigence of the Israel–Palestine conflict; Northern Ireland; the Balkans; Rwanda; Vietnam: these and many more bitter situations are all examples in which justice has been elusive and people have had to live their lives with unresolved anger and suffering. In theory we say God can forgive, but in practice we sometimes discover that the reality of that forgiveness is hard to handle. The Truth and Justice Commission initiated by Archbishop Desmond Tutu was a way to opening up the possibility of forgiveness which gives birth to new life.

It is Jonah's response at this point which requires us to look again at the meaning of the book. What has been his course so far? We have seen him first of all in silent opposition to God's call as he fled to Tarshish. On board ship he sought to hide himself away so that he could rest untroubled by life around him. Only the great storm and the dire needs of the ship's crew brought him to his senses, at which point his action brought deliverance. With the encouragement of the mariners, he finally declared himself to them before offering his life in exchange for theirs. Alone in the belly of the fish, he discovered himself in the presence of God and his faith was renewed to the extent that he went to Nineveh at the second time of asking. There he met with great success, to which he responded with correspondingly great fury. In the remainder of chapter 4 we see a faithful God alongside Jonah, seeking first to relieve him of his discomfort and then to challenge the basis of it.

We have seen extreme instability in Jonah during the story so far, shown most clearly by his response to God's second call being diametrically opposite to his first response. Some account must be made of this. We might say that after his return from *Sheol* he was a reformed character, a fact demonstrated by his willingness to go east, to the great city. We have seen that the people of Nineveh have heeded his message and turned to God. Jonah's obedience towards God met with a clear response. Why, then, was he so angry with God?

We could see his obedience as an act of supreme self-offering, or indeed compliance, for he was going against his own fundamental instincts and convictions. That is to say, Jonah's fundamental belief was that evildoers (i.e. Nineveh) should be punished. His underlying concern in proclaiming the message to Nineveh was that it should be destroyed. His own world view said that Nineveh should share the fate of Sodom and Gomorrah.

He could not accept what he knew would happen. When Yahweh repented in response to Nineveh's penitence, the prophet's real feelings broke through; he could no longer restrain them. This coincides with his own account to God in 4:2–3. He knew God would repent; he knew this was what God was like – but to experience it was more than Jonah could handle. He endured more than an intolerable threat to his world view: when God showed compassion on Nineveh, he suffered its actual collapse. His extreme anger is an indication of the depth of commitment Jonah, the son of faithfulness, had to his own fundamental beliefs which now lay shattered at his feet. An expression of the profound grief this causes him is his extreme anger towards God.

Cost of forgiveness

In the space of a brief text it can seem as though God's response to Nineveh's repentance was weak. How could people possibly know the truth of God's word unless they were made to suffer for their sins? Yet this punitive approach arises from a partial and therefore imperfect human understanding of sin and justice, presupposing a position of sinless perfection from whose lofty heights sinners must be judged. It is forgiveness that opens the way to new life. In as much as we refuse or are unable to forgive, we hold life at that point of offence, be it personal or national. By refusing to forgive, we say 'No' to new beginnings and a new creation.

Jesus Christ teaches us that it is those who have been forgiven who are able to forgive. Those who know their sin, and their susceptibility to sin, those who know how far they have fallen from God's ways, are the ones who may receive and experience the power of forgiveness. The cross of Christ teaches many things; among them is the truth that human beings, even religious human beings, prefer their own ways to the ways of God. That preference leads to the cross of Christ. Through Christ the Lord God gave power to human beings to reject and kill the Son of God. That can be seen as a weak thing for God to do. Instead of blasting sinful, selfish humankind with the full force of his righteous anger and unimpeachable justice, the Lord of all creates the possibility of new life by offering forgiveness and inviting the forgiven to his thanksgiving banquet. The central tenet of human righteousness is not sinless perfection but a self-awareness of our solidarity in human sin and dependency on God's forgiving grace. Out of such inconceivable divine grace and unimaginable generosity comes the impetus for gratitude, goodness, mercy and truth in human living.

While current attempts to account for human failure by analysing our genetic make-up, our diets, our parental inheritance, our social and economic environment, our lack of education, our religious upbringing, the government of the day, the media and many other things may have some value, only the acknowledgment of our human susceptibility to corruption, deceit, greed, envy, lust and hubris will account for our sin. Such moral failure can only be transformed by a God who takes on himself the cost of forgiveness as the price of new creation. We return to William Cowper's poem, 'Self-acquaintance':[1]

> Dear Lord! Accept a sinful heart,
> Which of itself complains,
> And mourns, with much and frequent smart,
> The evil it contains.
>
> There fiery seeds of anger lurk,
> Which often hurt my frame;
> And wait but for the tempter's work,
> To fan them to a flame.
>
> Legality holds out a bribe
> To purchase life from thee;
> And discontent would fain prescribe
> How thou shalt deal with me.
>
> While unbelief withstands thy grace,
> And puts thy mercy by,
> Presumption, with a brow of brass,
> Says, 'Give me, or I die.'
>
> How eager are my thoughts to roam
> In quest of what they love!
> But ah! when duty calls them home,
> How heavily they move!
>
> Oh! cleanse me in a Saviour's blood,
> Transform me by thy power,
> And make me thy beloved abode,
> And let me rove no more.

[1] See chapter 2, p. 82, footnote 80.

Jonah's prayer

> And he prayed to the LORD and said, 'I pray thee, LORD, is not this what I said when I was yet in my country? That is why I made haste to flee to Tarshish; for I knew that thou art a gracious God and merciful, slow to anger and abounding in steadfast love, and repentest of evil.' (v. 2)

Jonah's first prayer was from the belly of *Sheol* (2:1), his second from the depths of his burning anger. Neither place was comfortable. In both instances he had been 'consumed', first by the great fish and second by his great anger. In dire need he was drawn to prayer. Before making his desire known to God (v. 3), Jonah accuses him of goodness. Here the story-teller puts onto Jonah's lips the reason for his flight from God's presence. He had known all along what God was like; he knew how God might deal with Nineveh, and could not face the implications of that knowledge. Therefore he fled.

According to the rabbis of old, a possible implication of Nineveh's repentance in response to God's word was that shame would come upon Israel. They had a sharp exegetical insight when they interpreted Jonah's reasoning. They argued that the repentance of the heathen was a judgment on the unrepentant Israel. Jonah was therefore reasoning, 'Since the heathens are nearer to repentance, I might be causing Israel to be condemned. Rather I would die.'[2] In other words, recognizing that the heathens of Nineveh might repent in response to God's word, Jonah, aware of the failure of his own people to repent, resisted God's call to go to Nineveh. As an Israelite he would rather die than see the heathen Nineveh repent and shame his own people.

Jerome adopts a similar approach. He comments, 'Jonah's despair is about Israel's salvation . . . He is not saddened, as some think, by the salvation of pagan multitudes, but fears that Israel would perish.' Jonah fears that Israel's continued disobedience would lead her to shame and disaster, a fear compounded by the repentance of the pagan Ninevites.

A similar perspective is also seen in the words of Jesus when he says to an impenitent people, 'The men of Nineveh will arise at the judgment with this generation and condemn it; for they repented at the preaching of Jonah, and behold, something greater than Jonah is here.'[3] Nineveh's repentance will shame and condemn those of Jesus' contemporaries who failed to repent on hearing the teaching of the Lord.

[2] LaCocque and Lacocque, p. 138.
[3] Matt. 12:41.

A further possibility was that, while he knew that God was 'gracious . . . and merciful, slow to anger, and abounding in steadfast love, and repent[ing] of evil' (v. 2), Jonah believed these characteristics of the Divine belonged exclusively within the covenant relationship which existed between Yahweh and his people Israel. When dealing with his own people Yahweh would exhibit these characteristics, but when dealing with pagan nations he would be as *'ᵉlōhîm*,[4] bringing the desired and deserved judgment. Such an approach was especially appropriate when the pagan nations were also Israel's enemies. In this respect the prophet Jonah would gladly endorse the stern sentiments of Nahum, who inveighed against Nineveh. He would rejoice to see the defeat and humiliation of the 'great city' and the vindication of his own people. Jonah considered it unthinkable and intolerable that Israel's privileged enjoyment of the Lord – 'The LORD, the LORD, a God merciful and gracious, slow to anger, and abounding in steadfast love and faithfulness'[5] – should be mirrored in Nineveh; he simply could not accept Yahweh 'cheapening' his mercy by offering it to all and sundry.

The nature of God

It seems, therefore, that Jonah's distress arises out of the very nature of God and the implications of God's nature for Israel as well as himself. His responses are transparently honest, exposing human self-interest and the need for security. God's relenting over Nineveh undermines Jonah's security, forcing him to speak face to face with God himself. Jonah was called to push out the boundaries of his experience of God. He was called to teach the people of Nineveh about their Creator. Through the Ninevites, however, God teaches Jonah that he is at liberty to act as he will with whom he will. The story underlines God's freedom and the finitude of human beings in understanding the ways of God, even if, as 4:2 shows, Jonah already knew those ways in theory. Thus Jonah prayed to the Lord and said, 'I pray thee, LORD, is not this what I said when I was yet in my country? That is why I made haste to flee to Tarshish; for I knew that thou art a gracious God and merciful, slow to anger and abounding in steadfast love, and repentest of evil.'

In his 'own country' Jonah would have found many like-minded supporters of his view. In order to cope with the sheer mystery and complexity of life, most people need to fashion God in their own

[4]See chapter 4, pp. 102–104.
[5]Exod. 34:6.

likeness. Yet enemies, and others who do not fit into our scheme of understanding, have a particular role to play in God's gracious economy. They may well be God's way of opening us up to a greater God than we are able to perceive from within our own bunker of belief. The living Lord is always greater than we humans can know. A god 'like us' is a god limited by our experience and understanding. Those who believe in such a god are unlikely to say, 'Who knows? Perhaps God will do such and such.' Rather, they know what their god will and will not do. Such a belief is often characterized by pride rather than humility. To accept that in his freedom God may use our enemies to challenge and teach us, to enable us to grow into a deeper maturity and a greater likeness to Christ, may prove to be a most painful and humiliating growth point. The command to 'love your enemies',[6] to pray for them and be actively kind towards them, has never been easy or popular teaching.

In his angry cry to God, Jonah quotes some of the most gloriously beautiful words in the Old Testament. The phrase may have been part of an ancient Hebrew liturgy and is to be found in many other parts of the Hebrew Scriptures.[7] Jonah and those in his 'own country' would be well versed in the glorious vision expressed by these gracious words, but now he was being challenged to accept their truth in a different context.

Gracious

The word translated 'gracious' or 'compassionate' (*ḥannûn*) is used only of God in the Scriptures. A telling illustration of its meaning can be found in Exodus 22:26–27:

> If ever you take your neighbour's garment in pledge, you shall restore it to him before the sun goes down; for that is his only covering, it is his mantle for his body; in what else shall he sleep? And if he cries to me I will hear, for I am compassionate.

God hears the pitiful cry of the person who is friendless and cold because his only coat has been taken from him in pledge against his debt.[8] Here is a God who is touched by simple human need. However we may rationalize or regard the poverty resulting from international debt, we learn here of Yahweh's compassion towards

[6] Exod. 23:4–5; Prov. 25:21; Matt. 5:44; Luke 6:27; Rom. 12:20.
[7] Exod. 34:6–7; Num. 14:18; 2 Chr. 30:9; Neh. 9:17, 31; Pss. 86:15; 103:8; 111:4; 145:8; Joel 2:13.
[8] Amos 2:7–8 offers a graphic instance.

those in need. How easy it is for the self-righteous among us to be hard-hearted, rational Westerners.

Merciful

The word translated 'merciful' (*raḥûm*) is related to the word for 'womb' (*reḥem*) and therefore contains echoes of 'motherly love'. Once again this word always occurs in reference to God. Deuteronomy 4:30–33, addressed to a disobedient Israel, illustrates the sense of the word. Moses says:

> When you are in tribulation, and all these things come upon you in the latter days, you will return to the LORD your God and obey his voice, for the LORD your God is a merciful God; he will not fail you or destroy you or forget the covenant . . .

The waiting father's welcoming embrace of his younger son in Jesus' famous parable is a moving illustration of God's mercy.[9]

Slow to anger

Being 'slow to anger' is the opposite of having a quick temper. Positively it suggests the idea of patience and forbearance. As Jeremiah struggled in the face of persecution to proclaim God's word to the people of Judah, he pleaded in prayer for God to be patient with him:

> In thy forbearance take me not away;
> know that for thy sake I bear reproach.[10]

Forbearance is a key element in an 'abundance of steadfast love'. God shows his forbearance to Jonah. He does not blame him. Rather, the narrator paints a picture of a God who stays with the angry prophet. God does not desert his children in their suffering; like a good parent he stays with them through their struggles towards maturity.

Love

The Hebrew word *ḥeseḏ* is often translated 'steadfast love' and points to the quality of pledged love. It is this kind of love which characterizes God's commitment to his people. Marriage is an image

[9] Luke 15:11–32.
[10] Jer. 15:15.

of this love. In a wedding service the couple declare their willed intention to love one another 'till death us do part'. In a marriage the love of the heart may sometimes falter or fail; it may be severely tested in all kinds of circumstances. This pledged love of the will is the foundation of a secure relationship, come wind, come weather. It is also the kind of love seen in a parent's devotion to his or her child. The vivid imagery in Hosea 11 has this kind of love at its heart. Another key illustration from Hosea is shown in the prophet faithfully loving his wife back to himself, despite her infidelity and promiscuity. The Lord says to Hosea, 'Go again, love a woman who is beloved of a paramour and is an adulteress; even as the LORD loves the people of Israel, though they turn to other gods and love cakes of raisins.'[11] Hosea learns to love again because he sees that God's love for his faithless people does not fail.

Repent

Finally, God 'repents' (*nāḥam*) of the punishment he intends as the reward for sin. In Jeremiah 18:7–10 we find a divine dictum which has a bearing on this concept. God says:

> If at any time I declare concerning a nation or a kingdom, that I will pluck up and break down and destroy it, and if that nation, concerning which I have spoken, turns from its evil, I will repent of the evil that I intended to do to it. And if at any time I declare concerning a nation or a kingdom that I will build and plant it, and if it does evil in my sight, not listening to my voice, then I will repent of the good which I had intended to do to it.

These verses are set in the context of Jeremiah's visit to the potter's workshop. They complement the idea that God fashions the clay – that is, Israel – with the idea that a nation is free to do good or evil. A nation's attitude to God will affect how God deals with it. The first image shows God fashioning the people; the second shows God's openness to being influenced by the nation's response. By its repentance the evil city of Nineveh may be blessed, whereas by their failure to repent God's chosen people may experience disaster. Jonah works from the belief that God would show compassion on Nineveh, although, as we have seen, the king of Nineveh could make no such assumption. In turning from sin he could only hope for God's favour: 'Who knows?'

If Jonah's initial flight were caused by his belief that God would relent in response to Nineveh's change of heart, then we can only say

[11] Hos. 3:1.

that he did not want God to show pity on the great city. Certainly Nineveh could not have repented unless someone had proclaimed the word of God to them. Paul's reflections in Romans 10 come to mind here.

> But how are men to call upon him in whom they have not believed? And how are they to believe in him of whom they have never heard? And how are they to hear without a preacher? And how can men preach unless they are sent? As it is written, 'How beautiful are the feet of those who preach good news!'[12]

Moved by compassion (*nāḥam*) towards his people, God's will is that all should call on him, not just the chosen few. Jonah's anger at God's goodness is reminiscent of the parable in which those who had worked all day in the vineyard accused their employer of injustice when he paid them the same wage as those who had worked only an hour or so. They were angered by their employer's generosity.

Jonah's dialogue with God is similar to that between Job and God. Job affirms that we receive good at the hand of God and also evil. Even so, Job is deeply wounded and perplexed in the face of God's behaviour towards him. This is not unlike Jonah's situation. Both experience great upheaval in their lives, the outcome of which is a renewed knowledge of God. Whereas Job eventually accepts this, however, Jonah's resistance remains unresolved. A key feature of both books is that the main characters are angry at God's behaviour towards them, and both demand some kind of explanation from God. The writers of both books struggle with the theological implications of the nature of God for individuals and nations. The book of Jonah is a unique exposition of a belief that God relates to the nations of the earth in the same way that he relates to his chosen people. This implies that the chosen ones are not better than the others, but rather that they have a particular responsibility towards the others for articulating the ways of God to the world. The king of Nineveh was not only receptive to this; he was well along the way of understanding God's ways for himself. Jonah understood God's ways, but was unreceptive to them.

Jonah's despair

> Therefore now, O Lord, take my life from me, I beseech thee, for it is better for me to die than to live. (v. 3)

[12]Rom. 10:14–16.

In the Hebrew text a brief pause follows Jonah's petition. It is a literary device intended to give the listeners the time needed to absorb the shock of Jonah's request. His plea, 'O LORD, take my life from me', reminds us of his earlier instruction to the mariners, 'Take me up and throw me into the sea' (1:12). He seeks the ultimate escape from things which are too difficult for him. Yet already we know that he cannot escape God, and as God was unwilling to destroy Nineveh, so he was unwilling for Jonah to die or even to remain in a state of opposition towards him.

There is a definite allusion here to the account of Elijah's death wish:

> But he himself went a day's journey into the wilderness, and came and sat down under a broom tree; and he asked that he might die, saying, 'It is enough; now, O LORD, take away my life; for I am no better than my fathers.'[13]

The context, however, could hardly be more different. Elijah's suffering arose out of persecution, while Jonah suffered from unwanted success. It is easy to understand a death wish in the context of failure. Despite his success, Jonah failed to see that Yahweh could accept those who did not yet worship him. The repeated use of 'I', 'my' and 'me' in 4:2–3 suggests again his self-concern and resultant blindness towards Nineveh's change of heart.

The security of slavery

Jonah's plunge into the depths of despair was occasioned by the repentance of Nineveh. Whatever lay at the root of his concern, he was profoundly unwilling to acknowledge God's freedom in matters of salvation. Here he stands in the tradition of God's people through the centuries. The Israelites preferred the security of slavery in Egypt to the risks of freedom: 'Is not this what we said to you in Egypt, "Let us alone and let us serve the Egyptians"? For it would have been better for us to serve the Egyptians than to die in the wilderness.'[14] They were familiar with the cruel ways of their Egyptian taskmasters, the rules were obvious and the food was plentiful. Following God through a wilderness to the Promised Land, however, was no easy matter. Here they lost their ready-made security and were vulnerable, threatened by a law of grace which required them to learn to live from the heart.

[13] 1 Kgs. 19:4.
[14] Exod. 14:12.

Curiously, the Ten Commandments, associated with the wilderness wanderings in order to ensure that the newly liberated people of God remained free, became an instrument of bondage. This finely tuned moral compass which promised freedom became a weight leading to another kind of bondage which said that only through obedience to these laws can people be saved. Yet it was ever the case that God's people are rescued by God's grace and not by their self-righteousness. Jonah may represent this all-too-human spiritual legalism. Forgetting the eternal priority of God's life-giving grace, did the prophet build his own life on the foundation of obedience to the law? After all, he was the 'son of faithfulness'. To him it was outrageous that God should bless a nation which offered no such obedience to the moral code. From this perspective, Jonah could not see that God's response to his own earlier disobedience was proof that his own fundamental belief about God was wrong. After all, God had followed him, stayed with him and even gone ahead of him, despite Jonah's profound resistance to his call. He had sent the storm, addressed him through the sailors, and finally met him in the belly of *Sheol.* Paul crystallized the nub of this when he wrote in Romans 9:30–33:

> What shall we say, then? That Gentiles who did not pursue righteousness have attained it, that is, righteousness through faith; but that Israel who pursued the righteousness which is based on law did not succeed in fulfilling that law. Why? Because they did not pursue it through faith, but as if it were based on works. They have stumbled over the stumbling stone, as it is written,
>
> > 'Behold, I am laying in Zion a stone that will make men stumble,
> > a rock that will make them fall;
> > and he who believes in him will not be put to shame.'

This raises the question of the *raison d'être* of the 'chosen people'. In what way are they distinctive and how are they to live? As we have seen, they are formed by God's gracious call and teaching. Their purpose is to bear witness to the blessings of God's grace as they have themselves experienced it. In a world which seeks salvation through the security offered by systems and rules, God's people are those who resist creating security in anything other than God's grace. This is the gravitational pull on their moral compass. Those of us who seek, and sometimes find, security and meaning in life through the morality of 'the market', or middle-class values, or religious traditions, may need to be challenged by God's people to follow the way of freedom opened by God's grace. Faithfulness to God's call requires us to sit light to man-made religious systems and exposes us thereby to suffering insecurity and change. There will always be more to learn of our incxhaustible God. The people of God are those who hold out the hope that God will bring deliverance to all humankind. This is not to say that we do not freely acknowledge the limits of our humanity, particularly our human systems, but these things are transitional staging posts on the road to fullness of life and not our ultimate destinations.

Matthew's Gospel tells of Jesus' disciples out in a boat at night. They are caught in a storm and Jesus comes to them walking on the sea.

> But when the disciples saw him walking on the sea, they were terrified, saying, 'It is a ghost!' And they cried out for fear. But immediately he spoke to them, saying, 'Take heart, it is I; have no fear.'
>
> And Peter answered him, 'Lord, if it is you, bid me come to you on the water.' He said, 'Come.' So Peter got out of the boat and walked on the water and came to Jesus; but when he saw the wind, he was afraid, and beginning to sink he cried out, 'Lord, save me.' Jesus immediately reached out his hand and caught him, saying to him, 'O man of little faith, why did you doubt?'[15]

The story illustrates a life lived from the heart of faith. Life lived from a rule book could not have given us this story. Peter's spontaneous response to Jesus' call must be reflected by the church. In the storm it is called to step out of the safety of the boat into the waters of God's turbulent purposes, trusting only in the gracious, seemingly impossible call of its Lord. Like Jonah, Peter became afraid of God's unreasonable call and began to sink. Ensnared by a false security of his own making, he could not live in God's freedom. Jesus Christ embodies the climax of this gospel in his life and death: 'For Christ is the end of the law, that every one who has faith may be justified.'[16]

In his human life Jesus of Nazareth encountered the limitations of human understanding, frailty and sin. He lived within the constraints of particular religious traditions expressed through various systems. He did not set up his own opposing church or religious system. Rather, with divine authority he reinterpreted much religious tradition, all the while challenging those who put themselves in place of God. The profoundly challenging moral compass of his life was, like the Ten Commandments, shaped by the rule of grace. Moreover, it was this One who said that the disciple is not above his master.

[15] Matt. 14:26–31.
[16] Rom. 10:4.

God's response to Jonah's call (4:4–9)

And the LORD said, 'Do you do well to be angry?' (v. 4)

The Lord questions whether Jonah's anger is right or good. God's anger, as T. S. Eliot once said, is 'the unfamiliar Name' for his love. As Jürgen Moltmann writes,

> What the Old Testament terms the *wrath of God* . . . [belongs] in the category of the divine *pathos.* His wrath is injured love and therefore a mode of his reaction to men. Love is the source and the basis of the possibility of the wrath of God. The opposite of love is not wrath, but indifference . . . As injured love, the wrath of God is not something that is inflicted, but a divine suffering of evil. It is a sorrow which goes through his opened heart. He suffers in his passion for his people.[17]

God's anger finds the root of evil, 'not in passion, in the throbbing heart, but rather in hardness of heart, in callousness and insensitivity'.[18]

In this question God enquires of Jonah concerning the root of his own anger. What was it in Jonah which was angered by the goodness of God towards Nineveh? It is not consistent that a good person should be angered by a good event, for 'The LORD is good to all, and his compassion is over all that he has made.'[19] There may be a distant echo here of God's question to Cain: 'The LORD said to Cain, "Why are you angry, and why has your countenance fallen?"'[20] In Genesis the writer reflects on the inequalities of life. One person is killed and another escapes. Abel's offering is accepted while Cain's is refused. No explanation is given to account for these things. Instead, the writer shows considerable interest in Cain's response. Cain faced a choice: he could persist in the goodness he claimed, or he could allow his sense of rejection to lead him to do ill. In the event, instead of choosing to persevere in goodness, Cain decided to nurse his anger, and thereby gave opportunity for sin. The fruit of his angry response was the hatred which led to the murder of his brother, Abel. Does Jonah's anger stem from an inclination towards goodness, or from an inclination towards evil? Would Jonah's anger lead him towards God, or away from God? Would it become an opportunity for sin, or an opportunity for goodness?

[17] Moltmann, p. 272.
[18] Heschel, p. 224.
[19] Ps. 145:9.
[20] Gen. 4:6.

Jonah waits

> Then Jonah went out of the city and sat to the east of the city, and made a booth for himself there. He sat under it in the shade, till he should see what would become of the city. (v. 5)

In silence Jonah had fled God's presence. Now, in silence, he walks away from God's question and finds a more comfortable place to be. As Stuart suggests,[21] his sitting on the east (*qeḏem*) side of the city may simply point to the fact that he had entered the city from the west and, having gone through it, he left it on the east. On the other hand, the word *qeḏem* could also suggest that the prophet was looking 'forward', towards the east where the new day dawns with the rising sun, to see what God would do. He sits in the shade and waits. His very body language is his reply to God's question.

The three references to 'the city' in this verse remind the reader of the focus of attention. Inside the city walls, the king of Nineveh sits in great discomfort in sackcloth and ashes, hoping that, just perhaps, his city will be saved. Jonah, meanwhile, sits in silence outside the city walls, waiting for it to be destroyed. Despite his knowledge of God and God's disclosure to him (3:10), the prophet anticipates Nineveh's fate. The narrator is more interested in Jonah's fate, however, and so the story of Nineveh fades once more into the background.

The 'booth' (*sukkâ*) which Jonah made to shelter him from the heat was probably a temporary structure of leaves and branches. Such simple shelters were used by soldiers[22] and farmers.[23] They were also built for the celebration of the Feast of Tabernacles or Booths (*sukkôṯ*).[24] Jewish people even today erect such shelters as a reminder of how their ancestors lived during their wilderness wandering.[25]

God comforts Jonah

> And the LORD God appointed a plant, and made it come up over Jonah, that it might be a shade over his head, to save him from his discomfort. So Jonah was exceedingly glad because of the plant. (v. 6)

[21] Stuart, pp. 503–504.
[22] 1 Kgs. 20:12.
[23] Is. 1:8.
[24] Neh. 8:13–18.
[25] Lev. 23:42–43; Deut. 16:13; Neh. 8:14–18; Zech. 14:16, 18–19.

In the same way that God had 'appointed' a great fish to deliver Jonah, so now he 'appoints' a plant to shelter him. Jonah's wait outside the city was a long one. Maybe this delay aggravated his anger. Out of compassion for the distressed prophet, God protects him, saving him from his 'evil' (*rā'â*) or 'discomfort' (RSV). Jonah's response is telling: 'He rejoiced with a great joy.' The phrase immediately strikes us as being the opposite of his response in 4:1, where he was 'evil with a great evil'. God's gracious provision for him brought Jonah great joy; God's gracious provision for Nineveh brought him great anger. Despite this anger, God had not deserted his prophet. He came to comfort him. A Hebrew wordplay on 'shade' (*ṣel*) and 'save' (*lᵉhaṣîl*) hints at a deeper purpose in God's mercy. Maybe the pun could be expressed in English by saying that the plant was appointed to be a 'shade' to help him 'shed' his anger.

Were we to use joy and happiness to measure the high points of our experience, we would have to say that God's provision of a plant to shelter Jonah was the high point of the prophet's experience in this story. That he found no joy in the repentance of the great city of Nineveh points to his fundamental unease with God on this matter. Jonah and God did not see things in the same way; their goals did not coincide. In reflecting on Jonah's God, Paul writes,

> Love does not insist on its own way; it is not irritable or resentful; it does not rejoice at wrong, but rejoices in the right. Love bears all things, believes all things, hopes all things, endures all things. Love never ends; as for prophecies, they will pass away.[26]

The nature of the plant God provided is unknown. Some suggest a castor oil plant (RSV), others a 'vine' (NIV). The word *qîqāyôn* occurs only here in the Bible, making it impossible to know with any certainty what kind of plant was meant. Although the writer's interest was not primarily botanical, much plant imagery in Scripture relates to the gift of life: the plant would have been a source of hope to Jonah. Equally, however, plants were often images of decay and death: the plant offered only an uncertain hope. We discover here that Jonah's hurt was easily healed, but also that his joy was short-lived. The focus remained on Jonah's anger and God's response.

The worm

> But when dawn came up the next day, God appointed a worm which attacked the plant, so that it withered. (v. 7)

[26] 1 Cor. 13:5–8.

There were no early birds to catch this worm to prevent it from ruining Jonah's day! Again the stress is on God's ordering of creation. Sooner or later, worms destroy the things which bring us pleasure. The worm is the tiny, apparently insignificant creature of God which has been given power to ensure change in every situation. It represents death and decay, while its Creator and its God labours to bring forth a new creation. Here the tiny creature destroys a mighty plant. Most significantly for poor Jonah, it destroys his fleeting source of joy. A Jewish commentator writes,

> Jonah's joy in the gourd [i.e. the plant] is like the joy of men in the possessions of this world which do not persist, over the possession of which it is not worth rejoicing, nor is it worth being sorry for their loss. Then Scripture comes to show us the limitations of their benefits . . . And to explain this, it says, 'God prepared a worm' . . .[27]

No insurance policy will include the ravages of the worm. The worm is a symbol of the passing days and nights which secretly devour the life of all living creatures. Its voracious appetite is a ubiquitous fact of life. The worm is seen as an agent of God's judgment on the disobedient.[28] In some of Jesus' most severe teaching he urges the disciples to rid themselves of those things which, although they bring pleasure, may yet separate them from God: 'And if your eye causes you to sin, pluck it out; it is better for you to enter the kingdom of God with one eye than with two eyes to be thrown into hell [*gehenna*], where their worm does not die, and the fire is not quenched.'[29] Here, the insatiable appetite of the worm that 'does not die' is an image of the endless torments of hell.

The wind

> When the sun rose, God appointed a sultry east wind, and the sun beat upon the head of Jonah so that he was faint; and he asked that he might die, and said, 'It is better for me to die than to live.' (v. 8)

Soon after the plant died, the sun rose and a desert wind blew up. From the heights of joy, the combined forces of the worm and the wind conspired to bring Jonah once more to the very depths of despair. Ironically, Jonah had hoped the judgment from the east would fall on Nineveh. Instead, it is he who suffers its ravages, and

[27] Assembly of Rabbis, p. 1013.
[28] Deut. 28:39.
[29] Mark 9:47–48.

no reference is made to Nineveh being affected. On the east side of the city, Jonah would have no protection from this ennervating wind. Hot winds blowing off the eastern desert covered everything in sand and caused physical exhaustion. Stuart comments, 'In some Moslem countries, the punishment for a crime committed while the sirocco was blowing may be reduced . . . so strongly does the hot wind affect thinking and behaviour.'[30] Deprived of all comfort and suffering the effects of God's judgment without any protection, Jonah repeats his request to die.

The same image of the 'east wind' is used in Hosea to describe the terrible devastation that the Lord will bring on the callous and unbelieving Israel:

> Though he [Israel] may flourish as the reed plant,
> the east wind, the wind of the LORD, shall come,
> rising from the wilderness;
> and his fountain shall dry up,
> his spring shall be parched;
> it shall strip his treasury
> of every precious thing.
> Samaria shall bear her guilt,
> because she has rebelled against her God;
> they shall fall by the sword,
> their little ones shall be dashed in pieces,
> and their pregnant women ripped open.[31]

Here the Northern kingdom of Israel is compared to a plant that dies. The sirocco rising up from the wilderness would dry up its water supply. Deprived of its true Source of life, the land and its people would be deprived of every precious and desirable thing.

The prophet Ezekiel makes use of the same vivid imagery,[32] as does Jeremiah in describing God's judgment on his people in Jerusalem:

> At that time it will be said to this people and to Jerusalem, 'A hot wind from the bare heights in the desert toward the daughter of my people, not to winnow or cleanse, a wind too full for this comes for me. Now it is I who speak in judgment upon them.'[33]

[30] Stuart, p. 505f.
[31] Hos. 13:15–16.
[32] Ezek. 17:10; 19:12.
[33] Jer. 4:11–12; cf. 18:17.

The hot, sand-laden sirocco was too fierce and too hot to be life-giving in the fields or the cities. Its effects were indiscriminate in the same way that invasion destroyed the lives of both the righteous and the wicked. Jonah feels the full force of the wind. He knows the force of its power, and his discomfort is more than merely physical.

This is the second time we see Jonah at the mercy of the wind. The first great wind (1:4) stirred up the sea into a gigantic storm; now the second wind stirs up the scorchingly cruel heat of the desert. Both render life intolerable. In both instances the same Hebrew word, *rûaḥ*, is used. Is the scorching sirocco a reminder to Jonah of the great storm in chapter 1? Does it also express the heat of the returning storm within him? In the face of both, Jonah understandably seeks the oblivion he imagines death will bring. He has yet to answer the question put to him by God.

Jonah's answer

> But God said to Jonah, 'Do you do well to be angry for the plant?' And he said, 'I do well to be angry, angry enough to die.' (v. 9)

In asking the question a second time, God focuses it more sharply by referring to the withered plant. Jonah's answer is immediate: he is angry enough to die. He suffered the physical effects of the sirocco. It robbed him of his comfort and joy. His response showed self-concern at the heart of his faith. So absorbing was it that, when his faith was disturbed by God's response to the Ninevites and his body discomforted by the sultry east wind, escape by death seemed his only route to comfort. Edwin Good comments sympathetically: 'How can a man function with a God like this, who favours his enemies and who, as soon as he has given one little thought to his servant's comfort, promptly makes life miserable for him again?'[34]

The focus is clear. Jonah could not accept that the law of grace should work in favour of his enemies, but neither could he accept life without grace. God's graciousness to Nineveh was unacceptable. God's withdrawal of grace to Jonah was also unacceptable. He longed for a God who was partial like himself, instead of a God who was gracious, merciful and responsive to the cries of all creation. He wanted his own personal God rather than the God who made heaven and earth, the sea and the dry land.

[34] Good, p. 52.

The Lord's pity (4:10–11)

> And the LORD said, 'You pity the plant, for which you did not labour, nor did you make it grow, which came into being in a night, and perished in a night. And should not I pity Nineveh, that great city, in which there are more than a hundred and twenty thousand persons who do not know their right hand from their left, and also much cattle?' (vv. 10–11)

Jonah's pity, his heartfelt concern, that the plant was no longer there to shelter him, is contrasted with Yahweh's concern over Nineveh. Jonah's passion was activated when the plant perished. The word translated 'perish' is found also in 1:6, where the captain says to the sleeping Jonah, 'Arise, call upon your god! Perhaps the god will give a thought to us, that we do not perish.' It appears again in 3:9, where the king of Nineveh says, 'Who knows, God may yet repent and turn from his fierce anger, so that we perish not?' It is implied here that Jonah was more concerned about the plant which perished than about Nineveh. He was prepared to die for the comfort given him by the plant, but willing for the Ninevites to perish for lack of hearing God's word.

More important, however, is God's concern towards the people of Nineveh and their animals. The order of the Hebrew words at this point sharpens the contrast for us: 'You, you were concerned about the plant though you had not tended it nor had you made it grow ... but I, should I not be concerned about Nineveh the great city ...?' The Lord's question throws the spotlight on the big difference of attitude between Jonah and himself. Underlying God's question is an assumption that Jonah had the capacity to share in God's pity for Nineveh and that this would be more 'God-like' than the prophet's moralistic attitude. In his grief over the loss of the plant, Jonah was condemning himself out of his own mouth. He was no better than the Ninevites. He knew God, but had failed to work out the implications of that knowledge, both in his imagination and in his experience. His selfish anger signalled this failure. God reminds Jonah that he had not laboured for the plant: it had been a gift from God. Jonah has to understand that the essence of love is to labour for something and make it grow. Love and labour are inseparable. We love that for which we labour, and labour for that which we love.

The Lord's reference to the hundred and twenty thousand people of Nineveh 'who do not know their right hand from their left' comes as a reminder to Jonah that the people who inhabit the great city of Nineveh were ignorant. The city represented a great and powerful threat, but its people were ignorant. Jonah was heir to the revealed nature of God as presented in the Torah. In God's estimation, the most powerful culture of Jonah's world was marked by ignorance of God's ways. Their ignorance provokes 'pity' (*ḥûs*) in Yahweh.

God's gentle and persistent questioning was an expression of the divine pity and compassion for Jonah. In the way that God had laboured over Nineveh, so now we see him labouring to bring Jonah to repentance and new birth. By his own law of just deserts, Jonah should have been punished most severely for disobedience and evil. Without God's gracious mercy and compassion – the very qualities he so despised in God – Jonah was no different from Nineveh in his need of repentance.

Whether translated 'pity' (RSV) or 'concern' (NIV), the Hebrew word *ḥûs* means literally 'to have tears in one's eyes'.[35] In these final words of the text we are left with the image of the Lord being moved to tears of compassion as he looks on the ignorance of Nineveh. It is an image filled with the most sublime profundity, and one which we meet again in the pages of the New Testament as Jesus weeps over the city of Jerusalem.

> And when he drew near and saw the city he wept over it, saying, 'Would that even today you knew the things that make for peace! But now they are hid from your eyes. For the days shall come upon you, when your enemies will cast up a bank about you and surround you, and hem you in on every side, and dash you to the ground, you and your children within you, and they will not leave one stone upon another in you; because you did not know the time of your visitation.'[36]

A. J. Heschel writes,

> God's answer to Jonah, stressing the supremacy of compassion, upsets the possibility of looking for a rational coherence of God's ways with the world. History would be more intelligible if God's word were the last word, final and unambiguous like a dogma or an unconditional decree. It would be easier if God's anger became effective automatically: once wickedness had reached its full measure, punishment would destroy it. Yet, beyond justice and anger lies the mystery of compassion.[37]

[35] 'It is more reasonable to assume that the original meaning was "overflow" = "weep" when used of the eye. Weeping expresses emotion that can signify either sorrow for oneself or for others' (Wagner, in *Theological Dictionary of the Old Testament*, quoted by M. Butterworth, *The New International Dictionary of Old Testament Theology and Exegesis*, vol. 2 [Paternoster Press, 1997], p. 51).

[36] Luke 19:41–44; cf. Matt. 9:36; 23:27; Mark 6:34; 8:2.

[37] Assembly of Rabbis, p. 1016.

Even as we draw to the end of our story, God does not seek to have the last word. Is it not the case that the story continues even now not only to intrigue but to challenge God's people? In his graciousness the Lord leaves the last word for Jonah and for all of us who share some affinity with him. 'Should not I pity Nineveh, that great city?'

9. The repentance of Nineveh and the people of God

Did Nineveh repent?

The history books do not say so!

Biblical evidence

The Bible makes no other reference to the repentance of Nineveh, which, given the state of hostilities between Israel and Assyria, is curious. The books of Samuel, Kings, Chronicles, Nehemiah, Ezra and Esther are important sources for understanding the history of Israel and Judah and their relationships with other nations, but none refer to Nineveh's repentance. Had the great city repented, more could have been made of it by the prophets. Surely there would have been kudos for Israel in Nineveh's obeisance before Israel's God? The only mention of the story of Nineveh's repentance occurs in Luke 11:30 and Matthew 12:4, where Jesus uses it in upbraiding God's people, yet again, for their unwillingness to repent.

Extra-biblical evidence

Outside the Bible there is no documentary evidence for the repentance of the people of Nineveh. Perhaps it is hardly the sort of thing a nation would want to record in its own annals. Later, written evidence from the *Babylonian Chronicle* would record that Nineveh was destroyed in 612 BC. In 401 BC, when Xenophon and the retreating Greek army passed the ruins of Nineveh, the 'great city' was already an unrecognizable mass of debris.

Possible clues

Some evidence for the possibility of Nineveh's repentance has been accumulated by D. J. Wiseman. He describes how we now know that there was a total solar eclipse on 15 June 763 BC during the reign of the Assyrian king Assur-dan (793–753 BC), a contemporary of Israel's king Jeroboam II (781–746 BC). Wiseman has translated versions of omen texts from Nineveh, the *Enuma Anu Enlil,* which predict the sort of calamities which might well occur following a total eclipse. Included among them we find: 'The king will die, rain from heaven will flood the land. There will be famine,' and, 'A deity will strike the king and fire consume the land.' The Assyriologist W. G. Lambert finds evidence that not only did the kings take these omens seriously, they may even have abandoned the throne to a substitute king until the danger was over!

A further sign of divine anger in Assyrian religion was earthquake. Wiseman finds a record of an earthquake occurring during the reign of Assur-dan, although it is unclear whether or not this is the same Assur-dan, king of Nineveh, referred to above. Nevertheless, some accumulative evidence – that Assur-dan was a weak ruler, that cosmic happenings would be understood by the Ninevites as signs of divine wrath, that defeat in battle and loss of territory would create internal hardship and unrest – points to there having been a low time in Nineveh's life. It is possible that this occurred in the mid-eighth century BC and was followed by a turn in her fortunes during the latter half of that century.[1] This turn in her fortunes would have contributed to the resurgence of Assyrian power in the Ancient Near East.

Could it have happened?

If Jonah had gone to Nineveh at this time of Assyrian weakness, Nineveh's repentance in response to his preaching could have occurred before her resurgence. Alongside this possibility we need to set historical certainty. Ancient Near Eastern history would subsequently record Assyria destroying Israel's boundaries and taking her people into captivity in 721 BC, when, following a three-year siege, her chief city, Samaria, fell into the hands of the Assyrian king Sargon II.[2]

In Jonah chapter 3, the prophet's preaching to Nineveh results in the city's repentance, thus leaving the future open for her to recover

[1] For further detail see Stuart, and Wiseman.
[2] 2 Kgs. 17.

her imperialist strategy and, ultimately, to destroy Jonah's own unrepentant people, Israel. This historical possibility adds to the complexity of the Jonah story, giving rise to further speculations. Does the Jonah story attempt to account for Nineveh's resurgent strength, her prosperity and power? Was the writer of Jonah echoing the words of Isaiah[3] in suggesting that Assyrian power ultimately came from Yahweh?

The people of God

Israel's failure to repent

To this perspective on history needs to be added another. There is no shortage of evidence in the Old Testament concerning the consistent failure of Israel and Judah to repent in response to God's word to them through the prophets. The major prophetic voices of Amos, Hosea, Isaiah and Jeremiah were largely ignored. The fall of Israel in 721 BC and Judah in 587 BC to Assyria and Babylon respectively is attributed to the stubborn deafness of the people in failing to heed the word of the Lord. In 2 Kings 17 we have an account of the fall to the king of Assyria in 721 BC of Samaria, the greatest city in the Northern kingdom of Israel. Here the prophetic historian reflects on the cause of Israel's downfall.

> . . . the LORD warned Israel and Judah by every prophet and every seer, saying, 'Turn from your evil ways and keep my commandments and my statutes, in accordance with all the law which I commanded your fathers, and which I sent to you by my servants the prophets.' But they would not listen, but were stubborn, as their fathers had been, who did not believe in the LORD their God.[4]

Nineveh's immediate and wholesale repentance on hearing the word of Jonah makes a striking contrast. The response of the king of Nineveh, known also as the king of kings, is stunningly different from that of most of the kings of Israel and Judah.

The book of Jonah as a message to Israel

Is the prophetic writer of the book of Jonah addressing Israel? If so, does he speak to them by telling a story about Nineveh? Sometimes

[3] See, e.g., Is. 7:17.
[4] 2 Kgs. 17:13–14.

it is easier to receive a hard truth when it is given indirectly. After David's sin with Bathsheba, for example, the prophet Nathan tells a parable to David about the rich man with many flocks stealing the poor man's pet lamb. David immediately recognized that injustice had been done by the rich man and pronounced judgment. At this point Nathan said to David, 'You are the man.'[5] It was the king himself who was guilty of gross injustice. David recognized God's word in Nathan's parable and immediately repented.

Similarly, Amos addressed the people of Israel indirectly by focusing on the sins and afflictions of other nations.[6] Despite her own failing being set alongside those of others, Israel remained oblivious to her guilt. Israel's response to God's call through Amos was to assume that her prosperity and well-being were signs of God's blessing, and that her considerable religiosity was sufficient evidence of her total well-being. But God's people remained blind to their own evil and deaf to the prophet's call. Israel's stubbornness and ongoing failure to repent, even after suffering disasters intended to bring her to her senses,[7] may be being addressed in the book of Jonah.

In another example we see the prophet Ezekiel indirectly addressing the people with whom he was in exile in Babylon by speaking to them about the people who remained in Jerusalem.[8] Does the writer of Jonah use a similar strategy? Is he addressing Israel when he describes the repentance of Nineveh in response to the prophet's word? Could the repentance of the great city of Nineveh move God's people to repent?

Could Israel be scandalized into repentance?

Does the writer of the book of Jonah set out to scandalize Israel? Does he muse on Israel's readiness to turn away from God while the great Nineveh recognizes God's greatness and turns towards him? If God withheld judgment when Nineveh repented, how much more would he withhold judgment when Israel repented? Could Israel be scandalized into repentance by the repentance of Nineveh?

Alternatively, would Israel be scandalized when God dealt with her as she believed he should have dealt with Nineveh? How could God deliver Nineveh, yet allow Israel to be destroyed? How could God allow his own people to be destroyed by the wicked? In the story of Jonah we see a God who was set on the task

[5] 2 Sam. 12:7.
[6] Amos 1:3 – 2:4.
[7] Amos 4:6–12.
[8] Ezek. 8:5 – 11:13.

of salvation despite the reluctance of his prophet, a God who could not be manipulated by his own people. In 721 BC the Israel of the historical Jonah finally capitulated to Assyrian power. But Assyria's strength was from God. In the way that God had appointed the great fish and the tiny worm, so argues Jeremiah, he had also appointed Assyria for that purpose.[9]

Jerusalem, the 'great city' which failed to repent

Jerusalem, the city which epitomizes the very heart of God's people, is referred to by Jeremiah as the 'great city'. This designation is used after the destruction of Jerusalem in 587 BC, as people pass by the ruins asking one another the reason for the fall of Jerusalem:

> And many nations will pass by this city, and every man will say to his neighbour, 'Why has the LORD dealt thus with this great city?' And they will answer, 'Because they forsook the covenant of the LORD their God, and worshipped other gods and served them.'[10]

The fall of Jerusalem heightens the tension between God and his people. The city failed to respond to the preaching of Jeremiah in the same way that Israel failed to respond to Amos and Hosea. In a striking image of sheer contempt for God's word, we even see Jehoiakim (604 BC), the king of Judah in Jerusalem, responding to Jeremiah's words of impending disaster by slicing with a knife and burning the scroll on which the prophet's words had been written.[11]

As Ezekiel, a contemporary of Jeremiah, enumerates the terrible sins of Jerusalem, he begins by calling her 'the bloody city' or the 'blood guilty city',[12] where wickedness was unforgiven and cried for vengeance. In using this expression he equates Jerusalem with Nineveh, that whore and centre of pagan wickedness which Nahum had earlier condemned in very similar terms.[13]

All this foreshadows events in the New Testament. We know that Jonah did not speak out of any great love for Nineveh – indeed, he had resisted speaking at all. In the New Testament, however, Jesus' words over the great city of Jerusalem are given to us by Luke:

> And when he drew near and saw the city he wept over it, saying, 'Would that even today you knew the things that make for peace!

[9] 2 Kgs. 17:18; Is. 7:20, in reference to Judah.
[10] Jer. 22:8–9.
[11] Jer. 36:23.
[12] Ezek. 22:2.
[13] Nah. 3:1.

> But now they are hid from your eyes. For the days shall come upon you, when your enemies will cast up a bank about you and surround you, and hem you in on every side, and dash you to the ground, you and your children within you, and they will not leave one stone upon another in you; because you did not know the time of your visitation.'[14]

God's 'slowness to anger' is seen as Jesus, the Son of God, weeps over the city. Its religious leaders will seek to destroy the One who longs for their peace. Is the destruction of Jerusalem the inevitable consequence of Jonah's attitude? If so, herein lies a warning for all who claim to be God's chosen people, for all who cling to a belief system with all its trappings rather than to the mercy of the living God.

Jonah and idolatry

No serious reader of the Bible can be content to take the book of Jonah simply at face value. Its exquisite literary qualities alone draw us into the text in a way which shows the writer saying more than meets the eye.

Although, as we have seen, it is possible to accumulate plausible evidence showing that Nineveh did repent, the evidence cannot prove that Jonah's preaching was instrumental in its repentance, nor can it put the event into a historical or theological context which was significant for Israel. Despite the five verses describing Nineveh's response to Jonah's message, the reader is aware that by far the greater stress in the whole story is on the ongoing dialogue between Jonah and God. The book both opens and closes with the Lord calling Jonah.

To begin with, the focus of this dialogue is Jonah's unwillingness to go to Nineveh. We may rationalize it in terms of the prophet's unwillingness to face the enemy, his sense of outrage that Israel's God should show concern for the Gentiles, his reluctance to accept his vocation, yet this little book challenges us with something still greater. It concerns God's freedom and his people's bondage.

Jonah is not simply unwilling to go to Nineveh. The text points to Jonah's unwillingness to let God be God. As a result he himself was unable to be fully human, and became unable to see others as fully human. Instead, in Jonah's eyes they remained pagans who followed other gods, people outside the covenant mercies of Yahweh. Preferring the shadow to the real, the comfort to the struggle, the sense of having arrived to the perils of discovery, Jonah remained

[14] Luke 19:41–44.

cocooned in a belief system which protected him from the struggles and sufferings of others. Opting for the safety of being right rather than exposure to ridicule, for the predictable rather than the unpredictable, the prophet chooses security rather than risk. Such a choice inevitably limits his understanding of God.

To this extent Jonah is trapped into idolatry. The moral axiom of his belief was that God should reward the righteous (i.e. Israel) and punish the wicked (i.e. pagan nations). Confusion between the heavenly realities of God's nature and the earthly expression of God's rule was being resolved by Jonah resorting to the safety of his own understanding. To be cajoled by God into anything else was, for the faithful Jonah, to be unfaithful to the covenant God and his people. Like Job, Jonah was challenged and tested by this God, but unlike Job he was unwilling to break into a new understanding of God. God's freedom and compassion were opening new doors and bringing new worlds to birth, but, 'Jonah wants nothing to happen, certainly not a freedom that violates his own preconceived world, certainly not a compassion that will break the rigid calculus of his life.'[15]

Idolatry is not always expressed in the worship of strange gods or wooden images. It commonly takes the form of holding rigidly to a belief system which fails to recognize the loving freedom of the living God. A system of belief which offers security to its adherents while threatening those who cannot accept it is an idolatrous belief system. Jonah's belief, which ensured security for those who accepted it and threatened those who did not, was blown apart by God's freedom. In God's sight people have priority over belief systems, a theme powerfully fulfilled in Jesus of Nazareth.

Jonah and Judaism

Although Christian readers will want to bring to bear on their interpretation of this short text insights from the pages of the New Testament, it is also important to acknowledge that the roots of the Christian faith are inextricably tangled throughout the pages of what the church has traditionally called the Old Testament. These Hebrew Scriptures were, in fact, Jesus' Scriptures. From the Gospels we know that as a Jew he had studied its pages and, as we have already suggested, Jesus embraced a theological approach similar to that which underlies the book of Jonah. The word of the Lord through the book of Jonah was written by a Hebrew prophet for his own

[15] Brueggemann, p. 116.

people. How might the struggles and insights of God's ancient people nourish our Christian understanding?

In Jonah we see something of the twofold struggle of God's people, first with the problem of evil, and second with the relationship between the 'chosen people' and the peoples of the earth. These are familiar struggles for Christians in the New Testament and today.

The characteristic Jewish response to the problem of evil is that, in the last resort, God alone is responsible for evil. He could have created a world in which evil had no place; instead he created a world in which, in the words of the rabbis, 'the evil inclination' coexists with 'the good inclination'.

An illustration

To illustrate this approach, we take as an example a Jewish interpretation (that is, Midrash) of the story in Genesis 18. Here we read of God preparing to destroy the wicked cities of Sodom and Gomorrah, and Abraham arguing with God to exercise restraint. Jewish Midrash puts the following words into Abraham's mouth as he reasons with God:

> If Thou seekest strict justice there will be no world, and if Thou seekest to have a world, strict justice cannot be exercised. Dost Thou think to take hold of the rope at both ends? Thou desirest Thy world, and Thou desirest justice also. If Thou wilt not relent a little, the world will not endure.

'In other words', Hayman comments, 'the creation and the continued survival of the world requires God to achieve a balance between his attribute of justice, which if let loose would destroy the world, and his attribute of mercy, which on its own would exclude any kind of law of governance of the universe.'[16] Abraham pleaded for mercy to be shown in relation to the righteous inhabitants of the cities of the plain.[17]

Unlike Abraham, Jonah did not plead with God to have mercy on Nineveh. As far as Jonah was concerned, 'justice', seen as a principle of retribution, had to be done to Nineveh. Other rabbinic texts link Jonah's understanding of 'justice' with the traditional attributes of the Satan.[18] Both 'justice' and the Satan are depicted as accusing

[16] Hayman, pp. 461–476.
[17] Gen. 18:22–33.
[18] Meaning, in Hebrew, the 'accuser'.

humankind of evil and inflicting suffering, which is understood as retributive punishment. Thus Jonah is associated with the role of the Satan in relation to Nineveh. He accuses Nineveh of evil and wants to see the great city punished for her sin. On the other hand, God wants to show compassion to a penitent people. He adopts a position towards Jonah that Abraham had earlier adopted towards him in the story of Sodom and Gomorrah.[19] There, Abraham had pleaded with God; here, God pleads with Jonah and those whom he represents. As Abraham had pleaded with God to show mercy, so the Lord argues with Jonah, urging him to adopt a more compassionate attitude towards Nineveh. Without repentance of his accusatory spirit on Jonah's part, his attitude revealed that he had misunderstood the foundation of his own relationship with God. Such a fundamental misunderstanding not only undermined the order of creation, it also fatally flawed faith.

In both stories, God sends messengers to warn the cities of impending disaster. Albeit reluctantly, Jonah goes to Nineveh, but, unlike Abraham, his struggle does not refer to the 'judge of all the earth doing right'. From Jonah's perspective, the Judge of all the earth has presided over a miscarriage of justice in relation to Nineveh. As a religious 'insider' (someone at home in their understanding of God), Jonah believed that justice rather than mercy should be shown to the Ninevites, the religious 'outsiders' (those who, in the view of the 'insiders', had no claim on God and were ignorant of his ways).

Religious 'insiders', whether Christian or Jew, may find little difficulty in recognizing their own sense of outrage and injustice when they see those who have been in error given equal standing to those, often like themselves, who have striven, even suffered, for years to live according to the truth. In Acts 15:1–21 we see conflict between leaders of the early church struggling to adjust to a new understanding of God. Here was a God who 'made no distinction between us [Jewish Christians] and them [Gentile Christians], but cleansed their hearts by faith'.[20] It would be so much tidier for the 'insiders' if the 'outsiders' remained outside, but the God we meet in the book of Jonah seeks to bring the 'outsider' in. Some of Jesus' parables make precisely this point.[21]

Through Jonah the writer achieves a statement of great significance concerning God's relationship to the Gentile nations. The Lord is ready to respond to Gentile acts of repentance with compassion and

[19] Gen. 18.
[20] Acts 15:9.
[21] See, e.g., the parable of the good Samaritan, Luke 10:25–37.

mercy on the grounds that the penitent peoples of the earth are his handiwork. We see this thinking taken to its logical conclusion in Isaiah 19:24–25:

> In that day Israel will be the third with Egypt and Assyria, a blessing in the midst of the earth, whom the LORD of hosts has blessed, saying, 'Blessed be Egypt my people, and Assyria the work of my hands, and Israel my heritage.'

The Creator is compassionate, merciful and slow to anger. It is within this clear stream of theology that Jesus of Nazareth stands firm. The claim of the early Jewish people who recognized Jesus as Son of God was that the cross of Christ bears testimony to the anguish and passion in the heart of the Creator-Redeemer God. He it is who forgives those who crucify him.

Paul and the Jews

We return here to the problem discussed earlier, namely the failure of Israel, the people brought into being by the covenant grace of Yahweh, to hear his word through the prophets. We recall that the prophets of Israel such as Amos, Hosea, Isaiah and Jeremiah were given the task of calling back to himself God's own people, who in complacency, arrogance or ignorance had drifted away from him. Even John the Baptist and Jesus of Nazareth were prophets with the same calling, yet God's chosen people chose to follow their own lights and insights, refusing the God they claimed to love and serve. In Jonah we even see a prophet choosing to follow his own way in preference to God's call.

Paul, who claimed for himself a prestigious Jewish heritage, was himself initially among those who rejected God's word. Not until he met the risen Christ on the road to Damascus was his heart opened to God's word. Then, discovering for himself the inability of many of his fellow Jews to follow the Christ he proclaimed, Paul became an 'apostle to the Gentiles'. In his epistle to the Romans chapters 9–11, he struggles to understand the failure of God's people to accept his word, not only in his own day, but in the centuries before.[22]

After his paean of praise in Romans 8:38, Paul discloses his anguish over his own people:

[22] It is not the case that all Jews rejected the Christ. The earliest followers of Christ, the apostles and first leaders of the early church, were Jewish. Similarly, before the Christian era, by no means all God's chosen people were deaf to his call.

> I am speaking the truth in Christ, I am not lying; my conscience bears me witness in the Holy Spirit, that I have great sorrow and unceasing anguish in my heart. For I could wish that I myself were accursed and cut off from Christ for the sake of my brethren, my kinsmen by race. They are Israelites, and to them belong the sonship, the glory, the covenants, the giving of law, the worship, and the promises; to them belong the patriarchs, and of their race, according to the flesh, is the Christ. God who is over all be blessed for ever. Amen.[23]

He then begins his argument asserting that God's word had not failed. Some, both Jews and Gentiles, had responded to God's call, but their response depended not on man's will but on God's mercy. He uses Jeremiah's story about the potter who has freedom to make what he will out of the clay. He posits the possibility that even those who reject God's word nevertheless serve his purpose. Through them God's patience and mercy have been revealed for the benefit of both Jew and Gentile alike. He continues:

> What shall we say, then? That Gentiles who did not pursue righteousness have attained it, that is, righteousness through faith; but that Israel who pursued the righteousness which is based on law did not succeed in fulfilling that law. Why? Because they did not pursue it through faith, but as if it were based on works.[24]

He adds:

> I bear them witness that they have a zeal for God, but it is not enlightened. For, being ignorant of the righteousness that comes from God, and seeking to establish their own, they did not submit to God's righteousness.[25]

Recalling a passage from the Torah,[26] Paul speaks of the nearness of God to those who seek him:

> Do not say in your heart, 'Who will ascend to heaven?' (that is, to bring Christ down) or 'Who will descend into the abyss?' (that is, to bring Christ up from the dead). But what does it [i.e.

[23] Rom. 9:1–5.
[24] Rom. 9:30.
[25] Rom. 10:2–3.
[26] Deut. 30:11–13.

> righteousness based on faith] say? The word is near you, on your lips and in your heart.[27]

Drawing first on Moses, 'So I will stir them to jealousy with those who are no people; I will provoke them with a foolish nation,'[28] and then Isaiah, 'All day long I have held out my hands to a disobedient and contrary people',[29] Paul shows that God has not given up on his chosen people; he has patiently waited for them and, in the meantime, has drawn the Gentiles to himself. Finally, coming to the crunch question, Paul asks, 'Has God rejected his people?'[30] His response is unequivocal: 'By no means!' And again, 'Have they stumbled so as to fall? By no means!'[31] Reaching the climax of his argument, Paul continues:

> But through their trespass salvation has come to the Gentiles, so as to make Israel jealous. Now if their trespass means riches for the world, and if their failure means riches for the Gentiles, how much more will their inclusion mean! . . . If their rejection means the reconciliation of the world, what will their acceptance mean but life from the dead?[32]

The apostle is anxious lest Gentiles who accept the word of God in Christ should come to despise unbelieving Jews. He reminds the Gentile believers that the mercy which God has extended to them will be extended also to Jews. Significantly, he also reminds them that it is only through God's election of the Jews that his mercy is known at all. This is the same message of grace that God revealed to Jonah. He concludes with a further paean of praise: 'O, the depth of the riches and wisdom and knowledge of God! How unsearchable are his judgments and how inscrutable his ways!'[33] Paul, the Jewish apostle to the Gentiles, struggled to understand the response of some, though emphatically not all, contemporary Jews towards Jesus Christ. He would be cut to the quick by the way in which some, though emphatically not all, Gentile Christians have subsequently behaved towards Jewish people.

Long before Paul, long before the birth of Jesus of Nazareth, an earlier 'apostle to the Gentiles' addressed Israel's need of repentance.

[27] Rom. 10:6–8.
[28] Deut. 32:21.
[29] Rom. 10:21, quoting Is. 65:2.
[30] Rom. 11:1.
[31] Rom. 11:11.
[32] Rom. 11:11–12, 15.
[33] Rom. 11:33.

His reaction to God's dealings with the Ninevites brings into sharp focus the difficulty of repentance for religious people. The writer of the book of Jonah posits a conversation between Jonah and Yahweh, concerning the heart of God's good news of deliverance for all. The conversation continued into Jesus' day: as we have seen, many of his parables and encounters with Jewish leaders reflect the same struggle. At the beginning of the third millennium the people of God, like Jonah, still struggle to shun exclusivism and embrace the stranger.

> And the LORD said, 'You pity the plant, for which you did not labour, nor did you make it grow, which came into being in a night, and perished in a night. And should not I pity Nineveh, that great city, in which there are more than a hundred and twenty thousand persons who do not know their right hand from their left, and also much cattle?' (4:10–11)

You

Where I wander – You!
Where I ponder – You!
Only You, You again, always You!
You! You! You!
When I am gladdened – You!
When I am saddened – You!
Only You, You again, always You!
You! You! You!
Sky is You, earth is You!
You above! You below!
In every trend, at every end,
Only You, You again, always You!
You! You! You!

(Levi Yitzchak of Berditchev, 1740–1809)

Appendix: A possible chronology of Jonah's life and times

Dates BC	*Kings in Israel and Judah*	*Prophets*	*Events*	*Texts*
781	Jeroboam II			
		Jonah	Israel's borders strengthened.	2 Kings 14
762		Amos		Amos 6:13
760			Earthquake.	Amos 1:2
746	Zechariah			
745		Hosea	Revival of Nineveh under Tiglath-Pileser III.	
732	Hoshea			2 Kings 15
724			Samaria besieged for three years by Shalmaneser, king of Assyria.	2 Kings 18
721			Samaria falls to the Assyrians.	
701			Joppa in Philistia falls to Sennacherib. Nineveh becomes chief city under Sennacherib. Nineveh's borders extended.	
680			Nineveh chief city of biblical world's most powerful empire.	
671	Manasseh		Judah joins in unrest against Assyria.	2 Chronicles 33
		Nahum		
663			Fall of Thebes.	Nahum 3:8
640		Zephaniah		

Dates BC	*Kings in Israel and Judah*	*Prophets*	*Events*	*Texts*
612			Nineveh falls to Medes and Babylonians.	
605	Jehoiakim	Jeremiah	Jehoiakim burns the scroll.	Jeremiah 36
597		Ezekiel	First deportation to Babylon.	2 Kings 24
587			Jerusalem falls to Babylon.	

Map of places relevant to the book of Jonah

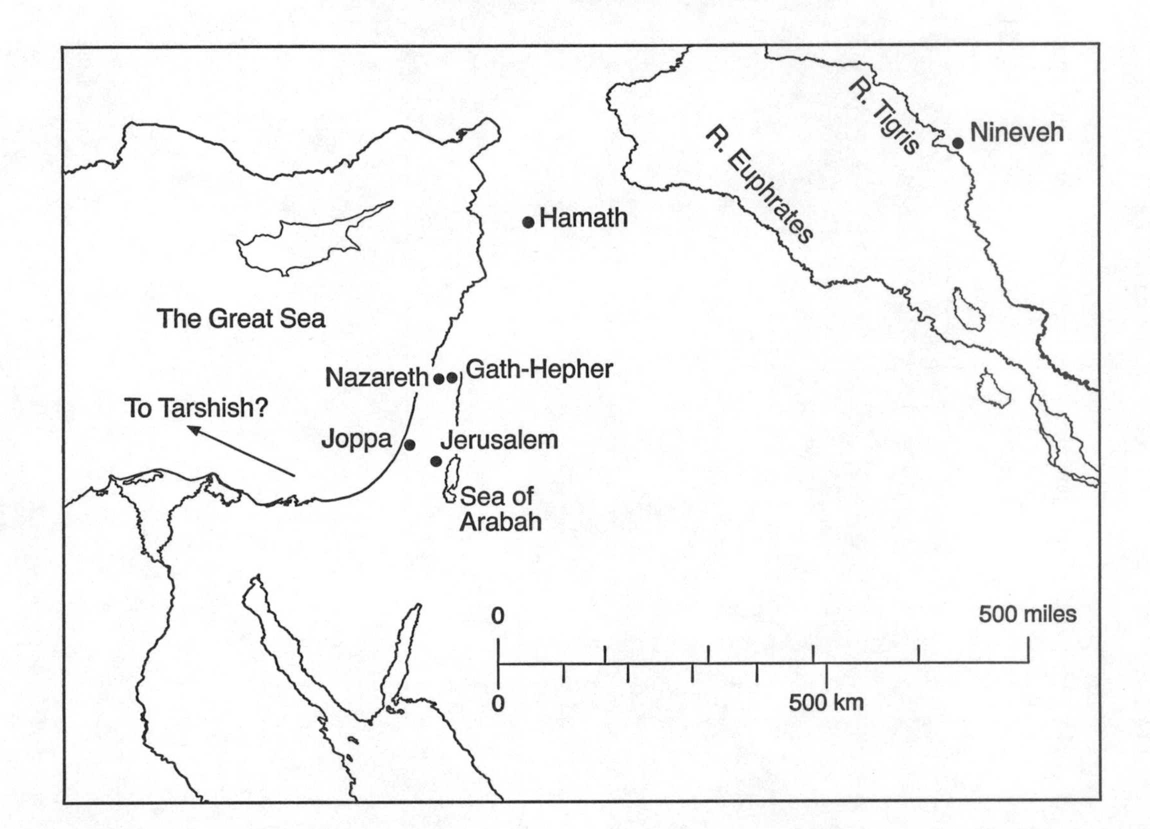

Other titles in The Bible Speaks Today series

New Testament

The Message of the Sermon on the Mount (Matthew 5 – 7)
Christian counter-culture
John Stott

The Message of Matthew
The kingdom of heaven
Michael Green

The Message of Mark
The mystery of faith
Donald English

The Message of Luke
The Saviour of the world
Michael Wilcock

The Message of John
Here is your King!
Bruce Milne

The Message of Acts
To the ends of the earth
John Stott

The Message of Romans
God's good news for the world
John Stott

The Message of 1 Corinthians
Life in the local church
David Prior

The Message of 2 Corinthians
Power in weakness
Paul Barnett

The Message of Galatians
Only one way
John Stott

The Message of Ephesians
God's new society
John Stott

The Message of Philippians
Jesus our Joy
Alec Motyer

The Message of Colossians and Philemon
Fullness and freedom
Dick Lucas

The Message of Thessalonians
Preparing for the coming King
John Stott

The Message of 1 Timothy and Titus
The life of the local church
John Stott

The Message of 2 Timothy
Guard the gospel
John Stott

The Message of Hebrews
Christ above all
Raymond Brown

The Message of James
The tests of faith
Alec Motyer

The Message of 1 Peter
The way of the cross
Edmund Clowney

The Message of 2 Peter and Jude
The promise of his coming
Dick Lucas and Christopher Green

The Message of John's Letters
Living in the love of God
David Jackman

The Message of Revelation
I saw heaven opened
Michael Wilcock

Bible Themes

The Message of the Living God
His glory, his people, his world
Peter Lewis

The Message of the Resurrection
Christ is risen!
Paul Beasley-Murray

The Message of the Cross
Wisdom unsearchable, love indestructible
Derek Tidball

The Message of Salvation
By God's grace, for God's glory
Philip Graham Ryken

The Message of Creation
Encountering the Lord of the universe
David Wilkinson

The Message of Heaven and Hell
Grace and destiny
Bruce Milne

The Message of Mission
The glory of Christ in all time and space
Howard Peskett and Vinoth Ramachandra